MOUSE
UNDER
GLASS

MOUSE UNDER GLASS

SECRETS OF DISNEY ANIMATION & THEME PARKS

by David Koenig

Foreword
by Richard M. Sherman and Robert B. Sherman

BONAVENTURE PRESS

For Anne Koenig,
who has been a blessing to as many as she has met,
especially one overly imaginative son.

Mouse Under Glass: Secrets of Disney Animation & Theme Parks by David Koenig

Published by
BONAVENTURE PRESS
Post Office Box 51961
Irvine, CA 92619-1961   USA

Cover art by Ray Haller

Excerpt from WOLFGANG PUCK'S MODERN FRENCH COOKING, copyright (c) 1981 by Wolfgang Puck. Reprinted by permission of Houghton Mifflin Co. All rights reserved.

Illustration by Mary Shepard from MARY POPPINS, copyright 1934 and renewed 1962 by P.L. Travers, reproduced by permission of Harcourt Brace & Company.

Illustration by Erik Blegvad from BED-KNOB AND BROOMSTICK, copyright 1957 and renewed 1985 by Mary Norton, reproduced by permission of Harcourt Brace & Company.

Richard Huemer quotations excerpted from Richard Huemer Oral History by permission of Department of Special Collections, University Research Library, UCLA.

This book is in no way authorized by, endorsed by or affiliated with the Walt Disney Company. References to Disney trademarked properties are not meant to imply this book is a Disney product for advertising or other commercial purposes.

Publisher's Cataloging in Publication Data
Koenig, David G.
     Mouse Under Glass: Secrets of Disney Animation & Theme Parks / by David Koenig.
          p. cm.
     Includes bibliography and index.
          1. Walt Disney Company. 2. Animated films—United States—History.
          I. Koenig, David G., 1962- II. Title.
NC1766.U52D5   741.5'8'0979493   96-78506

ISBN 0-9640605-0-7 (hardcover)

ISBN 0-9640605-1-5 (softcover)

Printed in the United States of America
97 98 99 00 01 / 10 9 8 7 6 5 4 3 2

Menu

Acknowledgments

One goal in compiling information for this book has been to unearth fascinating tid-bits to inform even the most MENSA-calibre Disneyphile. A sizely portion of such never-before-published information comes from those who graciously consented to interviews, (and I sincerely thank) Tony Baxter, Carol Connors, Will Finn, Vance Gerry, Joe Grant, Terry Gilkyson, Ryan Harmon, Huston Huddleston, Mrs. Richard Huemer, Steven Hulett, Al Kasha, Earl Kress, Peggy Lee, Mel Leven, James Lopez, Fred Lucky, Malcolm Marmorstein, Jeffrey Price, Maurice Rapf, Terry Rossio, George Scribner, Peter Seaman, Tom Shaw, Tom Sito, Linda Woolverton, a few anonymous you-know-who-you-ares, and, most gratefully, Richard M. Sherman and Robert B. Sherman.

Many of these interviews would never have taken place without the assistance of these agents and accomplices: Paul Cacia, Dave DiMello, Alan Glisch, Dodie Gold, Rick Green, Jeff Lenburg, David O'Connor, Kevin Plunkett, DreamWorks' Terry Press, Jack Rapke, Steve and Sue Tunstall, Lew Weitzman, the staff at ASCAP, and Disney's Howard Green, who after 47 phone calls is probably still having nightmares about dancing message pads with my name on them.

Research assistance was provided by Sam Gill and the staff of the Academy of Motion Picture Arts & Sciences' Margaret Herrick Library, the UCLA University Research Library, Dave Smith of the Walt Disney Archives, Jane Newell and her assistants at the History Room of the Anaheim Public Library, the trademark research staff at the Los Angeles Public Library, and Rob Ray and the Rob Ray Collection.

Help with permissions came from Teresa Buswell of Houghton Mifflin Co., Ellen Goulet of Harcourt Brace & Company, Charlotte Brown of the Department of Special Collections at UCLA's University Research Library, and Joe Adamson.

Friends and family members provided insight, advice, assistance and support: Bill Bax, Charles Christ, Jason and Shannon Clark, David Cutler, Sara Daly, Kevin Duarte, Larry, Sheryl, Garth and Mimi Hamlin, Tim and Kimberly Hensley, Julie Howard, Bill Jagielski, David and Laura Keefe, Deanna Keefe, Anne, Gerald, Joe, Paul and Maryanne Koenig, Rita Pipta, Michelle and Paul Roden, Brent and Chris Walker, and Jordan Young.

The wonderful artwork is the work of wonderful artist Ray Haller, while the extra polish on the prose is courtesy of editor extraordinaire Randy Skretvedt.

No one helped more than my wonderful wife, Laura, who served as official photographer, assistant blooper catcher, chief advisor and supporter, and virtual co-author. Without her assistance, encouragement and patience, this book would still be in my head, taking up increasingly scarce storage space.

But my greatest thanks are to my Lord and Savior Jesus Christ, to whom I owe everything. I can never sufficiently repay Him for what He does for me and especially for what He did for me—and for you.

Foreword

By Richard M. Sherman and Robert B. Sherman

It was the spring of 1961. We were in Walt Disney's office demonstrating a song we had just written for a film treatment of a book about an English nursemaid named Mary Poppins. The song, "Jolly Holiday," contained a section in which Mary Poppins would order tea for herself and her friend Bert, whereupon a quartet of tuxedoed waiters would reply in song, "...order what you will, there'll be no bill, it's com-pli-men-ta-ry." Suddenly, Walt said, "Hold it! You know, waiters always remind me of penguins. The waiters should be penguins!" We were stunned by this incredible remark and asked, "How can you train four penguins to sing?"

Then Walt said rather matter-of-factly, but with a twinkle in his eye, "We'll animate them... in fact, we'll animate the whole sequence—except for our principals."

This was the birth of one of the most outstanding and magical sequences in any Disney film. Yes, Pamela Travers created the characters. Yes, Don da Gradi designed the sequence. Yes, we wrote the song. But Walt Disney's innovative genius provided the magic touch that inspired his animators, actors, choreographers and musicians to heights of which they never dreamed.

As Walt Disney's staff songwriters since 1960, we were accustomed to being called in to "troubleshoot" a story or park attraction. If the boss felt a song could clarify a title or a scene, we wrote it. Examples of this are "The Tiki Tiki Tiki Room" (which explained what the Enchanted Tiki Room was all about), the theme song for *The Wonderful World of Color*, "There's a Great Big Beautiful Tomorrow" for the Carousel of Progress, and "It's a Small World (After All)," which Walt asked us to write when the original concept—national anthems of two dozen countries played simultaneously during the ride—proved to be a disaster.

Another example of the Disney magic touch occurred at a time when we were riding high. It was the spring of 1965. We had just won two Oscars for the song "Chim Chim Cher-ee" and the score from *Mary Poppins*. No sooner did we sit down in Walt's office when he asked, "Have you boys read Kipling's *The Jungle Book?*" We replied that we hadn't but we did remember seeing the Korda movie starring Sabu. He said, "Good, that's enough. You know the basic story." He then went on to explain that he had had an entire treatment, script, storyboards and songs prepared and he was very disappointed. It was too true to the book, too somber and intense. It lacked fun. He wanted us to come in with a new team of storymen and animators to lighten up the story, to "Disneyfy" it.

Our first of five *Jungle Book* songs was written for perhaps the most frightening sequence in the story. Little Mowgli is kidnapped by a band of marauding monkeys and brought before the terrifying king of the apes. Following Walt's order to "Disneyfy" it, we turned the scary king of the apes into the hip "King of the Swingers" and his band of monkeys into a swingin' Dixieland band. The first time Walt heard "I Wan'na Be Like You," he said, with that same twinkle in his eye, "That'll work. You're on the right track." It was his track. It was his last great film.

To say that it was a privilege to work for and with this insightful and inspiring man is a great understatement. His like may never come again. But, now and then, it is thrilling to see glimmers of his vision shining through.

Richard M. Sherman and Robert B. Sherman
Beverly Hills, California
August 1996

Preface

Most everyone who worked directly for Walt Disney had the same goal: to produce a story or a drawing or a song or a theme park attraction that the boss would like. For many, it continued to be their primary motivation even after the boss had died. Writer Bill Peet was the rare exception. He wasn't near as concerned with pleasing Walt, as he was with writing the best story that he could. Walt would yell at him. Peet, daringly, yelled back. More than once, Walt demoted him. More than once, Peet quit. Finally, after 25 miserable years, Peet walked out for good. He was about the best storyman Disney ever had.

But, to Walt, himself a master storyteller, writers were dispensible and only as good as their last story. His admiration—and the fame—went to the animators, who possessed a skill he did not. Upon his favorite artists he bestowed the crown "The Nine Old Men," giving rise to the false impression that there were only nine animators and they did all the work. That's the impression one might get from *Disney Animation: The Illusion of Life*, a book written by two of the Nine and devoid of any mention of the Story Department. When the book came out, Bill Peet phoned one of the authors and yelled at him.

As Peet told the animation trade magazine *Hogan's Alley*, "There has to be a brain. The humor rarely comes from the animation. It has to be on the boards. *Illusion of Life* doesn't even suggest any thought behind it. For a feature to hold together as a drama and have a continuity with personalities, it has to be very carefully worked out."

To me, what separates Disney animation from that of rival studios is not so much the animation as the thought that goes into it long before any artist picks up a pencil. It's the thousand words that each picture signifies. For Disney's celebrity may be in its cartoon characters, but its cultural and historical significance is its role as our national storyteller. The animation, then, is the illustrations of that story.

Here, I trace the development of Disney's 30 best known features, from first inspiration through final film and ultimately into theme park attraction. Note the company's secret formula that distinguishes its features and parks from others' lies not only in what it uses but in what it does not—the characters, gags, scenes, songs and other ideas that don't survive the editor's cut. Usually, the difference is that Disney's competitors are content to settle for those first or second ideas.

In the same way, there's as much to learn about what makes a film great from the best Disney films as from the worst, how the charm of *Snow White* became the schmaltz of *Fox and the Hound*, and the non-stop insanity of *Aladdin* matured from the please-stop inanity of *Robin Hood*. At the same time, the rides at Disneyland and Disney World which often grew out of these movies also had their ups and downs.

Disney learned the hard way not to take itself so seriously and that pretty pictures are worthless without an entertaining story. I have, too. So, dear reader, be forewarned. This is not one of those official Disney tomes that doubles as a coffee table and features more backpatting than a Jerry Lewis Telethon. The tone is slightly less solemn. I ruminate. I explicate. I divulge. I even nitpick a little, and the purchase price doesn't include a lithograph or commemorative watch.

David Koenig
Newport Beach, California
October 1996

I

The Disney Cookbook
Introduction

"Cooking is creation; a collaboration of the cook, his ingredients, and, for me, a great deal of love. Fine food flows from the heart. Mastery of the craft is achieved through practice, experience, and feeling."

– Wolfgang Puck,
Wolfgang Puck's French Cooking for the American Kitchen (1981)

t first glance, the recipe for cooking up a Disney classic does not appear too complicated. Start with one classic tale of adventure featuring an attractive, heroic youth with a dream and a dilemma. For a dash of humor, throw in a couple of mischievous sidekicks, preferably furry. Make the villain more outlandish. Stir with a little romance. Mix in a generous helping of catchy music. And bring to a boil with beautiful animation.

The recipe seems simple enough, the ingredients sufficiently available. But then realize that no one else has been able to duplicate Disney's creations. Watch another studio's animated features, visit another conglomerate's amusement parks, you immediately sense something's missing. They don't feel Disney.

Competitors have tried. There have always been those who figured if they knew Disney's secrets, their tricks, they could produce the same quality entertainment. They might recruit comparable talent, often away from Disney, but there remained something they couldn't imitate, the guiding principle. In the beginning, that principle was the principal, Walt Disney. He shared the same tastes as America's masses; he understood what excited them, what made them laugh and cry and sigh. His genius was a perfectionist drive to delight the public's appetites, whatever the cost.

To prepare an animated feature, the master chef would take as his first ingredient an **Original Tale**, some fairy tale or storybook audiences might be familiar with, a reference point. But as once-cherished as these tales may have been, by the time Disney was through with them, he had made them his own.

Nowadays, more people are familiar with the **Disney Version** than the classic tale that inspired it. First, Walt disassembled the story to locate its heart or, if it didn't have one, to install one. In an entertaining way, Disney's movies would teach a life lesson about honesty, responsibility, friendship or some other core value. "Walt felt every story should have a moral," explains storyman Joe Grant, who started at the Disney Studios in the early 1930s and at age 87 still reported to work five days a week. "Then you had to create reasons for each character to act a particular way. You introduced humor, and so on."

After adapting or creating and then fleshing out the characters, the writers and sketch artists went to work on the story, piling idea on top of idea. The picture grew like a snowball, drifting into often unexpected directions. "One of (Walt's) tricks was to never leave a thing until it had been milked in every possible way, and worked out in the best possible way no matter how much time it took or how much money it cost. He built his pictures that way," according to Grant's partner in the Thirties and Forties, the late Dick Huemer. "He made many sequences just to see if they would work. Even though they weren't essential to the story, he'd go ahead just to see, to try, always to try for the touchdown play."

Disney held gag contests, offering cash prizes to anyone who could come up with funny bits that got used. Week after week, the studio gardener went home with the most money. (He never became a gag man because, according to Huemer, he was a heck of a gardener.)

Walt served not only as participant but also judge and jury. "The story for *Snow White*, in a sense, was written in Walt Disney's head," Grant says. "He was a storyteller, and he'd go from room to room. Everybody knows the story; it's a simple outline. But as Walt went he added the Dwarfs and so on. That method died with him. Today, the writers in here—we use them up like Kleenex. The process is long and tedious. (Features) take three years each to make, sometimes a full year in preproduction alone. There's much more reliance on individuals. Walt's control was total. Nothing got too far away from him. In order for Walt to put his thumb on everything, he had separate departments. He had to know where everything was." Usually that meant going through everyone's work after they had gone home, sometimes salvaging crumpled-up drawings from their wastebaskets.

Huemer recalled, "He was always working on story. He was forever picking your brain, even if you were at a social affair with him or something. Anything you said he'd be listening to, cocking his ear, you know, and remembering *everything* you said with that marvelous brain that never forgot a thing. Not a single thing! This I venture to guess was at the core of his genius, this wonderful memory, and, of course, his way of reaching back into that memory and picking out things and applying them right to the heart of any subject. He could go right to the nub of the problem, no matter what it was. Even if it was the design of a uniform for the employees at Disneyland, he would have an opinion on it. Nothing was too small for him to venture an opinion on and his was generally the best one."

Even today, the films are still crafted by committee during meeting after meeting. Disney features are not written on a laptop computer by a lone scribe reclining on the beach at Malibu. It's a battle of friendly fire, with dozens of staff members trying to come up with the best idea.

"It's always a contest to see how much of your material makes it into the picture and what is the response. And if you've got a laugh, you've got a jewel. If something of yours doesn't go over, well, it's sort of embarrassing," Grant says. "There's as much taken out as is left in. You have a time limit and the time limit is audience endurance. (So) we're never at any point positive what's going to be in the picture. Everything's built out of sand."

Often those who start out as animators, like Huemer, gravitate to the story department. "I think we enjoy having more and more creative influence," speculates animator Tom Sito, who headed the story crew on *Pocahontas*. "In animation they say here's your character, here's what he does, here's what he says, here's how much time he has. The actor has accents in his voice. (The animation) is still a performance. It's like Hamlet. Everybody knows what he says, what he does, what he wears. Yet what makes Mel Gibson different from Laurence Olivier different from Nicol Williamson different from Kenneth Branagh? Animation is performance art."

A background as an animator provides a writer with a sense of what will work on film. "Writing is much more intuitive than animating," adds Will Finn, animator turned writer turned director. "In animating, so much work has been done, the pipe has been laid, the track's there, so you're not worrying about trying to concoct the idea, all your energies are going toward executing it."

Professional writers, as a rule, are a sensitive, protective lot; their words and ideas are their children. They aren't comfortable tossing up their offspring like clay pigeons. But proficient animation writers must be thick-skinned, open to give and take. They are collaborators on a constant search for answers, visualizing scenarios to help their director, producer and fellow writers discover what direction to follow. And, when all is said and drawn, the final decision comes down to personal taste.

Ultimately, that decision is the director's. In the old days, no matter whose name appeared on the credits, the real director was Walt, who thought even the best ideas could be improved. "You have to sell (your ideas) to the one who makes the decision," says animation writer Steve Hulett. "We always said, 'There's no point having a great idea before the director's ready for it.' The timing has to be right. He has to see there's a problem, or he would say, 'Nah, we don't need that.'"

Since an animated story is best told visually, the writing process traditionally began with a basic treatment followed *not* by assigning a screenwriter to draft a full screenplay, but by pinning series of drawings and captions onto six-foot sheets of corkboard. These "storyboards" helped everyone to better visualize characters and sequences and allowed ideas to be easily added, subtracted or rearranged. Visual impact was always a higher priority for Walt than the story. During planning for one picture, after viewing more than half the storyboards, volatile animator Milt Kahl exploded, "Come on, Walt, what the hell's the story about?" "Don't worry about it," Walt replied. "It'll come."

Even when that story finally came, Walt dwelled on impact and emotion, even at the cost of coherency. More than once during the creation of *Pinocchio*, animator Ward Kimball complained that a major plot point didn't make sense, but Walt remained unperturbed. As another of his Nine Old Men, Frank Thomas, quoted Walt's credo: "To heck with the logic if it got in the way, go for the entertainment." Even the tightest of classic Disney narratives contains its share of nonsensical or contradictory **Plot Holes**.

Although the story remained subservient to the entertainment, it was honed over and over again, often taking years to flesh out. If the plot or characters weren't developing to his liking, Walt might drop the project entirely, even after years of work. What makes for great storytelling is both a great story and great telling; carrying audiences on an exciting adventure, climbing to greater and greater heights without a lot of detours, yet not giving away the destination, however inevitable. "It's difficult to take a fairy tale that everyone knows how it turns out. You gotta surprise them," says writer Maurice Rapf, who decided for one Disney film that just before Cinderella heads out the door for the ball, resplendent in a beautiful gown, her stepmother and stepsisters should tear the dress to shreds. "Otherwise, it's too easy."

Even after the formal writing is complete, the story, characters and even dialogue continue to be shaped by the directors, producers, composers, lyricists, voice actors, character animators, layout artists and effects animators. Giving screen credit to 28 writers on *The Lion King* seems a vast underestimate.

The end result is typically more Broadway than Brothers Grimm. "For anyone who's ever seen these pictures, the formula is very obvious," Grant says. "They are based directly on musical theater. Musical theater is not dead, as far as Disney is concerned."

Walt's dreams, though, were bigger than Hollywood. Long before Virtual Reality, he dreamed his family audience could not only experience these timeless tales but interact with them, personally stepping into his worlds of fantasy and adventure, and he created a Disney Land for them to step into. Walt's first theme park designers, or "Imagineers," were artists originally hired for animation projects. With this new medium, the designers used their same skills—concocting fantastic ideas, crafting detailed art, telling fascinating stories, pleasing a diverse audience—but quickly discovered the vast difference in translating a story into three dimensions to produce **Attraction Offspring**.

"The movies develop the personalities, the rides are centered on environments," explains Tony Baxter, senior vice president of creative development for Walt Disney Imagineering (WDI). "We can't do characters like the movies can. We take the visitor into the environment. It's like when you go to church, it's not the statues that are important but what they represent."

WDI goes through as many ideas as the Feature Animation division. "Ninety percent of the concepts we develop for a theme park never make it past the 'blue sky' phase," admits writer/creative director and former Imagineer Ryan Harmon. "But we never throw them out!" When Disneyland Paris was deciding recently how to follow-up Space Mountain, 30 to 40 old concepts were dusted off for a fresh look.

"Our brainstorming sessions begin with the premise that there are no bad ideas," Harmon explains. "Everyone in the room, no matter what their specialty, is encouraged to participate. We weed through the results, develop the best through treatments and artwork, then pitch them to management. If we're successful, we're funded to continue developing in a specific direction."

As with a not-yet-realized Winnie the Pooh dark ride Harmon developed for Disneyland in the early 1990s, the goal is to come up with an attraction that compliments the film property. "After viewing the three classic Pooh shorts over and over, I asked myself what I, as a guest, would hope to see in the ultimate Pooh attraction," he says. "Because you can't tell a linear story in a ride-through attraction, I started listing all the different environments the films took us to. I then borrowed the simple umbrella concept of most Pooh tales: Pooh wants honey, Pooh tries to get honey, Pooh gets honey. Next, I chose what I felt were the most exciting and diverse environments—permitting us to see all of the beloved characters, and placed them in a sequence that fit the most basic story structure."

Harmon wrote very brief dialogue and looping song edits. An artist designed a track layout and created color storyboards, while a model maker recreated their ideas in three dimensions. Over the following weeks, the designers made numerous presentations, and tweaked the ride accordingly. In the end, the attraction lost its spot in Mickey's Toontown to Roger Rabbit's CarToon Spin.

While a ride can be much more physically stimulating than sitting in a movie theater, like movie audiences, theme park guests are traditionally passive, willing to let the medium do the thinking for them. Disney attractions take advantage of that surrender, manipulating what guests see, hear, even feel. Consequently, complicated scenarios, such as the set-up for the Twilight Zone Tower of Terror at the Disney-MGM Studios, are often lost on an audience. "Sometimes designers forget that guests check their brains at the gate," Harmon says. "We might develop the coolest story or mythology for an attraction that goes right over their heads!"

Many dark rides, unable to carry a coherent narrative, instead string together the best scenes from a well-known movie. "Sometimes we rely on the guest having seen the film and provide an opportunity to relive the most memorable moments," explains Harmon. "When you're working with a classic film in the dark ride medium, you typically don't want to stray from the story. No one will get it."

Harmon cites the E.T. attraction at Universal Studios as one that tried to be a sequel to the movie. "You find yourself in a psyche-delic world where dozens of tiny E.T.s are singing and dancing. I always ask myself, 'Did I miss that scene in the movie?'"

Pinocchio's Daring Journey, on the other hand, seems to make sense because the images are familiar: Pinocchio dances with the marionettes, a giant cage drops over you, Lampwick turns into a donkey at Pleasure Island, a signpost points away from the sea and towards "Pinocchio Village," Monstro lunges at you, Geppetto searches the streets with a lantern, Pinocchio is reunited with Geppetto at his toy shop by the Blue Fairy.

Unlike film, attractions can be tinkered with even after they're unveiled to the public—making the Indiana Jones Adventure vehi-cles run more smoothly, rewriting the Jungle Cruise spiel (which every captain does, anyway), even just adding a few new charac-ters outside the Alice in Wonderland ride. However, once an ani-mated feature is released, it's finished, **Bloopers** and all. Conse-quently, especially since full animation is so expensive and time consuming, most of the editing takes place with the storyboards so everyone is pretty confident in his work before committing it to film. Occasionally scenes do end up on the **Cutting Room Floor**, usually to pick up the pacing. Songwriter Richard Sherman, who has seen more than one of his numbers cut, says the decision is a difficult and sometimes controversial one: "Sometimes it's mone-tary, sometimes it's artistic. Nobody's trying to ruin a picture, but as they say, the road to hell is paved with good intentions."

Sometimes the filmmakers edit out seemingly good material. Sometimes they leave in material which most of us never see any-way, split-second **Hidden Images** placed inconspicuously on a cel or two by prankish animators. Asked if animators try to get away with including subtle extras, one said, "Whenever we can." Yet officially, they're discouraged because they can be distracting; audiences will watch the background for little in-jokes and not the movie. "The problem is you can't scene steal in animation," says animator Tom Sito. "(We animators) like all the in-gags, but I don't know. Cracking each other up in dailies is an easy joke. The idea is to entertain the audience."

The practice first surfaced in the late 1980s, after a few animators on *Who Framed Roger Rabbit* added little extras, some naughty, some silly, others private in-jokes. Or maybe it just seemed to start then because of the advent of laser discs which permitted the public to view individual frames in the privacy of their own homes. Legend has it that mischievous Disney animators have been slipping in inconspicuous additions as far back as a chipmunk subtly defecating in the forest in *Snow White and the Seven Dwarfs.*

Unfortunately, good-natured fun has turned into paranoia, leading viewers with overactive imaginations to visualize sexual or otherwise strange images and messages in completely innocent places. For while with the release of each new feature, we can expect the usual byproduct of children laughing, adults smiling, and critics reaching for their thesaurus to find new synonyms for "masterpiece," there are sure to be a few **Strange Reactions**, as well.

II

Disney Developed
Salad Days
1922-1942

"Neither knowledge or diligence can create a great chef. Of what use is conscientiousness as a substitute for inspiration?"

– Sidonie Collette,
Prisons and Paradise (1932)

Through the 1920s and early 1930s, Walt Disney pioneered, popularized and revolutionized animation. Viewing the fledgling medium not as a novelty but as serious entertainment on par with the live action comedies of Charlie Chaplin, he introduced careful planning and meticulous attention to detail in every phase of producing his cartoons.

The quality gap between Disney cartoons and the primitive products of other studios was not lost on audiences, who demanded movie theaters show only Disney, giving rise to the slogan, "What—no Mickey Mouse?" Noted Dick Huemer, who animated his first character for the Raoul Barré Studio in 1916: "Disney was the first person who really analyzed cartoon action. Old animation was done from pose to pose without much thought. It was almost like it was a design. Without any weight. Whereas Disney immediately gave his characters weight, and life and breath, and naturalness. In Disney, it flowed from thing to thing, and (other studios') stuff went from extreme to extreme."

While live action studio heads looked down on Disney, calling him the "Mickey Mouse Man," Walt tried to bring respect to the craft of animation. But, into the 1930s, even live action shorts were looked down upon. One by one, the movies' great comedians made the switch to features. Chaplin hadn't released a short since 1923. If anybody could make a 90-minute cartoon, it was Walt Disney.

He saw feature length as another way to make his work better. "When he first started as a young man," Joe Grant remembers, "he did a series of *Alice* comedies, then *Flowers and Trees* and other Silly Symphonies. Everything became something else: the Silly Symphonies became *Fantasia, Alice* became *Alice in Wonderland*. Everything had some connection to his past, something he wanted to complete."

But could Walt sustain an audience's attention, let alone entertain them, for more than ten times the length of his other cartoons? "*Snow White* was his adventure," Grant recalls. "People were afraid the audience would run into the lobby, that an hour of color would make them dizzy."

The actual repercussions of his experiment were far more profound.

- 1 -
Snow White and the Seven Dwarfs

The Original Tale

Although they are known as history's most prolific writers of fairy tales, brothers Jacob and Wilhelm Grimm were, more accurately, folk tale collectors, the first to compile and preserve on paper centuries of stories. The first edition of their multi-volume *Nursery and Household Tales* (1812) contained more than 200 stories, including arguably their most famous, "Little Snow-White."

The tale concerns a king who, a year after his wife dies giving birth to a beautiful "snow white" daughter, marries again, then promptly drops out of the story himself. The new Queen is beautiful yet proud and haughty, and has a looking glass to tell her each day she's the fairest in the land. But as Snow-white grows, she becomes even more beautiful, and the mirror finally breaks the news to the Queen. Envious, she commands a huntsman to kill Snow-white. But the hunter pities the girl and allows her to escape into the woods, assuming the wild beasts will devour her. To convince the Queen he has done her bidding, he kills a boar and gives his Majesty its lung and liver, which she salts and eats.

Meanwhile, Snow-white, after a terrifying flight through the forest, finds a cottage, small but neat and clean. She has a bit to eat then falls asleep on one of seven small beds. They belong to seven interchangeable dwarfs, who return from mining and discover Snow-white, but allow her to stay if she'll keep everything neat and clean.

When the mirror reports that Snow-white still lives, the wicked Queen goes to the cottage disguised as an old peddler woman. She sells Snow-white a bright silk lace, ties it on her too tightly, and the girl falls as if dead. The dwarfs return and cut the lace, reviving Snow-white. The peddler woman returns the next day and sells Snow-white a poisoned comb. The dwarfs again return to find their housekeeper on the floor and awaken her by removing the comb from her hair.

The next day, the peddler woman has an apple, half white, half red. To assure Snow-white it's harmless, the Queen eats the white half. Snow-white bites the poisonous red half and drops. When the dwarfs return, they look everywhere but can't find anything poisonous. They unlace her, comb her hair and wash her, but she doesn't stir. They cry for three days and, unable to bury her because her cheeks are so rosy red, they place her in a glass coffin on top of a mountain.

One day, a bypassing prince spends the night at the dwarfs' cottage and notices the encased beauty. He must have her and the dwarfs finally relent. As his servants carry her coffin away, they stumble and the shock dislodges the chunk of apple from her throat. Snow-white awakens, marries the prince, and at their wedding the wicked Queen is forced to put on red-hot iron slippers and dance until she drops dead.

The Disney Version

Walt recognized that "Snow White" provided everything he wanted in an animated feature: drama, action, pathos and perfect opportunities for music and humor. Its singular shortcoming was a dearth of fully defined characters to carry the story. From the time he had a small group of artists and writers first begin work on the project in 1934, Walt realized that what would give "Snow White" the most color would be turning it into "Snow White *and the Seven Dwarfs*." His idea was to endear the nameless, faceless dwarfs to audiences by giving them personalities. The storymen came up with more than 50 different names that would dictate their personalities (see chart at right). Since they were named after basic, obvious moods, the first five came quickly. The last thought of were Doc, the bungle-tongued leader, and Dopey. Many actors auditioned for the part of Dopey, but every voice killed the character, so finally he was given none, which fit the silly simpleton perfectly.

Walt was so intent on displaying the Dwarfs' different natures that during a 1936 story conference he suggested that their chairs be carved to fit their personalities, with Dopey in a high chair. For a scene in which the Dwarfs entertain Snow White, the writers suggested they sing a song like "Little Brown Jug," "Three Blind

Eeny, Meeny, Miny, Doc

• Silly	• Deafy	• Shorty
• Sappy	• Daffy	• Shifty
• Scrappy	• Doleful	• Thrifty
• Snappy	• Woeful	• Nifty
• Snoopy	• Wistful	• Neurtsy
• Goopy	• Soulful	• Hotsy
• Gloomy	• Helpful	• Hungry
• Gaspy	• Awful	• Hickey
• Gabby	• Graceful	• Hoppy
• Blabby	• Tearful	• Jumpy
• Flabby	• Tubby	• Jaunty
• Crabby	• Weepy	• Chesty
• Cranky	• Wheezy	• Busy
• Lazy	• Sneezy-Wheezy	• Burpy
• Dizzy	• Sniffy	• Baldy
• Dippy	• Puffy	• Biggy
• Dumpy	• Stuffy	• Biggy-Wiggy
• Dirty	• Strutty	• Biggo-Ego

Mice" or "Frére Jacques," but again, Walt saw another chance to bring out the Dwarfs' characters. A simple new ditty, "The Lady in the Moon," was penned, then another, "You're Never Too Old to Be Young," which was finally replaced by "The Silly Song," that similarly highlighted each Dwarf.

The first outline from August of 1934 closely followed the original tale, with a few fanciful embellishments. Before discovering the Dwarfs' cottage, Snow White would travel through the Morass of Monsters, Upsidedownland (where the trees' roots stick in the air), and, foreshadowing *The Wizard of Oz*, poppy-filled Sleepy

Valley. Instead of succumbing to the tightly laced bodice, Snow White would only fall for the poisoned comb and apple. One idea was that after Snow White recovers from the poisoned comb, the magic mirror informs the Queen, who flies into a rage and smashes the mirror to pieces. The mirror then reassembles itself, mocking the Queen and prophesying her demise. The storymen eventually deemed it more dramatic to have Snow White "die" just once and more romantic for her to be awakened by a kiss. That way, Snow White would also come off as a lot less gullible.

It also seemed more romantic to have Snow White and the Prince meet well before the climactic kiss. In the final film, they meet briefly in the castle courtyard, but in early treatments Prince Charming played a much more prominent, flamboyant role, as did his horse. In the Prince's first scene, he vaults the courtyard wall and gives Snow White a kiss by the wishing well. After she runs off, he serenades her, singing and playing the mandolin, but becomes so excited he falls into a fountain and exclaims, "She loves me!" All this is being watched by the Queen who, jealous, has her guards arrest the Prince and drag him to the dungeon. There, the Queen proposes marriage, but, for some reason, he refuses. Using magic, she manipulates some chained skeletons like marionettes to amuse him. She points to one skeleton chained to the wall, a "Prince Oswald" (a jab at Oswald the Lucky Rabbit, Walt's first successful character, the rights to which he lost), and exits with a dirty laugh. She later returns disguised as the witch and attempts to kill him by flooding the dungeon. The birds come to the Prince's rescue to free him from his chains. He gets into a Douglas Fairbanks-style sword duel with the guards, including swinging from the chandelier; he then calls his horse, and the horse informs him of Snow White's predicament. The prince rides off in pursuit of the witch.

Walt had long wanted to work a fantasy dance in the clouds into a Silly Symphonies short, and when he heard the song "Someday My Prince Will Come," he thought he'd finally have the chance. As Snow White finishes telling the Dwarfs a story, she would begin to daydream. In would sail the Prince on a winged horse or in a swan boat with heart-shaped sails, singing and playing an instrument. The dozens of onlooking stars encourage Snow White and the Prince to waltz in the clouds. The cherubic stars also dance, then shoot little cupid arrows. Snow White and the Prince run back to the swan boat together and depart.

It was among the many scenes the animators storyboarded that were cut, typically to keep the story moving. Other deleted scenes included:

• Snow White's mother dying in childbirth.

• Snow White in her room making fun of her stepmother by asking "Mirror, mirror on the wall..." to her own cracked little mirror.

• The Huntsman taking Snow White on horseback to pick wildflowers and returning alone.

• The Huntsman being dragged away by Nubian torturers.

• The birds helping Snow White mend the Dwarf's pants.

• Countless Dwarf gags, such as Dopey falling in a river and almost over a waterfall.

Cutting Room Floor

Full Disney-style animation is so expensive and time-consuming that rarely are entire scenes completed and then cut. But since there had never before been an animated feature, Disney had no standard to gauge pacing and length. To tighten the film, Walt ordered the most extraneous sequences, including several featuring the Dwarfs, to be deleted.

In the first, after the Dwarfs discover Snow White sleeping in their bedroom, Grumpy argues with Doc over if she should stay. Finally, Grumpy begrudgingly gives in: "She can stay till we get our gooseberry pie!" With all the bickering and a shot of Grumpy tweaking Doc's nose, Walt thought the sequence made too much of the Dwarfs' argumentativeness.

In the final film, Snow White cooks supper for the Dwarfs and sends them out to wash up, but, except for Dopey swallowing some soap, they never get to eat. Actually, a fully animated sequence followed, with the Dwarfs sloppily slurping soup, and Snow White attempting to show them how to eat it with a spoon. Happy then sings lead on "The Music in Your Soup," during which Dopey swallows his spoon and again gets the hiccups. Happy kicks Dopey in the rear, expelling the spoon and the soap he swallowed in the previous scene.

Two other deleted sequences occur after the Dwarfs are sent off to work. First, they are outside the mine trying to decide what to give Snow White as a gift. One proposes a crown, another a coach, another a harp. Grumpy suggests a mop. Characteristically, Sleepy mentions a bed which, considering their own sleeping quarters the previous night, sounds like the perfect gift.

In the next extensive, nearly completed scene, the Dwarfs begin building the bed with the help of the animals. Squirrels, chipmunks, rabbits and bluebirds deliver fluffs of dandelions to Sneezy, who stuffs them into the mattress. Sleepy, while carving a bedpost, is buzzed by a fly. He swats at it furiously with chisel and mallet, inadvertently sculpting a rabbit. As a running gag, Dopey goes around cutting Doc's and Happy's shirt tails. The sequence ends with more animals arriving to warn that the witch is at the cottage.

The scene of the witch brewing a potion in her cauldron was also trimmed by 31 seconds, deleting a shot of her adding an ingredient and, after a skull-shaped cloud of smoke rises from the brew, dipping in the apple.

Many countries thought the film too terrifying, so foreign prints had to be edited even further. On initial release, England banned the film for anyone under 12. An uncut version wasn't released in Sweden until 1992, when it was okayed for kids under seven with a parent. In that country, it had been cut by eight minutes in the 1960s and four minutes in the 1980s, trimming Snow White's escape through the forest, the witch's transformation and the thunder-and-lightning finale.

Plot Holes

• Snow White is as stainless as her name. During her mad, terrifying dash through the woods, despite falling on the ground and into water and snagging her clothes on trees, she and her outfit remain perfectly clean, dry and untorn. She also runs rather well in heels.

• If the Dwarfs are content to live in the middle of nowhere, couldn't they have settled on a cottage a little closer to the diamond mine? And what do they do with all these diamonds? Couldn't they have invested in a maid some time ago?

• If the Queen wished to appear a "harmless old peddler woman" whom Snow White would welcome into the cottage, why did she make herself so scary looking?

• Obviously the Dwarfs had good intentions in not burying the life-less Snow White, but didn't they think she would rot?

Bloopers

• Perhaps it's the early animation, but ever-smiling Snow White and Prince Charming just can't keep their mouths shut, literally. In the opening scene, Snow White hums with her mouth open. And to end the scene, a bird kisses Prince Charming on the teeth.

• At work in the mines, with diamonds sparkling everywhere, the Dwarfs seem to be picking at barren rock.

• During the Dwarfs' first trek home from the diamond mine, Dopey suddenly has a lantern which he didn't have when he started the trip.

Hidden Images

Although Disney cut the poisoned comb scene from the movie, an illustration of a comb does appear at the end of the film on the final page of the storybook.

Strange Reactions

Snow White and the Seven Dwarfs cost a then-astounding $1.5 million to produce, yet proved to be the one of the top grossing films of the year. It charmed audiences and critics alike, and the Academy of Motion Picture Arts and Sciences even presented Walt with a special Oscar and seven little miniature Oscars. The relationship between Disney and the Academy remained amiable until 50 years later in 1989, when Snow White made an unsanctioned appearance at the Academy Awards ceremony, to everyone's embarrassment. Dressed in Disney's trademarked outfit, a singer played Snow White as a whining, would-be starlet in a dreadful musical number with Rob Lowe. Disney sued. The Academy, sur-prised that someone would take exception since they had been staging dreadful musical numbers for years, issued a formal apology.

To show there were no hard feelings, four years later, Snow White returned to the Academy Awards broadcast. Disney volunteered to animate Snow White announcing the winner for Best Animated Short. But when the segment aired, the equipment malfunctioned and made it sound as if, midway through her presentation, Snow White burped.

Attraction Offspring

What makes *Snow White* an ideal theme for an amusement park attraction isn't its exciting narrative nor its endearing characters. When designers began detailed planning of Disneyland in 1954, they quickly discovered that translating a Disney film into a Disney theme park attraction is primarily about atmosphere and secondly about story. The goal became making the guests feel as if they were actually a part of the story. Snow White's most spectacular setting was the Dwarfs' diamond mine. So, in the original Snow White attraction, guests traveled in mine cars through gem-covered caverns that stretched nearly half the ride's length. From there, riders passed through the forest, approaching the Dwarfs' cottage in the distance, but at the last minute veered toward the witch's castle. Guests moved through the grasping trees to see the witch first in the cottage doorway and then on the cliff.

Exciting, guests no doubt thought, but there was one thing missing... Snow White. The early dark rides were designed for visitors to imagine themselves in the place of the main character. You weren't supposed to feel as if you were with Snow White, you *were* Snow White. Unfortunately, nobody got it and instead wondered where she was. One reason for completely remodeling Disneyland's Fantasyland in 1983 would be to add Snow White to the Snow White ride, Peter Pan to the Peter Pan ride and Alice to the Alice in Wonderland ride.

Age was an even bigger reason for the overhaul. After nearly 30 years, the carved dummies, wearing mops for wigs, had been repainted so many times they no longer resembled the characters. The entrance to the attraction featured a mural of the Dwarf's house that was painted in incorrect perspective so that the back of the house was in front. At one point, signs in the ride were accidentally repainted "To the Witch's Cottage" and "To the Dwarf's Castle."

Nevertheless, the main Fantasyland courtyard looked pretty much the way it did on Opening Day in 1955, and for those who loved the place, it would be difficult to bulldoze history. "I was nervous. It was Walt's thing and here I was tearing out the heart of Disneyland," remembered Imagineer Tony Baxter. "So one goal I had was all the rides would have 25 percent more track. I reasoned, 'Well, even if a ride's not better, I can say at least it'll be longer.'"

The new Snow White's Scary Adventure starts off on a happy, musical note in the Dwarfs' cottage before plunging guests into terror. Yet the Imagineers still didn't have enough room for the planned last scene designed to finally give the ride a happy ending. They wanted to end with the prince on horseback, the Dwarfs going up a bridge and Snow White above on the bridge. Instead, as in its original form, the witch dies and story stops cold. Artists grudgingly painted a sign reading, "And they lived happily ever after..." Oh, well, they must have figured, at least it's better than Mr. Toad's Wild Ride, which ends by sending all the riders to hell. But there would be a happy ending. Nine years later, the Imagineers installed an exact replica of the Snow White attraction at Euro Disneyland, but with the final scene intact.

- 2 -

Pinocchio
_____

The Original Tale

Using the pen name Collodi, journalist Carlo Lorenzini began
the serialized "Tale of a Puppet" in 1881 for a children's illustrated
weekly in Florence, Italy. The installments drew to a close two
years later and were compiled into a book, *The Adventures of
Pinocchio: Tale of a Puppet.*

This bizarre, disjointed morality play alternates between seeing
how rude and obnoxious the author can make his hero and then
how severely and strangely he can punish him. Let's hope Collodi
never worked at a day care center. The story begins with penniless
old Geppetto, who hopes to strike it rich by touring the world as a
puppeteer. He goes to a carpenter to get some wood, they get into
a fight, and the carpenter finally gives the old man a strange log
that cries when struck. Geppetto takes the piece of wood home but
as he begins carving it, the puppet torments him. After Geppetto
teaches Pinocchio to walk, the puppet runs out of the house. A
policeman catches him by the nose, but jails the bad-tempered
woodcarver instead.

Pinocchio returns home to find a large Talking Cricket, who lec-
tures him on the perils of disobeying his parents and not studying.
When the puppet has heard enough, he throws a mallet at the
insect, smashing it against the wall. The brat then goes out to look
for food, only to have a bucket of water dumped on his head. He
returns home and falls asleep warming his feet on the furnace.
Geppetto arrives to find Pinocchio has burned his feet off. He
promises to make him new feet if Pinocchio will go to school, and
the old man pawns his jacket to buy him a schoolbook.

The next day, Pinocchio heads for school but ends up at the puppet theater, where he trades his primer for admission. The puppets
on stage recognize their brother Pinocchio and call him to join
them. But their heartwarming reunion doesn't make for a very

exciting show and the ugly puppet master, Fire-Eater, hangs Pinocchio from a nail in the kitchen. The ogre threatens to toss Pinocchio into the fire, but has a change of heart and instead gives him five gold coins to take home to his papa.

En route, Pinocchio is diverted by the Fox and the Cat, who tell him of a magic meadow in Foolville, where he can plant his five coins in the ground and have them grow into two thousand. After dinner and a nap at the Red Crab Inn, Pinocchio continues his trek to the Field of Miracles and passes the cricket's ghost, who warns him to go to school and avoid thieves. Pinocchio then runs into the Fox and Cat, with sacks over their heads, who demand his money or they'll kill his papa. The puppet puts up a fight, bites off the cat's paw and escapes.

He reaches the cottage of a beautiful, blue-haired girl, who explains that everyone there is dead and she's just waiting for her coffin. There, the hoodlums catch up with the puppet, hang him from a tree and plan to return for his coins in the morning. But the blue-haired girl has a giant falcon untie him and a poodle coachman bring him to her. She lays Pinocchio in bed and calls three doctors: a crow, an owl and the Talking Cricket, who tells her how naughty the puppet is. In his defense, Pinocchio lies, causing his nose to grow longer and longer. The girl beckons thousands of giant woodpeckers to fly into the room and peck his nose back to normal size.

She wants Pinocchio and Geppetto to live with her, but the puppet again meets up with the Fox and Cat. They take him to Foolville, a land populated with beggars who have been conned— sheep of their wool, butterflies of their wings, etc. Pinocchio buries his coins and when he returns they are gone. He informs an ape judge, who imprisons him. He's released after four months and heads for the blue-haired girl's house, only to find in its place a marble tombstone saying she died of sorrow. An enormous pigeon then reports that Geppetto is building a boat to look for his missing puppet in the New World. The bird takes the puppet to the seashore, only to see the old man disappearing into the rough waters. Pinocchio dives into the sea, and after swimming all night arrives at an island. There lives the Blue Fairy, now a woman, who will allow Pinocchio to stay if he behaves and goes to school.

Pinocchio becomes the hardest-working student, but one day is tricked by seven friends into going to the beach. They fight and one classmate, hit in the head with a giant math book, drops as if dead. The children flee, leaving the police to find only Pinocchio at the boy's side. A vicious policedog chases the puppet into the sea but can't swim, so Pinocchio rescues him. Pinocchio continues swimming but is caught up in a net by a hideous green fisherman. Mistaking him for a puppetfish, the fisherman rolls Pinocchio in flour and is about to toss him into a sizzling frying pan when the policedog rescues the puppet.

Pinocchio returns to the fairy, who says if he behaves, tomorrow he'll be a real boy. He decides to invite all his friends to the next day's festivities, but his most mischievous pal, Candleflame, convinces Pinocchio to catch a coach to Funland, where there's no school, only fun. The boys go, but after five months of playing, they awaken to discover they've grown donkey ears. They soon turn entirely into donkeys and are sold by the Coachman.

A ringmaster buys Pinocchio to perform at the circus. On opening night, Pinocchio twists an ankle jumping through a hoop, so the ringmaster sells his lame beast to a man who plans to drown him and use his skin for a drum. The man ties a heavy rock to the donkey's neck and throws him in the sea. But the fairy sends a school of fish who eat his flesh and hoofs, revealing wood instead of bones. Pinocchio swims away and spots a blue goat on a rock. But before he can reach it, he's swallowed by a gigantic shark. Inside is a starving Geppetto. Pinocchio leads the old man out of the sleeping shark's mouth and helps him swim to safety. ˙

They find a thatched hut, which had been given to the Talking Cricket a day earlier by the blue goat, heartbroken she would never again see Pinocchio. The puppet goes to get his papa a glass of milk. A farmer offers him a glass if he'll pump water, since his donkey Candleflame is dying from overwork. Pinocchio returns every day for five months to earn milk for Geppetto and learn other tasks. He makes enough to buy a new outfit, but instead gives all his money to the fairy's snail, who says the fairy is penniless and dying. That night, Pinocchio dreams the Blue Fairy forgives him. He awakens to see his former wooden body lifeless in a chair and that he has turned into a real boy.

The Disney Version

Collidi's tale certainly provided the Disney crew with plenty of exciting adventures to animate. But along with all the action came a selfish, mean-spirited hero and an odd lot of supporting players. Perhaps Collodi had the right idea when he tried to kill off the malicious brat by hanging him after fifteen installments. He only invented the guardian fairy to appease the public and his editor.

Disney's storymen would have to sand out the characters' rough edges. They originally conceived their puppet as a similarly sarcastic, rambunctious, Charlie McCarthy-type wise guy. He looked like a real wooden puppet, with a long nose, peaked cap, shoestring tie, bare wooden hands and dwarf shoes. But, after six months of work, Walt realized the lack of appeal of such an unsympathetic title character and scrapped all drawings.

Before the animators returned to work, Walt wanted characters the audience cared about and a story with heart. Pinocchio's cockiness gave way to innocence and curiosity. He was drawn more like a real boy, with a button nose, bulgy cheeks, big eyes, big ears, child's Tyrolean hat, round tie, four-fingered gloved hands and regular shoes.

They also gave him a conscience. At first, Pinocchio's conscience was to be shown by splitting his personality and showing him arguing with himself. The role was then given to the beleaguered cricket. Jiminy started as a true cricket—a cross between a cockroach and a grasshopper, with toothed legs and waving antennae. He was a pompous old fellow given to flowery speeches and mixed metaphors. Again, Walt demanded a more likeable, more accessible character. Animator Ward Kimball did drawing after drawing, gradually excising all insect appendages and basically ending up with a little man in spats and a tailcoat. As his appearance became more humanized, Jiminy Cricket became more cheerful and spry. He sang, danced and traded in his cane for an umbrella. And he would never be too far from Pinocchio to remind him to behave. He became the puppet's—and the movie's—compass.

As originally conceived, Geppetto combined the mannerisms of the dwarf Doc with the look of the voice actor, character actor Spencer Charles, crotchety yet with a heart. After shooting nearly

100 feet of experimental animation, Walt thought the character came across as too strong and abrasive, just as in the book. A mellower, more innocent voice was found in Christian Rub and a charming new character emerged, one who believably yearned for a son of his own.

Even Geppetto's mischievous cat, Figaro, was transformed into a fluffy kitten.

The number of villains was condensed, but their personalities were more fully realized and their motives more believable. Menacing Stromboli the puppet master wouldn't want to punish Pinocchio for ruining his show, but would want to keep him for accidentally improving it. The flamboyant, smooth-talking Fox and the inept Cat would strike a deal with the sinister Coachman to lure Pinocchio to Pleasure Island. Mel Blanc recorded a full voice track for Gideon the Cat, but as with Dopey, whose whimsical, Harpo Marx-like persona made him *Snow White's* most comic and popular creation, Disney decided to make the Cat mute. All that remains of Blanc's work in the film is a single hiccup.

The storymen boiled the plot down to a handful of the book's key adventures, then began adding cute Disney touches, many of which were dropped anyway. Early treatments are filled with scenes and bits of business that didn't make it to animation:

• After Pinocchio sets his finger on fire, Geppetto explains in a bedtime story, "The Mighty Tree," that the boy is made of wood and that his grandfather was a proud monarch of the forest.

• The climax of the marionette show was to be a jungle scene "in which the music is treated in an unusual modern manner, building up to a strong climax of banging Ubangi puppets and Pinocchio finishing up as the star of the show."

• A slightly different montage would show the forbidden things to do on Pleasure Island: smashing lampposts and windows, tracking mud into model homes, carving names on furniture, breaking up effigies of school teachers and teachers' pets, gunning down effigy cops in a shooting gallery.

• Pleasure Island also had a darker adjunct, Bogyland, filled with all sorts of bizarre-looking monsters.

• Geppetto, Figaro and goldfish Cleo, sailing over the choppy sea to rescue Pinocchio, take a short cut through the Narrows; it's dangerous but they have to get there quickly. Within sight of Pleasure Island, Geppetto says, "Nothing can stop us now," when they are swallowed by Monstro, guardian of the Terrible Straits.

• After Pinocchio escapes from Pleasure Island, the Coachman tells the Fox and the Cat he will pay plenty for the lad dead or alive so the law doesn't learn of their business. Another montage would show Jiminy and Pinocchio, trying to cover up his ears and tail, as they battle their way home through a snowstorm, hiding by day, traveling by night, like hunted criminals. The Fairy informs Pinocchio and Jiminy of Geppetto's fate by reading them a letter that washed up in a bottle. The Fox and Cat then intercept him on his way to rescue Geppetto and, learning of his ambition to be a real boy, promise they can arrange it. Pinocchio won't be swerved. They struggle, Pinocchio runs away, the Fox and Cat give chase and run right into the arms of the law.

• After bringing home the now human Pinocchio, Geppetto gives him a birthday party and a gift—a cute little puppet in the likeness of his former self. Figaro and Cleo feast on cake, while Jiminy dances for them.

At least three songs were recorded but not used: "As I Was Saying to the Duchess," a ditty sung by Walter Catlett as Honest John the Fox; "I'm a Happy-go-lucky Fellow," sung by Cliff Edwards as Jiminy Cricket and included seven years later in *Fun and Fancy Free*, and "Three Cheers for Anything," sung by the boys on the coach as they head for Pleasure Island. Lampwick (Frankie Darro) supplied the catchiest lines, with an at-first-reluctant Pinocchio (Dickie Jones) finally joining the chorus.

Disney also had songwriters work on ideas for at least two other numbers that changes in the story would make unneccessary, for when the marionettes warn Pinocchio to flee and for a lie Pinocchio would sing as his nose grew.

Plot Holes

• Geppetto has a reputation as a lovable, old toymaker, yet he's actually a little twisted. He torments his cat with the puppet, smokes in bed, snores, packs a gun under his pillow, and is so lazy he makes the cat walk across the bedroom and open a window that is within his own reach.

- Funny that Honest John should be so surprised to see a talking puppet—he's a talking, upright-walking, fully dressed fox!

- Just curious. Shouldn't Pinocchio turn into a *wooden* donkey?

- Two inconsistencies, in particular, always bothered Ward Kimball. First, after helping Pinocchio escape from Stromboli, the Blue Fairy says it is the last time she can help him. Yet later, as a dove, she provides the note filling him in on Geppetto's whereabouts. Second, Pinocchio spends forever on the bottom of the ocean, with no obvious side effects. Then, once he finally gets out of the water, he drowns.

Bloopers

- Geppetto paints Pinocchio's eyebrows black, then dips his brush in water to clean it. He next dips his brush in red paint and paints the puppet's mouth black.

- Jiminy Cricket cozies up to sleep on the end of a fiddle and kicks his shoes off in front of him. He is roused by the arrival of the fairy and goes to get his shoes, which are some distance away, and sitting neatly heel to heel.

- In shots of Geppetto in bed, there is a window right above it. Yet in long shots the window is well to the right of his bed.

Strange Reactions

Although *Pinocchio* is one of the most beautifully animated films ever made, it flopped in its first release. Due to its tremendous production cost of $2.6 million and the closing of overseas markets due to World War II, *Pinocchio* initially lost more than $1 million.

To make matters worse, Collodi's nephew implored the Italian Ministry of Popular Culture to sue Walt Disney because Pinocchio didn't look Italian enough. He claimed the character was depicted "so he easily could be mistaken for an American." No mention was made as to whether brash Pinocchio acted Italian enough.

Attraction Offspring

In early Disneyland designs, *Pinocchio* was planned to be represented by a water chute thrill ride. Passengers in small crafts would ascend the interior of Monstro, then enjoy a breath-taking slide down his tongue into a pond. Instead, a kinder, gentler canal boat ride was built which began by entering Monstro's mouth. Although when the attraction first opened there was little to see, a year later the barren banks would be adorned with miniature settings from Disney classics. Storybook Land's charm lies in its hand-crafted detail. Tiny toys are barely visible through the opalescent front windows of Geppetto's Woodcarving Shoppe. The miniature mailbox even has Pinocchio's name on it.

A full-scale dark ride was designed for the park in 1976 to fit in the Fantasyland Theater. Guests would ride through the Adventures of Pinocchio in vehicles designed after Geppetto's wood-carved toys. But everything was put in storage for a few years, before being revived for the grand opening of Tokyo Disneyland. The following year, a new, improved Pinocchio's Daring Journey was built as part of the entirely remodeled Fantasyland at Disneyland.

Hidden Images

Next to Disneyland's new Pinocchio ride would be a Pinocchio-themed Village Haus restaurant. After the structure was entirely built, glowing green exit signs had to be placed over all the doors. Unfortunately, there was a structural beam directly over the center of the main doors, blocking installation of a light. A light could placed to the right or the left, but either way it would look like the electrician was drinking and accidentally put it off center. Tony Baxter had an idea to provide balance: painting Figaro on one side holding a rope that draped over the beam and hooked onto the tilted exit sign. When building a replica of the Village Haus restaurant at Euro Disneyland, there was no structural beam over the door. Instead, Baxter put the exit sign over the center and Figaro off to the side with a knowing, satisfied expression that says, "We got it right this time!"

- 3 -

Fantasia

The Disney Version

Walt was fond of saying, in regards to his entertainment empire, that it all started with a mouse. *Fantasia* certainly did. The idea of an extended Silly Symphony originated as a two-reel Mickey Mouse cartoon version of Paul Dukas' famous piece of classical music *The Sorcerer's Apprentice*. After a chance meeting with Walt, Leopold Stokowski agreed to conduct the orchestra for the short, but suggested making it an entire *Concert Feature* demonstrating various pieces of classical music. Walt passed on the feature idea, until he saw the production costs rise on *The Sorcerer's Apprentice*. He would have to expand it if he ever hoped to recoup his investment.

Looking for suitable music, Walt, Stokowski, the writers and story artists considered and developed concepts for dozens of possibilities, including Wagner's "The Ride of the Valkries" and "Pilgrims' Chorus," Stravinsky's *The Firebird, Petrouchka* and *Reynard*, Von Weber's "Invitation to the Dance," Mozart's *The Magic Flute*, Debussy's *La Mer*, Holst's *The Planets*, Saint-Saëns' *Danse Macabre*, Weinberger's *Schwanda the Bagpiper*, Strauss' *Don Quixote* and "Till Eulenspiegel," Kodály's *Háry János*, Prokofiev's *The Love for Three Oranges*, Berlioz's "Roman Carnival Overture," Rimski-Korsakov's "Flight of the Bumblebee," and even "Pop Goes the Weasel."

At each story meeting, new selections were substituted and the order reshuffled. The final program featured Bach's *Toccata and Fugue in D Minor*, Tchaikovsky's *Nutcracker Suite*, Beethoven's *Symphony No. 6*, *The Sorcerer's Apprentice*, Ponchielli's *Dance of the Hours*, Stravinsky' *Rite of Spring*, Mussorgsky's *Night on Bald Mountain*, and Schubert's "Ave Maria."

Each piece suggested a different storyline. "*Fantasia* did have a book," said Joe Grant. "The book was the music. We had to find a story in there. We were on a quest. Dick (Huemer) and I would listen to the music for months and months. Everything was found in the music."

When Walt asked for music to accompany an evolutionary look at the origins of life, Stokowski suggested the controversial *Rite of Spring*, originally composed to depict caveman rituals. Huemer recalled the translation from music to pictures: "There's nothing to start with, except for the music, only blank boards and a lot of dinosaurs. What do they do? What does this music suggest to you? It suggests a fight. This wailing music suggests the trek of the dinosaurs seeking water from the dried land where the mountains have risen and the earth has dried, the swamps drained...they have to find water. Stravinsky's music suggested this eerie, mournful scene of staggering through the swirling dust. You see some fall dead and others struggle on. They become silhouettes in the murk. We envision their extinction to the strains of the music."

Other selections, such as *The Sorcerer's Apprentice* and *Night on Bald Mountain*, were composed with established narratives in mind. After deciding on "Entrance of the Little Fauns" from Pierné's *Cydalise et le Chevre-Pied*, Huemer and Grant began designing a host of Greek mythological characters—fauns, centaurs, cupids, Bacchus, Minerva, Jupiter. But in trying to construct a narrative, they found the music provided no visual contact, no contrasting phrases, no pauses, nothing to hook the animation on. "This music would just go straight ahead. We couldn't stop it, we couldn't cut it, and here come the fauns, and here come the centaurs, and here comes Jove throwing thunderbolts...we couldn't find a place to put all this fine pictorial material in," Huemer said, noting that they "had assembled a cast with no place to go if we dropped the idea of *Cydalese* entirely... So Joe and I looked around for another piece of music and decided on Beethoven, the 'Pastoral Symphony,' which is about someone's feelings on their journey into the country, and other bucolic matters. So we went ahead and laid it out and presented it to Walt and he went along with it. But Stokowski didn't like it at all. He said, 'Beethoven didn't mean this, he meant human reactions and their salubrious feelings.' But somehow we brushed aside his objections and went ahead."

Initial sketches for the scene depicted languorous, bare-breasted nymphs reclining by rainbow-colored pools. Walt, though, wanted something a little more upbeat, and the beauties were recast as centaurettes as part of a drunken romp.

The Hays Office didn't like either approach. In a November 24, 1939 letter, the Censor Board warned Disney "against the possibility of too realistically portraying some of your characters such as for instance, in the second movement of Beethoven's symphony, 'By the Brook,' the characters described as female centaurs, or centaurettes, should not be part the body of a horse and part a beautiful female body showing breasts. In the third movement, please avoid showing anything sensually suggestive in the action of Bacchus chasing one of the centaurettes. In the Arabian dance, care should be used in the portrayal of the shy harem girls, and in their oriental dance, there must be no forward or excessive body movements. Care must so be used in the bubble dance in the *Dance of the Hours*."

After viewing the scenes, censors demanded that the animators go back and add flower bras to cover some centaurettes' breasts. But the scene remained somewhat risqué—and ripe for reproach.

Undeterred, Walt's plans for *Fantasia* grew greater and greater. He considered using 3-D glasses for *Toccata and Fugue* and spraying appropriate scents and perfume in the theaters during suitable moments in the film. Stokowski suggested gunpowder as "a very exciting smell" to accompany the magical incantations of *The Sorcerer's Apprentice*. The main obstacle to smell-o-vision would be airing out the auditoriums between performances.

Walt also wanted to use a projector that could project 180 degrees around a theater, so when the enchanted brooms went out of control, their shadows would would march down each side of the theater. Instead, he settled for Fantasound, a forerunner of Surroundsound.

As his excitement for the project grew, Walt wanted to issue a partially new *Fantasia* each year, every few months replacing an old number with a newly animated one. That way, people would look at it not so much as music frozen on film, but as live and constantly changing, like a concert or ballet. They would have to ask not only where and when *Fantasia* was playing but *what Fantasia* was playing.

Disney got as far as animating one whole sequence for inclusion in a future *Fantasia*, set to the tranquil "Clair de Lune." Six years later, the animation was reset to "Blue Bayou" and inserted in *Make Mine Music*, along with another previously scrapped idea, "Peter and the Wolf." "Flight of the Bumble Bee" was finally used as a swing version, "Bumble Boogie," in *Melody Time*.

Cutting Room Floor

"The Pastoral Symphony" continued to come under attack not just for its sexual images but also for featuring some offensive racial characterizations. Bacchus is attended by two Nubian centaurettes who have the bodies of zebras instead of horses. The pair was edited out in later rereleases of the picture, expect for a brief glimpse when they first enter with Bacchus. Even worse was a servile, bare-breasted black centaurette who polished the hooves of the white centaurettes. All traces of her were eliminated by reframing four shots and trimming others.

Strange Reactions

Walt's bravest, most ambitious experiment turned out to be his most sensational flop. Critics and audiences, perhaps expecting a Mickey Mouse cartoon, didn't know what to make of it. But there were other reasons: foreign markets still closed due to the war, the limited number of theaters that installed the expensive Fantasound equipment, and, frankly, many people found the film pretty dull.

It sounds almost sacrilegious, but as one anonymous old-timer explained, *Fantasia* is boring for three reasons: (a) It has no continuity. Compilations rarely do, but a lack of flow and direction is especially deadly for feature animation. As soon as you grow attached to one character, he's out of the movie. There's no continuous story to carry audiences anywhere and, as a result, no momentum. The movie stops and starts again every ten minutes. Worst of all are the long interludes with musicologist Deems Taylor. I want school credit the next time I have to watch his scenes without a fast-forward button.

(b) *Fantasia* is lo-o-o-o-o-ong. On opening night, it clocked in at 135 minutes plus an intermission. *Snow White* set the standard at 87 minutes; you'll see a lot of animated features shorter but few longer. Disney quickly re-edited *Fantasia* to 120 minutes and then 82 minutes, deleting *Toccata and Fugue*, numerous shots of Stokowski conducting, and the special stereophonic soundtrack so it could play in more movie theaters. But no matter how Disney sliced it, audiences still required a post-"Ave Maria" wake-up call.

(c) *Fantasia* is scientifically engineered to induce sleep. Watch the movie sometime and count the yawns. Various fairies and wood nymphs yawn. Dinosaurs yawn. Mickey yawns. The Sorcerer yawns. Zeus yawns. A pegasus yawns. A centaurette yawns. A cherub yawns. Ostriches yawn. A hippo yawns twice. From *The Nutcracker Suite's* drowsy-eyed fish to Chernobog's big stretch after a hard day of demonizing, it's one character after another waking up and going back to sleep again.

In hindsight, it sounds better to say the film was simply ahead of its time. As the years passed, *Fantasia* began receiving the recognition its artistry deserved. But the complaints also kept coming, over everything from the topless cupids to accusations that the dancing hippos and elephant made fun of overweight people. Classical music purists complained about the textural editing and deletions in "The Pastoral Symphony" and how in *The Nutcracker Suite*, the original order of the movements was altered and the first two movements were omitted entirely. And Stravinsky, in his later years, objected to everything about *The Rite of Spring*, including the rearrangement and editing of the score, the dinosaurs and the performance itself.

"Who cares what they think," huffed Huemer. "I mean we're in the entertainment business, and music's a very arbitrary thing, isn't it? You can say this music represents a storm; the next guy says no, it represents a battle, or another guy says it represents an earthquake—and they would all be right, because who's to say? So we say that Beethoven music reminds us of fauns cavorting and centaurs. So go prove it doesn't!"

Then, after the film's 1969 rerelease proved a cult hit among college-age kids looking for a hallucinogenic experience, conservative groups began picketing movie theaters for screening Disney's animated "drug fantasies." Hippie-era moviegoers liked to sit in

Disney Tragedy Trivia Quiz

(Answers on next page)

1. In *Snow White and the Seven Dwarfs*, number of times Snow White screams in terror:
(a) 3. (b) 6. (c) 9.

2. In *Pinocchio*, number of instances of violence or other unfavorable behavior, as cited by *Playboy*:
(a) 19. (b) 31. (c) 43.

3. In Disney animated features, number of villains who plummet presumably to their death:
(a) 3. (b) 6. (c) 9.

4. Number of Disney fully and partially animated features that show heavy drinking or drunkenness:
(a) 4. (b) 8. (c) 16.

5. In *101 Dalmatians*, number of times someone is called an idiot:
(a) 0. (b) 7. (c) 14.

6. In Disneyland, number of graveyards:
(a) 2. (b) 5. (c) 8.

7. Number of types of deviant behavior promoted by "Yo Ho (A Pirate's Life for Me)," the Pirates of the Caribbean theme song:
(a) 10. (b) 20. (c) 30.

8. In Disney animated features, number of climactic forest fires:
(a) 2. (b) 4. (c) 6.

9. In *The Aristocats*, number of scenes in which we see the butler's underwear:
(a) 4. (b) 6. (c) 8.

10. In *The Lion King*, number of major characters who violently attack their co-stars:
(a) 7. (b) 9. (c) 11.

Disney Tragedy Trivia Quiz Answers

1. (b) 6. Snow White shrieks once when she sees the huntsman about to stab her, and five times during her flight through the forest. When she awakens to see the animals surrounding her in the forest and the Dwarfs surrounding her in their bedroom, she yelps more in surprise than terror.

2. (c) 43. The August 1993 issue of *Playboy* noted 25 instances of battery, nine acts of property damage, three slang uses of "jackass," three acts of violence involving animals, two shots of male nudity, and one instance of implied death.

3. (c) 9. Fatally falling are the witch in *Snow White*, Lucifer in *Cinderella*, the bear in *Fox and the Hound*, Ratigan in *Great Mouse Detective*, Roscoe and DeSoto in *Oliver & Co.*, McLeach in *Rescuers Down Under*, Gaston in *Beauty and the Beast*, and Frollo in *Hunchback of Notre Dame*.

4. (c) 16. *Pinocchio* (at Red Lobster Inn and Pleasure Island), *Fantasia* (Bacchus, Jacchus), *Dumbo* (Dumbo, Timothy), *Saldos Amigos* (Donald Duck), *Make Mine Music* (Grandpa Coy), *Adventures of Ichabod & Mr. Toad* (Weasels at Toad Hall), *Sleeping Beauty* (the kings, lackey), *Sword in the Stone* (at dinner table), *Aristocats* (Uncle Waldo), *Robin Hood* (Sir Hiss), *Rescuers* (hillbilly Luke), *Pete's Dragon* (Red Buttons, Mickey Rooney and drinking buddies), *Great Mouse Detective* (Dawson), *Who Framed Roger Rabbit* (Roger), *Beauty and the Beast* (during "Gaston"), *Hunchback of Notre Dame* (during "Topsy Turvy"). The three chugs in *Pocahontas* don't qualify as heavy drinking.

5. (b) 7. Cruella calls Roger and Anita idiots, Cruella calls Horace and Jasper idiots twice, Jasper calls Horace an idiot twice, Anita calls Roger an idiot and Roger calls Pongo an old idiot—not to mention the use of witch, devil, clod, blockhead, fool, imbecile, twerp, lummox, weasel, scoundrel, horrid man and crazy woman driver.

6. (c) 8. There's the main graveyard scene inside the Haunted Mansion, a pet cemetery in front of the Mansion, a human graveyard to the left, the original pet cemetery behind the right side of the Mansion, the tombstone set of the Frontierland Shooting Gallery, a miniature cemetery next to the Alice in Wonderland church on Storybook Land, Tom Sawyer Island's graveyard (formerly in the Indian Village), and the Submarine Voyage's graveyard of lost ships.

7. (b) 20. Although many of these deeds seem redundant, the ditty celebrates plundering, pillaging, rifling, looting, kidnapping, ravaging, extorting, pilfering, filching, sacking, marauding, embezzling, hijacking, kindling, charring, inflaming, igniting, burning up the city, begging and, of course, drinking up, me hearties, yo ho!

8. (b) 4. There are curtain-closing infernos in *Bambi, Jungle Book, Lion King* and *Fox and the Hound* (the one blaze that's purposely set and the one blaze that we never see extinguished).

9. (a) 4. The old lawyer exposes the butler's boxers on the staircase, the butler's pants drop when he announces the lawyer's arrival at Madame's door, he irons his jacket without his trousers, and his underwear is bared several times during his first encounter with the farm dogs. Coincidentally, some years ago a psychiatrist, after intensely analyzing Disney cartoons, noted a remarkably high number of gags involving characters' posteriors.

10. (c) 11. Except for pacifist Zazu, every major character has at least one violent outburst (the 3 hyenas, Mufasa, Scar, Timon, Pumbaa, Nala, Simba, Sarabi, Rafiki).

Scoring: This is real life. Get used to going unrewarded for a job well done.

48

the front row, even on top of each other, smoking pot and offering advice to Mickey.

One movie house chain, National General Theaters, tried to brace its theater managers for a different type of Disney audience. "Don't get uptight about the potential audience," advised a corporate memo. "These are nice, unwashed, pot-smoking citizens. They like to buy tickets by the bundles and there is no report to date that any theater has had difficulty with crowd control." The company asked the theaters to promote the film not as typical Disney fare, but "now you sell *Fantasia* as you did *Easy Rider*. Hip youngsters come to see it as a special kind of trip." Disney didn't exactly discourage the connotation. Psychedelic posters and other ad materials featuring Chernobog and the dancing mushrooms called it "The Ultimate Experience," while the promotional kit quoted one underground review: "Disney's *Fantasia*: A Head Classic: Representation of sound as color does resemble tripping on STD, LSD, THC and various other letters in the alphabet."

The company's official position was that while *Fantasia* was still a family film, "it has Now Power to attract all types and ages of audiences, but especially the highest segment of all, the teens-to-30 group."

In 1982, Disney tried to update *Fantasia* for audiences accustomed to stereophonic sound by rerecording the entire soundtrack. Stokowski remained as the onscreen conductor, but offscreen Irwin Kostal led a new 125-piece orchestra, including four musicians who had participated in the original sessions 45 years earlier.

Kostal's new score would correct a two-frame lag that resulted from the primitive recording techniques of the 1930s, as well as transitional problems in the music caused by editing out the black centaurettes. Kostal restored a few bars of music, retimed it and smoothed it out. He also reorchestrated certain segments, such as *Toccata and Fugue*, to correspond with current tastes in music and the trend towards returning to the original composer's sketches. Unlike the sweeter, more romantic Stokowski version, Kostal's *Night on Bald Mountain* more closely reflected Moussorgsky's original, bolder composition. The narrator, musicologist Deems Taylor, was also cut.

By this time, though, Walt's oft-maligned experiment had come to be regarded as a masterpiece. The public, after years of decrying some modern movie for tinkering with revered classical music, was outraged that some modern classical musicians would tinker with a revered movie. For *Fantasia's* 1990 theatrical reissue and 1991 video cassette release, the original Stokowski-led tracks were restored and digitally remastered.

Consequently, Walt's dream of an ever-changing *Fantasia* is near. The next time you see it in theaters, it will be *Fantasia Continued*, featuring about a half dozen new sequences, including a long-ago-scrapped idea, Hans Christian Andersen's "The Steadfast Tin Soldier," and "Pomp and Circumstance" featuring Donald Duck as Noah.

Attraction Offspring

It would seem impossible to create a coherent theme park attraction from a movie filled entirely with unrelated sequences that focused not on story, character or setting, but on music, sound and color. Music has always been a key ingredient in theme parks' overall "show," but in the Fifties its role on attractions was limited to background music or accompaniment. In the Sixties, Imagineers began coordinating the music with rides' settings and making it a part of their show, using repetitious theme songs such as for It's a Small World, Pirates of the Caribbean and the Carousel of Progress.

Then, in the 1970s, advancements in audio-animatronics allowed attractions to become even more musically based; the music could be coordinated with the action. In 1971, Walt Disney World's Magic Kingdom opened with Country Bear Jamboree, a country western concert by robotic bears, and the Mickey Mouse Review, with Mickey conducting a large orchestra of characters and introducing set pieces from *Snow White*, *The Three Caballeros*, *Song of the South*, *Cinderella* and *Alice in Wonderland*. (Twelve years later, the Mickey Mouse Review was moved overseas lock, stock and audio-animatronic barrel for the opening of Tokyo Disneyland, where it plays to this day.) Disneyland soon added its own Country Bear Jamboree and replaced the Carousel of Progress with America Sings, a look at America's musical heritage.

After America Sings closed in 1988, one of the projects considered to move into its carousel theater was a Greatest Moments in Disney Musicals attraction that presented a medley and a setting from a different Disney classic on each stage. Designers especially liked the concept, even considered as a Fantasyland dark ride, since it could be constantly changed and updated by including characters and songs from the latest Disney release.

It took the Imagineers until 1992, but they finally captured a *Fantasia*-like, mixed media blend of music, sound, stunning visuals and fantastic effects in Fantasmic!, a night-time extravaganza over Disneyland's Rivers of America. A step beyond EPCOT's water/laser/fireworks show IllumiNations, Fantasmic! deftly blended movies, music, a slim storyline, fireworks, lasers, smoke, fire, mechanical characters and live performers led by the Sorcerer's mousy apprentice. Live theme park entertainment would never be the same.

- 4 -

Dumbo

The Disney Version

Pinocchio and *Fantasia* were elaborate, expensive and, on initial release, extravagant failures at the box office. *Dumbo* would be simple, streamlined and surprisingly successful.

It was even based on the thinnest of original stories, a glorified comic strip given away in a cereal box, that turned up at Disney's Story Department in the spring of 1939. "A man and his wife had written this little book that wasn't even a book. It came on a scroll that you turn," explained storyman Joe Grant. "It was about an elephant with big ears in a circus. Dick (Huemer) and I saw him as a handicapped individual and thought it would be a fun story to do."

Walt, preoccupied with more ambitious features, a bitter strike by his employees, and an impending trip to South America that would result in *Saludos Amigos* and *The Three Caballeros*, wasn't too interested in the character, but thought he might make for a nice short. Grant and Huemer had bigger, feature-length plans yet knew their boss, already turned off on the idea, would never sit still long enough to read a lengthy story treatment. So, they devised an installment plan, submitting their scenario episode by episode. One early chapter closed: "Dear Reader, if you are at all faint-hearted, or impressionable, we earnestly advise you to stop right here. Read no further! Do something else! Go to the movies—or to bed—anything; but skip the rest of this chapter." The writers were barely a quarter of the way through their treatment when Walt, the latest installment in hand, tramped into their office one morning. "This is good!" he said. "What the hell happens tomorrow?"

Grant and Huemer's script had at least the germ of every important episode that would make it to screen. Originally titled "Dumbo of the Circus," the ugly duckling story follows the baby elephant as he is ridiculed by others, separated from his mother and finally hailed as the star of the show when it is discovered his enormous ears enable him to fly.

At first, Dumbo was going to speak, but the writers quickly recognized that taking his voice away made him appear more childlike and endearing. For emotional support, they gave Dumbo a spunky little mouse and five jazz-singing crows. In the first draft, Dumbo was to consult a psychiatrist owl, Dr. I. Hoot. In the end, the writers decided to have Timothy Mouse give Dumbo a magic feather to alleviate his fear of flying.

The original ending was also condensed. The newly decorated Casey Jr. was to chug over the landscape, pulling the little circus train toward the Rocky Mountains. Inside, the gossipy elephants decide to make Dumbo the leader of the herd. One elephant tries to jump off a tub and fly with her ears, but lands on her nose. Timothy Mouse, on a big desk, manages Dumbo's contracts, signing some, tearing up others. Dumbo, in helmet and flying goggles, reclines in his private streamlined car, surrounded by a bevy of beauties who manicure him and massage his ears. His proud mother sits in an easy chair knitting him a special sweater with Dumbo's insignia and wings. The train steams toward a glorious sunset beyond the mountains. The picture dissolves to a night shot of the California and Rocky Mountain area, showing Hollywood glistening in the distance as the train wends its way toward the city of the stars.

The last sequence of the finished film was abbreviated to a quick montage of newspaper headlines, the redecorated train heading for the hills with Dumbo and the crows flying behind, and Dumbo joining his mother in the back of his private car.

Plot Holes

• The elephants' pyramid act looks pretty complicated. Shouldn't they have practiced it first? Actually, the elephants seem to know what they're doing, but they obviously have never tried it with Dumbo before.

Bloopers

• When Mrs. Jumbo goes into a rage, her shawl momentarily vanishes after a rope is thrown around her neck.

• The ringmaster has a pretty ambitious imagination. "One elephant climbs on top of another elephant until finally all *seventeen* elephants have constructed an enormous pyramid of pachyderms," he says, even though he doesn't own half that many elephants. He does proceed with the act using seven elephants (although at the start of the act he's circled by eight).

• When Dumbo and Timothy awaken to find themselves up a tree, Timothy takes a look down and sees the trunk is relatively free of branches and there is no pond or fence below. Yet when he and Dumbo fall, they break through two branches and somehow land in a pond near a fence. When we look back up at the tree, we see the broken branches—on opposite sides of the tree.

• The five crows seem to have a puzzling effect over Dumbo's orange collar with the big yellow stripe. In three shots, the collar's yellow stripe disappears, while in two other shots, the entire collar is missing.

• Alert Oliver Stone: there may be a sixth crow on the grassy knoll. After singing "When I See an Elephant Fly," the five crows fall to the ground laughing their heads off. When we see them laughing on their backs, one of the crows looks like suspiciously like the leader, but his jacket is brown instead of blue, his shirt has no red stripes, his spats are brown instead of light purple and the sprig in his hat is light purple instead of blue. And in the next shot his cigar disappears. Then he and the other crows are quieted by the real lead crow, leaning against a fencepost back with his cigar and traditional outfit.

Strange Reactions

Dumbo is the white elephant of Disney classics. The film was rereleased infrequently to theaters and was one of Disney's first features shown on television and released on video. Quality was never the problem; the movie is funny, sweet, exciting and has catchy tunes. Opening to audiences staring down the barrel of World War II who yearned for the triumph of good over evil and underdogs over bullies, it charmed about every everyone...except Walt. With *Pinocchio* and especially *Fantasia*, Walt seemed intimately involved with every frame, betting his finances, reputation and future on bold experiments that extended the boundaries of animation, art and filmmaking. Audiences, for their part, went nuts over a shorter (63 minutes), cartoonier, low-budget quickie that Walt, frankly, wasn't too involved with. He was especially angered when *Time Magazine* ran a big feature story on the Dumbo phenomenon—knocked off the cover after the bombing of Pearl Harbor—in which his crew made it sound, Walt thought, like he had nothing to do with the picture. When Walt first aired the film on TV, it ran seriously edited, minus most of the credits.

Huemer imagined Disney didn't actually come to grips with the movie until the animators, in effect, paid homage to *Dumbo's* surrealistic "Pink Elephants on Parade" by plagiarizing the concept as the "Heffalumps and Woozles" nightmare in *Winnie the Pooh and the Blustery Day*, released two years after Walt's death. "Walt was that way," Huemer said. "He had to own lamb. Until the mother licks the lamb clean and makes it hers, she won't nurse it."

Attraction Offspring

A month after Opening Day in 1955, Disneyland visitors could commandeer their own airborne pachyderms on a carnival-type Dumbo the Flying Elephant attraction. Interestingly, original plans called for all the elephants to be painted pink, simulating Dumbo's drunken nightmare.

In the 1970s, the flying elephant nearly got its own area at Disneyland. Dumbo's Circus, though light on the Dumbo and heavy on the circus, would feature acts performed by the least qualified character: acrobatics by Goofy, ballet by Hyacinth Hippo, and so on. Guests could meet Pegleg Pete in the cook tent. A Pleasure Island-themed section would lead to the then-proposed Pinocchio's Daring Journey ride.

Dumbo's Circus was designed as an adjunct to Discovery Bay, an entire new land based on an upcoming science fiction film. "Discovery Bay was banking on *Island at the Top of the World*," explained Imagineer Tony Baxter. "We thought this would make our mark in science fiction and put us back in the live action business, but it was a terrible movie. It bombed and it killed Discovery Bay (and Dumbo's Circus) along with it. We did get some ideas from (Discovery Bay), like the airship, into Euro Disney's Discoveryland."

And there's at least one sign of Dumbo's Circus now at Disneyland. While rebuilding the Dumbo the Flying Elephant ride for the remodeling of Fantasyland, the Imagineers remembered that an elaborate, two-foot-tall model had been built of Dumbo's Circus, with its centerpiece a pile of collapsed elephants. They used one elephant to make a mold to cast the finials that surround the new Dumbo ride. "We never throw anything away," Baxter smiled.

- 5 -

Bambi

The Original Tale

Felix Salten's *Bambi: A Life in the Woods* (1928) is a coming-of-age story of survival for the title deer, who is about the only character still standing by the last page. Newborn Bambi, inquisitive about all the sights and sounds of the forest, meets up with birds, insects, the sincere old Hare and the vain old Owl. He meets his cousins, shy Faline and thin, weak Gobo, and sees some silent, aloof stags. And he learns of Man and the necessity of being ever cautious, alert and ready to run.

Nearing adolescence, Bambi, Faline and Gobo often find themselves abandoned by their mothers. Once while crying for his mama, Bambi is chastised by the old Prince, the largest, oldest, most mysterious stag in the woods.

The first winter is a harsh one. Hunters come and all the animals flee. One shot kills Bambi's mother, and Gobo, exhausted, falls to the ground, a sure victim.

Bambi grows older and grows antlers. He develops romantic feelings for Faline and fights off two older stags for her. He occasionally runs into the old Prince, who one day saves Bambi from a hunter imitating Faline's voice.

Months later, a fatter, cockier Gobo returns to the forest. He impresses the others with tales of how wonderful Man is, how Man fed and cared for him. But the old stag pities Gobo. A few weeks later, the now fearless Gobo is out in the open and shot.

Bambi begins spending less time with Faline and more with the old Prince. Once, Bambi is shot by a hunter but the stag prods him to continue running. He leads him to safety, to rest and recuperate. Later, the great stag takes Bambi to see the body of a freshly slain poacher, illustrating that Man is not all powerful. With Bambi near full maturity, the aging Prince bids a final farewell to his son.

The Disney Version

Walt first considered *Bambi* as an animated feature in 1935, but there was one problem. Live action director Sidney Franklin had bought the rights two years earlier. Disney, despite having no intention to present a realistic portrayal of deer living in a forest, was able to persuade Franklin to allow him to make it, with Franklin's input, of course.

Walt's primary desire was to transform the beautiful words into beautiful pictures, even though it would take the fast-evolving art of animation seven years to catch up with him. His would be a distilled beauty of nature, intensified by a feeling of realism, yet with no sign of ugliness, cruelty or dying animals.

His plan of attack was first to get a solid grasp on the characters and then build the story. In early 1937, he appointed Perce Pearce and Larry Morey to head up the story crew. They discovered that although the animals spoke to each other in the original, Salten had tried to keep the anthropomorphism to a minimum, making the animals true to their natural attitudes and behaviors. Disney's characters became much more anthropomorphic, as did the storyline. Salten attempted to maintain a distance between the sexes and the species. Disney's fuzzy creatures would be part of one big forest family.

Bambi's love interest, Faline, was in, but her pathetic brother, Gobo, was cut entirely. The annoying rabbit who is killed near the end of the book was initially recast as Mr. Hare, head of a large family and well respected in the forest neighborhood. He would be a well-mannered philosopher, ever trying to tell Bambi a story, but always chased off by a fox before he can finish it. During the climatic run through the forest, in which many animals are slain and Bambi eventually is shot, the hare would lie dying, and Bambi would wait to finally hear the end of his story before running off, moments before the hunter arrives.

For Bambi's childhood pals, the artists drew a cute squirrel and chipmunk. In one planned sequence, Bambi was to meet an ill-tempered bee on the meadow who warns him to watch where he's eating. Soon after, Bambi tells his pals he thinks he's swallowed a bee. He has a buzzing in his tummy and soon starts hiccupping.

His friends try comedically to dislodge it, and finally the bee shoots out of Bambi's mouth, with hiccups of his own.

Eventually Bambi's buddies evolved into a skunk, Flower, who originated as a gag during Bambi's introduction to the forest, and a precocious bunny, Thumper. Thumper started as one of Mr. Hare's children and eventually assumed his father's place in the story. The story crew even considered giving him dad's death scene. In the first treatment, Bambi's mother introduced him to the wonders of nature, a charming scene but a dull one. As Thumper's part grew, he took over this function as well.

Even the unseen villain, Man, got off the hook, to some degree. One scene in the book has the hunters' dogs cornering a fox, holding it prisoner until their masters arrived, as the animals of the forest taunted the dogs for being mindless slaves to cruel Man. Disney had planned to have an owl, squirrels and other critters torment the dogs as they kept Faline at bay, but changed it so Bambi comes to the rescue and heroically fights off the dogs.

One area of disagreement was how to depict the slain hunter. The artists storyboarded all sorts of possibilities, from a hazy shot of a hand near a rifle to an explicit full body shot. The subtle approach might have less impact, yet the excessively graphic might prove too unsettling. Walt put it up to the audience. The boards were filmed into a "storyreel" and screened in front of a test audience. When it came to the shot of the dead man in the forest, director Dave Hand had included the strongest drawing. The audience of 400 gasped in horror, and Walt demanded the entire sequence cut from the picture.

The film would be sweet—and simple. The original novel contained 223 pages of text with 10,000 words of dialogue, and the first screenplay draft came in at 5,000 words. "The characters talk too much," Walt noted. "In the book, it's different. We're working with a medium that calls for action, so let's cut all unnecessary conversation." Every word that could be cut was, such as the Old Prince's scripted farewell to Bambi: "The time has come for you to take my place in the forest. Goodbye, my son." Their exchange of looks, the father walking off and the son stepping confidently to the foreground said it all. In total, the finished film contains 950 words of dialogue.

Bloopers

• While investigating the wonders of nature, Bambi happens upon a mother possum to the right of her three babies, all hanging upside down by their tails from a tree branch. Bambi turns his head, and we then see the possums as he does—rightside up. Except that the mother remains on the right, so that her babies are now to her left.

• Faline's eyes are blue, except during the forest fire sequence when she is pursued by the hunting dogs and saved by Bambi, when her eyes are brown.

• After the fire, a raccoon is on the riverbank licking its young. The child suddenly vanishes, and the parent continues licking air.

Attraction Offspring

Fortunately, the Imagineers were wise enough never to give any of the rides a *Bambi* theme, since the most logical attraction would be the shooting gallery.

III

Disney Discouraged
Potluck
1943-1949

"It is a fundamental fact that no cook, however creative and capable, can produce a dish of a quality any higher than that of its raw ingredients."

– Alice Waters,
Chez Panisse Menu Cookbook (1982)

The Thirties for Walt was an unbroken string of successes, capped by the triumph of *Snow White*. Then, in the space of a few short years in the early Forties, came the disappointing reactions to *Pinocchio*, *Fantasia* and *Bambi*, projects into which he had invested incredible amounts of time, money and energy. His goal of one day producing an animated feature a year now seemed financial suicide. The market for short subjects was also drying up, and most of his resources were being tied up with war film assignments for the government. So, he began dabbling in live action mixed with limited animation and resigned himself to making less expensive, less ambitious compilations or "package features," often musically based.

Since package features were not much more than collections of featurettes and shorts (which Walt had been making with nothing but acclaim for twenty years), they seemed safer. "He didn't like the criticism of *Pinocchio* that it was really three different movies done by three different (animation) units. He was very sensitive to that," says writer Maurice Rapf. "Each unit could do twenty minutes in a year. A feature was too much for any one unit, so it was divided up among five units or so with a separate animation director for each. So he started to do anthologies. They were cheaper, and he could divide them up (among the units)."

Another reason, adds Joe Grant, was the studio "had a lot of people come off (after World War II), and we had to find work for them. There was no money in shorts, so we did those mini-*Fantasias*, though on a much smaller scale."

Disney also desired respect from his peers. It was time to try his hand at live action combined with increasingly less animation.

- 6 -

Song of the South

The Original Tale

Starting in 1880 with *Uncle Remus: His Songs and Sayings*, Joel Chandler Harris began collecting popular folk tales of the Old South as told through a kindly old black carpenter to the son of a plantation owner. The stories feature a wide variety of mostly animal characters, such as Brer (dialect for Brother) Possum, Brer Coon, Brer Wolf, Brer Lion, the gullible Brer Bear, the wily Brer Fox and, most often (appearing in nearly three-quarters of the 185 tales), the rascally Brer Rabbit.

Usually Brer Rabbit would be found playing pranks on the other animals, such as when he had Brer Bear stick his head in a honey tree, only to be stung by so many bees, his head swelled up and he couldn't remove it.

Brer Rabbit about to help Brer Bear get a swelled head in one Uncle Remus tale.

In Harris' most famous story, Brer Fox creates a Tar Baby to trap his nemesis.

Another time, all the four-footed creatures were arguing over who could laugh the loudest. Brer Rabbit said he could laugh the loudest because he had a laughing place, which he consented to show each of them one at a time. He took Brer Fox first, but when the fox didn't see anything, Brer Rabbit had him run back and forth through the vines and bushes. In doing so, the fox ran into a tree and jammed his head in a hornet's nest—and naturally still wasn't laughing. Then Brer Rabbit explained that's because it was *his* laughing place, not the fox's.

Often, Brer Fox tried to trap Brer Rabbit. Once the fox created a tar dummy and placed it along the side of the road. When Brer Rabbit passed by, he greeted the tar baby, but it wouldn't respond. Growing frustrated, the rabbit began pummeling the dummy, got stuck and was apprehended by Brer Fox. The rabbit pleaded to be thrown anywhere but the briar patch, which is where the fox tossed him. But, born and bred in a briar patch, Brer Rabbit escaped.

In another tale, Brer Rabbit had wandered into the fox's pea patch and was caught up in a trap. He saw the bear approaching, told him he was making a dollar a minute keeping the crows away and invited him to take his place. Brer Rabbit then ran to tell Brer Fox that his trap had caught the one stealing from his pea patch. The fox returned to batter Brer Bear with his walking stick.

The Disney Version

Although Disney had experimented mixing small amounts of live action footage with animation, he had never before made a predominantly live action feature. But he realized that to get the full impact and maximum entertainment out of the animated Uncle Remus parables, they should play off of live-action situations.

He enlisted Southern novelist Dalton Reymond to create a story to bridge the animated lessons. It quickly became apparent that not only had Reymond never written a screenplay before, but he would also need delicate assistance in handling the sensitive subject matter.

Reading an early treatment of *Uncle Remus*, the Censor Board projected that just about everyone would be offended. They said religious people wouldn't like the expressions like "Lord knows." Brits would object to the words "sissy" and "bloody." And the city of Atlanta, its Chamber of Commerce, mayor and other civic groups would protest the line "Atlanta! Dat's er mighty tur'ble place." To appease the latter, artist Mary Blair was sent on a ten-day trip to Atlanta to visit a noted local artist and historian.

Brer Rabbit, furious that the Tar Baby won't pay him any attention, soon finds himself attached to the Baby, to Brer Fox's amusement.

Most sensitive was the portrayal of blacks. The censors suggested Disney seek counsel with "some responsible Negro authorities," cautioning, "our Negro friends appear to be a bit critical of all motion picture stories which treat of their people." For good reason. Hollywood had a long history of condescending portrayals of blacks, and Reymond's and Harris' writing wasn't any more sympathetic. Both would refer to blacks as "darkeys" and had a fondness for scenes of stereotypical funny business.

So Disney hired Maurice Rapf, known for his screenwriting abilities as well as for his progressive views, to work with Reymond. But Rapf thought this was absolutely the wrong picture for him—or Disney—to be associated with. "I went to Walt and told him I didn't think he should make it, that he would get into trouble," Rapf said. "With the growing consciousness of blacks, I thought it might bring down a lot of trouble and he said, 'That's why I want you to work on it.' He knew I was a leftist."

Rapf finally relented. "What prompted me to work there was B.A. Botkin in *The Treasury of American Folklore*, which included the Uncle Remus tales. In his preface, which was about 20 pages long, he said if you read the fables carefully you find they're stories of slave resistance. Brer Rabbit symbolized the smaller, less powerful black man. Brer Fox, Brer Bear and Brer Coon were the oppressive whites, and the stories were all about how to outwit the masters," he explained. "With that in mind, I thought, 'I can make something of this,' but it quickly became muddled because Reymond had Brer Rabbit as the alter ego of the little white boy."

In his approximately 65-page treatment, Reymond had constructed a story around three Brer Rabbit fables, teaming the ruthless fox with the witless bear in pursuit of the prankish rabbit. The trouble was in the live action story. Although Reymond had set the action in the Reconstruction period, there was little evidence of it. Rapf insisited "it had to be absolutely clear it wasn't slavery. I put the situation in my story that the plantation was left to the father and mother not the grandparents, and they had no money. They couldn't pay Remus, and that's why the father left—he was supposed to be Joel Chandler Harris—to work as a journalist and send money home. He even says, 'We gotta pay these people. They're not slaves.' The plantation was supposed to look run down; the

whites' clothes were left over from more prosperous times."
Rapf also developed Uncle Remus as a much stronger character.
"I always believed in rebellion," he said. "So when Remus is told
he can't read any more stories to the boy, he packs up his things.
He's mad. He's not going to get the father, he's leaving. He says,
'I'm a free man, I don't have to take this.' And the kid isn't going
for the father, he's going for Remus. The father doesn't come until
after the kid gets hurt by a bull."
Finally, in Rapf's ending, Uncle Remus has to tell the injured
boy a story to revive him. Little Johnny would have stayed in a
coma, but comes to when he hears a story about Brer Rabbit getting hurt and getting better.

But the considerably older Reymond disagreed with most of
Rapf's suggestions. The tumultuous team eventually dissolved
when Rapf found out the married Reymond was using Rapf's name
to chase a studio mail girl. Rapf was reassigned to *Cinderella*,
Morton Grant was named Reymond's new partner, and many of
Rapf's changes started to unravel. In the finished film, the whites
become wealthy again, the boy runs away and Uncle Remus follows, and the father revives the boy.

Writing for live action did present one constraint that wasn't as
much a problem for animation, since color movies were still the
exception in Hollywood rather than the rule. "At that time there
were only three Technicolor cameras, so as soon as the cameras
would become available, that's when the screenplay would be finished," Rapf said. But Walt had one advantage. "Disney had the
inside track because everything he did was in color."

Strange Reactions

If the movie proved successful, Walt had considered it as just the
first of a series of Uncle Remus pictures. Yet, despite its rich, criti-
cally-acclaimed animation and profitable run at theaters, *Song of
the South* ended up presenting some less-than-flattering characterizations of blacks, which have hindered rereleases of the picture.

The NAACP picketed the movie in New York and other cities,
mistaking the characters for happy slaves. They also singled out
Butterfly McQueen as a hysterical Stepin Fetchit-type, a little black
boy who gets scared and rolls his eyes when he thinks he sees a

ghost, and a scene in which the plantation workers gather at the injured boy's window to sing Negro spirituals, which they saw as "Uncle Tomming."

Rapf, who tried desperately to get away from the connotations of happy slaves and other offensive stereotypes, suddenly found himself associated with what was perceived as an anti-black movie. He admitted, "It was written in 1945 and we weren't really as sensitive as we should have been."

Walt, on the other hand, was thoroughly surprised by the reaction. "Walt wasn't racist, he was hoping not to offend the blacks," Rapf said. "He had a theory that the reason why the film was picketed and particularly attacked by the Los Angeles chapter of the NAACP was because the head of the local chapter was actor Clarence Muse. He knew that Walt Disney wanted to do a Remus story, and Muse wanted to play Remus. He was a standard serious black actor, but Disney got someone else. Now others said that couldn't be true, because Muse was a technical adviser on the film, though I think if that's true he didn't do a very good job advising."

Attraction Offspring

Song of the South got its own attraction almost by accident. Three factors led to Splash Mountain, nearly 45 years after the release of the movie that inspired it. First, theme park head Dick Nunis was constantly urging the Imagineers to design a flume ride. The designers weren't as enthusiastic. After all, all the other amusement parks already had a log ride, and Disneyland would be the last one in the water, so to speak. "So, we didn't want to do it unless there was a great reason beyond a log in a flume," Tony Baxter said.

Second, into the 1980s, with the Bicentennial long gone, Disneyland's red, white and blue audio-animatronic revue America Sings was falling victim to low attendance, the same problem which had befallen its predecessor, the Carousel of Progress.

"And finally," Baxter said, "if you snapped a picture of Disneyland at a moment in time you'd see about 2 percent of all the visitors in the park in Bear County. So I had the idea of taking the characters from America Sings and putting them in a *Song of the South*-themed flume ride. We'd only have to create about ten new Brer characters and we'd have 75 to 80 figures for virtually free. In fact, several of the America Sings characters, such as Mother Possum and her babies, are on model sheets for *Song of the South*."

The Great Mr. Toad Mystery

In 1941, the studio began work on *The Magnificent Mr. Toad*, an animated featurette based on Kenneth Grahame's *The Wind in the Willows*. It was bright, lively and humorous, but after three-quarters of an hour it just ran out of gas. Disney shelved the entire picture for years, before finally deciding to trim it from 48 minutes to a half-hour and combine it with "The Legend of Sleepy Hollow" into *Two Fabulous Characters*. The film was released in 1949 as *The Adventures of Ichabod and Mr. Toad*.

But actually *Mr. Toad* was in jeopardy before it was even photographed, when one day all the elaborate background paintings for *The Wind in the Willows* mysteriously disappeared. Dick Huemer noted, "It was a great mystery and manhunt for a number of weeks with staked out cops and decoys, etcetera. Not a trace! Not a clue! Then in came a mysterious phone call tipping the studio off to go to the home of one of the gardeners, a little, shriveled, Nazi-looking guy. There they found the backgrounds all wrapped up in a big roll. He explained he found them up against the fence way over on the other side of the lot and, thinking they had been thrown away, had taken them home in the interests of the preservation of art. They believed him. Now the theory is that some shrewd character (a maniac, I presume, who is queer for backgrounds) stashed them away over there meaning to come around on the outside some dark night and complete the deal."

Some maniac. The artwork is now priceless.

IV

Disney Delighted
Classic Cuisine
1950-1959

"I feel a recipe is only a theme, which an intelligent cook can play each time with variation."

— Madame Jehane Benoit,
Enjoy the Art of Canadian Cooking (1974)

For Walt, making package features like *Make Mine Music, Fun and Fancy Free* and *Melody Time* was probably about as exciting as taping together a bunch of shorts he'd made fifteen years before. If he was going to make an animated feature, he wanted to make it his way, stretching the medium to its boundaries, opening it up and exploring all it could do. He was a sports car throttled in a school zone.

The war had forced him to put his efforts and resources into propaganda pictures, which actually kept the studio afloat; Disney produced more feet of film for training soldiers, selling bonds and lifting morale than he ever had for entertainment. Now he had the time, if not the money, to try one last time to find out if *Snow White* was a fluke: put the fairy tale formula to work one more time. Tell a story about a lovely heroine, harassed by her evil stepmother, befriended by a collection of diminutive cuties who help her overcome the forces of evil and find true love with Prince Charming. Only this time the princess-to-be would be named Cinderella.

- 7 -

Cinderella

The Original Tale

Arguably the most famous fairy tale of all time, "Cinderella" was written by Charles Perrault in the 1600s, about a nobleman who has a beautiful, kind-hearted daughter and remarries a proud woman with two equally haughty daughters. As soon as father drops out of the picture, the stepmother enslaves his daughter, who becomes known as *Cinder*ella because she often sits near the fireplace.

One day, the prince of the kingdom throws a ball and invites everyone of position, including Cinderella's stepsisters. Cinderella helps them get ready but, after they leave, she bursts into tears. Her Godmother appears and puts her magic wand to work. She turns a pumpkin into a coach, six mice into horses, a rat into a coachman, six lizards into footmen, and Cinderella's rags into a beautiful gown. The only stipulation is Cinderella may not stay out past midnight.

At the ball, the prince quickly takes to the lovely stranger. Cinderella leaves at 11:45, but returns to a second ball the next night. She enjoys herself so much that she loses track of time. Fleeing in panic as the clock strikes twelve, she loses a slipper. The prince salvages the shoe and vows to marry the girl whose foot it fits. His attendants try it on everyone in the kingdom, even the lowly Cinderella, whom it fits. Everyone is astonished, especially when she pulls the second slipper from her pocket. Her Godmother appears and magically transforms Cinderella's clothes. The prince and Cinderella marry, and she forgives her sisters, marrying them off to two great lords and giving them apartments at the palace.

The Disney Version

Whereas most of the stories on which Walt based his animated features had to be trimmed of unnecessary story elements, "Cinderella" is such a simple, straight-forward tale that it required more addition than subtraction.

The first known script was written in 1940 by Dana Cofy and Bianca Majoli. They added a few characters and gave almost everyone a fancy name: Cinderella's stepmother became Florimel de la Poche; her stepsisters, the short Wanda and the tall Javotte; her pet mouse, Dusty, and pet turtle, Clarissa; the stepsisters' cat, Bon Bon; the Prince's aide, Spink, and the stepsisters' dancing instructor, Monsieur Carnewal.

In their version, the King, Queen and Prime Minster decide to hold a ball so the Prince can meet a bride. Cinderella, after singing a work song and watching the animals stage a little acrobatic show, sees the Prince and his entourage returning to the palace. The Prince arrives at the palace, learns of the ball, and refuses to have anything to do with it until the King commands him to attend by royal decree. Spink, delivering the invitations to the ball, knocks at the de la Poche chateau, interrupting a painting class. Cinderella receives the message and hands it to Madame. A song accompanies a montage of ladies at various homes as they search for wardrobe, closing on the three de la Poches saying, "We haven't a thing to wear."

Except for some business with the mice outwitting the cat so the feline ends up wrecking the kitchen, the treatment then sticks rather close to the fairy tale, until Cinderella arrives home late from the second ball. Her stepfamily pounces on her and drags her to a dungeon in the chateau's cellar. The cat scatters the mice and lizards. Imprisoned, Cinderella sings a song about clocks (naturally). When Spink and his troops arrive at the de la Poche chateau, Dusty the mouse steals the slipper and leads everyone to Cinderella's cell. Spink wrests away the key and discovers the princess-to-be. After the big wedding, we close on Dusty in a gem-encrusted mouse hole.

Work intensified on the project in the mid-1940s, in the hands of various writers. To make the mice more a part of the story, they would make Cinderella's dress. To heighten the drama and pick up the pace of the story, the writers condensed the action from two fancy dress balls into one. Cinderella would be a much less passive character than Snow White, actually going out and getting her own Prince, but still not as bold as she could have been. "My thinking," said writer Maurice Rapf, "was you can't have somebody who comes in and changes everything for you. You can't be delivered it on a platter. You've got to earn it. So in my version, the Fairy Godmother said, 'It's okay till midnight but from then on it's up to you.' I made her earn it, and what she had to do to achieve it was to rebel against her stepmother and stepsisters, to stop being a slave in her own home. So I had a scene where they're ordering her around and she throws the stuff back at them. She revolts, so they lock her up in the attic. I don't think anyone took (my idea) very seriously."

In 1946, storyman and part-time lyricist Larry Morey joined studio music director and occasional composer Charles Wolcott to pen six songs. Cinderella would sing the hopeful "Sing a Little, Dream a Little" while overloaded with work, and "The Mouse Song" as she dressed the mice up in tiny clothes. In "The Dress My Mother Wore," she fantasizes about her mother's beautiful, old wedding dress. In an effort to resurrect the fantasy sequence deleted from *Snow White*, "Dancing on a Cloud" would accompany Cinderella and the Prince waltzing at the ball, as she imagines they are dancing on clouds. After the ball, she would sing "I Lost My Heart at the Ball," and the Prince would croon "The Face That I See in the Night."

All the songs were dreadful and, mercifully, none was used. Two years later, Walt finally called for outside help. Tin Pan Alley tunesmiths Mack David, Al Hoffman and Jerry Livingston would write all the songs that were eventually included in the movie, and a few that weren't. For the work song, Cinderella would sing "I'm in the Middle of a Muddle," in which she complains about wanting to have fun but can't because the work is piling high. The storymen then decided to turn the work scene into the fantasy number, having the overloaded Cinderella split into two and then four and eight and finally an entire regiment to do all the work. They completely storyboarded the scene, and David, Livingston and Hoffman wrote a new "Cinderella Work Song."

In the end, economy won out. The work song evolved into a number for the mice, "Cinderella," in which they decide to make the dress.

Financially strapped, Walt felt *Cinderella* might be his last chance. In a 1948 letter to a friend and fellow writer, Dick Huemer wrote: "Walt suddenly decided to hold up work on the music lesson sequence. Fergy (Norm Ferguson) and I had practically readied it for animation. In fact, he's holding up on all but a few absolutely essential story-progressing sequences."

Fully storyboarded, the music lesson sequence featured a flamboyant French music teacher who grows increasingly exasperated as one stepsister tries to play the flute and the other attempts to play the harp. At the last minute, Walt decided the sequence was extraneous and just slowed down the story, so he excised the music teacher and the harp. The scene was simplified to one stepsister on the flute and the other warbling "Sing, Sweet Nightingale" only to be interrupted by the arrival of the invitation to the ball.

Plot Holes

• What are the odds that Cinderella is the only one in the kingdom who wears that particular size shoe?

Bloopers

• The Case of the Disintegrating Milk Dish: Early on, Jaq the mouse kicks Lucifer the cat in the rear, knocking the cat's face into his milk dish. After the puss raises his puss, the dish seems to have dissolved into a puddle of milk.

• When the stepsisters hear that the just-arrived message is from the palace, they run across the room to grab it from Cinderella, with Anastasia evidently leaving her flute behind. The girls struggle over the invitation, and the Stepmother finally snatches it away and begins to read it. When we take another look at the girls, Anastasia has her flute back in hand.

• Cinderella pulls out of a chest her mother's plain old dress, which she hopes to wear to the ball, and spins it around. When birds lower the gown onto a mannequin, the dress gradually sprouts a big pink bow on the back.

• Hurriedly trying to escape Lucifer with what's left of a broken necklace, Jaq strings three beads onto Gus' tail. We cut to the cat, and then when we cut back to the mice, Jaq is only stringing bead number two onto Gus' tail.

• When the giant palace clock strikes eight, the eleven appears to read XII.

Strange Reactions

During one staff meeting, Walt announced, "Boys, if *Cinderella* doesn't make it, we're through." *Cinderella* made it, proving a smash critical and financial success that allowed Disney to continue producing feature-length classics filled with rich, beautiful, full animation through the 1950s, while other studios were cutting back in terms of output and quality.

Hidden Images

For the centerpiece of Walt Disney World's Magic Kingdom and Tokyo Disneyland, the Imagineers designed an ornate Cinderella Castle and decorated its main walkway with a big, colorful mosaic of scenes from the movie. In designing the mural, artist Dorothea Redmond looked to some co-workers for inspiration. In the scene where Cinderella is trying on the glass slipper, the page kneeling at her feet is a caricature of veteran Disney artist Herb Ryman, while the other page looking on is longtime Imagineering executive John Hench.

Imagineers also pop up in the Hall of Presidents film at the Magic Kingdom (in the gallery during the Congressional debate) and in paintings adorning EPCOT Center's American Adventure. "It's not uncommon for artists when they need a face to use one around them," explained one Imagineer.

- 8 -

Alice in Wonderland

The Original Tale

Charles Lutwidge Dodgson was a minister, mathematician and serious author who was taken most seriously when he wrote nonsense. Published under the pseudonym Lewis Carroll, his *Alice's Adventures in Wonderland* (1865) opens with Alice and her cat Dinah sitting on a riverbank listening to her sister read a book which, lacking pictures and dialogue, bores Alice. She spies an anxious White Rabbit in a waistcoat and follows him down a hole, tumbling from dull, prosaic reality into a nonsensical dream world. After falling past bookshelves and cupboards, Alice pursues the rabbit down a hall of doors. Behind one tiny door is a lovely garden, so Alice drinks from a bottle labeled "Drink Me" and shrinks to the door's size—only to realize she left the key on the table. She nibbles from a cake marked "Eat Me" and her neck shoots up like a giraffe's. She cries, the rabbit appears and, startled, he drops his gloves and fan and flees. Alice picks them and shrinks.

She then finds herself swimming desperately in her own tears with other creatures, including a mouse, parrot and dodo, who organizes a Caucus-race, a special competition in which every participant wins a prize. Alice suddenly finds herself with the White Rabbit who, mistaking her for his servant Mary Ann, orders her to fetch his gloves and fan. In his house, she sips from another "Drink Me" bottle and grows so big the rabbit can't come in. He has Bill the Lizard slide through the chimney to evict her, but Alice kicks him back out. The rabbit and his servants begin pelting the giant with pebbles, which magically turn into cakes when they hit the floor. Alice eats one, shrinks and escapes.

After eluding a monstrous puppy, she meets a large, rude caterpillar smoking a water-pipe. When Alice nibbles at one side of his mushroom, her neck again grows and an angry pigeon attacks, mistaking her for a snake. After regaining her size, she arrives at the

Sir John Tenniel's original illustrations of the White Rabbit and other characters in Lewis Carroll's book were a great influence for the Disney artists.

Duchess' house, where the Queen's Fish-Footman is delivering an invitation for a croquet party to the Duchess' Frog-Footman. Inside, the foul-tempered Duchess abuses a baby, who cries and sneezes from the pepper being tossed about by the Cook. After she tosses the baby to Alice, it turns into a pig. She then meets the grinning, occasionally invisible Cheshire Cat. Alice goes to the March Hare's house, where the mad hare, Mad Hatter and drowsy Dormouse are having a wild tea party.

Finally, she finds herself in the Queen's garden, where people-sized playing cards are painting the white roses red. The roaring Queen of Hearts arrives with the subordinate King and orders the gardeners to be executed, but Alice saves them. During a croquet game with no rules, the Cheshire Cat is sentenced to death for insulting the King, but all but his head vanishes, thwarting the beheading. Alice later meets the Mock Turtle, who sings a sad tale of his mock education and teaches her and the Gryphon the "Lobster-Quadrille."

Next, Alice arrives at the chaotic trial of the Knave of Hearts, accused of stealing tarts. The White Rabbit is the court herald, while the Duchess' cook and members of the tea party serve as witnesses. Alice, frustrated that the trial lacks rules, evidence and justice, finally rebels against the nonsense and awakens to reality.

In Carroll's sequel, *Through the Looking Glass, and What Alice Found There* (1872), Alice steps into a large mirror and enters another land where everything seems backwards. The countryside is laid out like a giant chessboard, and scenes abruptly change as she crosses over a brook into the next square. On her way to the final square where she will become a queen, she encounters the Red and White Queens and Kings, the clumsy White Knight, a garden of live flowers, and strange insects such as a rocking-horse-fly, snap-dragon-fly and bread-and-butter-fly. She also meets a host of nursery rhyme characters, including the battling Lion and the Unicorn, bickering mirror-image twins Tweedledee and Tweedledum, who tell her a twisted version of the "Walrus and the Carpenter," and Humpty Dumpty, who translates the nonsensical "Jabberwocky" and tells the joys of unbirthdays. Alice's adventure ends when she gets fed up at a chaotic dinner party in her honor.

Although Disney's storymen had difficulty deciding which of Carroll's sequences and characters to delete, they always planned to include the Mad Tea Party.

The Disney Version

At first glance, *Alice in Wonderland*, a classic of Nineteenth Century children's literature, seems a natural for Disney, the most popular children's storyteller of the Twentieth Century. After all, Walt achieved his first success in the mid-1920s with a series of silent *Alice* comedies, placing a live action girl in an animated world. In 1931, he purchased the rights to Sir John Tenniel's original illustrations and over the next two years developed ideas for a feature starring a live action Mary Pickford in an animated Wonderland. He shelved the idea after Paramount released an all-live action *Alice in Wonderland* in 1933, but resumed interest in 1937. The next year, Disney officially registered the title *Alice in Wonderland* with the Motion Picture Association of America and began work on hundreds of story sketches and paintings.

Yet the studio quickly realized that Carroll's work would not fit quite so easily into the Disney mold. Not without a fight, anyway. The book really has no story or logical progression of events, in fact, most everything that happens is illogical. There are countless characters who come and go, few of them very sympathetic, and they spout long sililoquies and engage in odd conversations and intricate wordplay.

"I wouldn't work on it," said writer Maurice Rapf. "It couldn't be done. It depends too heavily on the imagination of the reader."

In fact, one storyman, in his 161-page analysis of the book to aid development of the feature, noted, "We are going to have to change it radically, all the way through... and forget almost all of Carroll's stuff."

That wasn't really an option, either. Unlike brief fairy tales, Carroll's *Alice in Wonderland* was a full-length, well-known classic work of literature that purists would readily defend against excessive tampering. Walt, reflexively antagonistic to restraints on his creativity, seemed resigned to making the movie more out of duty than desire. "I think he felt he had to do it. People were always writing in and saying, 'Why don't you do this, why don't you do that?' I myself asked him back in 1938, 'Why don't you do *The Hobbit*?' He couldn't see it. But people constantly were saying, 'Walt Disney simply must do *Alice in Wonderland*!'" recalled

Dick Huemer. As a result of his heart not being in it, "Walt wasn't with it; he wasn't interested. He often withdrew from things he didn't quite dig."

As long as the outside world was telling him what to do, Disney might as well look beyond his gag men for input, so he enlisted respected literary luminaries to offer suggestions or write treatments and scripts. "Walt had always been the darling of the intellectuals," said Joe Grant. "He brought in Aldous Huxley, Frank Nugent and other New York literary types."

According to Huemer, Huxley silently sat in on the first five story meetings and was never seen again. "It's my personal opinion (Walt) thought (Huxley) would be a great name to associate with the picture," he said. "Walt was always very conscious of publicity and the effect of things. I don't know any other reason why he picked *Alice*; it was simply a great classic and incumbent upon him to do it."

All through the 1940s, Disney enlisted dozens of in-house and outside writers to work on the project. The main problem they encountered with the original was its lack of a cohesive storyline; all they had to work with was the series of unrelated events and characters that Alice encounters as she wanders through Wonderland. The first series of storyboards, completed in 1939, remained fairly faithful to the book, but included a few additions to move the plot along. In place of a long narrative voice-over, the "Drink Me" bottle would talk and fill Alice in on what was going on. The character eventually evolved into a talking Doorknob.

For the sake of continuity, the White Rabbit would crash the tea party, falling from a bicycle and breaking his glasses, so Alice would take him back to his house to find another pair.

A later idea for Alice's motivation for exploring through Wonderland was to recover her cat. In one late 1945 screenplay by Cap Palmer that reads more like *The Wizard of Oz* than *Alice in Wonderland*, live action Alice is playing dress up with her cat, Dinah, and when the feline tries to escape, she tells it to go away and never come back. The cat follows the White Rabbit down the hole, and Alice pursues Dinah. The ground beneath her gives way like a trap door and she plummets past a mole, a diamond mine and a "Center of the Earth" signpost, before Alice, having now turned into a cartoon character, hits the bottom. There, through one of a long row of small doors, she can see her live action self sleeping, but resolves not to awaken her until she recovers Dinah. Later we discover that Dinah has become the Cheshire Cat ("When you shrink beyond nothing, you become a Wonderland creature"). The pair set out to find the Queen, who is the only one who can break the spell, and are joined on their quest by the Mad Hatter and March Hare. When they finally arrive at the garden party, Alice pleads with the Queen to assist her cat, but instead gets blamed for some stolen tarts. She spends a lonely night in prison, where through a tiny door she can see her live action self, still asleep. She calls for help, but can't stir her flesh and blood alter ego.

The trial is performed as a broad comic opera. The Knave testifies against Alice, while the Mad Hatter and March Hare try to help, but gum things up. At the last minute, the Cheshire Cat materializes to pin the guilt on the Knave. Because this is an unselfish act, it breaks the spell, enraging the Queen and the mob. Alice eats a last bit of mushroom she has saved and shrinks. She races through a forest of legs down the Great Hall and tugs at the tiny door, now enormous. She then loses her balance, falls upwards through the rabbit hole, faster and faster, the cards close behind, until she crashes at the top and all goes black. Live action Alice awakens under a tree, as the cartoon cards turn into falling leaves. "It was all a dream," she muses, then fingers the White Rabbit's watch in her apron pocket. "Or... was it?" The movie fades out on the kitten's mischievous grin.

Palmer later revised his script so that instead of chasing the White Rabbit and then turning into the Cheshire Cat, Dinah is in cahoots with the rabbit. The White Rabbit shows up after Alice has drifted to sleep, checks his watch and beckons Dinah. "Oh dear! Oh dear!" the rabbit moans. "I thought she'd never go to sleep. We must hurry or we shall be late."

Yet another idea was for the whole dream to be a nightmare caused by Alice eating too many tarts. In the end, the storymen figured it was easier to have Alice's motivation for continuing through the wild just be to follow the White Rabbit.

Off and on, the story crew continued exploring the idea of a live action Alice in an animated Wonderland. In 1945, the studio announced that Ginger Rogers would star; a later release stated that the film would be built around Disney's new child star, Luana Patten, who had appeared in *Song of the South*.

Before deciding in late 1946 to go all cartoon, Disney also considered using live actors as Alice and her sister in the introduction and conclusion, with the dream sequences fully animated. In another early 1946 draft by Palmer, a live actor would portray Lewis Carroll, ill at ease at a garden party in his honor. He hears a small girl's voice and slips away from the party. He moves down to the riverbank, where behind a hedge, in a grassy dell he meets a girl having a tea party with two dolls, a stuffed mouse, and, at the head of the table, her kitten, Dinah. Alice's conversation reveals that she wants to be a grown-up. After conversing with Carroll, she falls asleep, into Wonderland, where Carroll continues as narrator.

Near the end of the dream, Alice is on trial, accused of being a child. The White Rabbit, last to take the stand because he's late, testifies that he saw Alice playing with dolls and her kitten. Alice is sentenced to grow up and promptly begins growing up, right through the roof of the castle, the clouds and against a map-like sky, which begins stretching like rubber to its breaking point. Alice moans, "Oh, if only I could be myself again, I'd never..." and—bam!—she's back at the riverbank, opening her sleepy eyes as Carroll finishes up his story.

Unfortunately, the screenwriter's new twist worked against the fabric of Carroll's book and the very purpose of Wonderland itself. Instead of a childish girl who's bored by reality until she sees the inanity of 100-proof fantasy, this Alice wants to be an adult from the start, so she has nothing to learn from being frustrated by all the nonsense and certainly no reason to want to be a kid again!

As if Carroll's first book didn't provide enough material to sift through, by late 1945 it was decided to include a sampling of characters from *Through the Looking Glass*. An early idea was for when Alice returned to her normal size inside the White Rabbit's house, she would escape into a mirror, leading to a "sequence of the best stuff in the other book," where she would encounter a hideous Jabberwock, Humpty Dumpty, the White Knight, the Lion and the Unicorn, Tweedledee and Tweedledum, and the Walrus and

In 1946 Disney decided to add Tweedledee, Tweedledum and other characters from Carroll's sequel, *Through the Looking Glass*, into the mix.

the Carpenter. The last two twosomes actually made it.

The one easy thing about adapting *Alice in Wonderland* into a Disney movie was that its episodic nature, filled with colorful characters and incidents, provided natural moments for musical numbers. Often in musicals, characters are forced into unnatural plot turns as an excuse to work in a song; Carroll's characters, who didn't necessarily have any connection to the storyline, already were popping out of nowhere and saying (or singing) clever things that didn't necessarily have any connection to the story. In their treatments, the writers spelled out certain places that would be ripe for a musical number and often suggested "song angles," or specific ideas from which to build them. The seemingly countless suggestions included:

• For the opening of a live action Alice playing dress up with her cat, a theme song called "Let's Pretend."

• An "Echo Song" would accompany Alice and the White Rabbit falling down the rabbit hole.

• As Alice plummeted down the rabbit hole past bookshelves, a fat, jovial encyclopedia and an ensemble of famous literary characters would sing "Getting to the Bottom of It All."

• After she lands, a reception committee of famous Wonderland characters greet her with signs, a brass band and a rendition of "Welcome to Wonderland."

• The series of increasingly small doors would be replaced by a Hall of Mirrors, so Alice sees hundreds of images of herself distorted as in a fun house, with her voice equally altered. She sings "Who Am I?" joined by a chorus of her reflections, who also do a ballet.

Hearing Voices

In designing their characters, the storymen often had in mind particular actors, each suggesting a different way the character could be played. Below are the story department's 1946 voice casting suggestions for each *Alice In Wonderland* character (the actor who got the part is in parentheses):

White Rabbit (Bill Thompson) Ray Bolger, Charles Winniger, Victor Moore, Frank Morgan, Spencer Tracy

The Mouse Donald Meek, Irving Bacon, Henry Travers

Gryphon Jack Carson, Arthur Treacher, Alec Templeton

Mock Turtle Richard Haydn, Rudy Vallee

Dodo (Bill Thompson) Nigel Bruce, Reginald Owen, Percy Kilbride

Cheshire Cat (Sterling Holloway) Peter Lorre, Edgar Bergen as Charlie McCarthy, Phil Silvers, Claude Rains, Reginald Gardiner, Allyn Joslyn

March Hare (Jerry Colona) Ed Wynn, Phil Silvers, Red Skelton, Hugh Herbert, Stan Laurel

Mad Hatter (Ed Wynn) Raymond Walburn, Danny Kaye, Reginald Gardiner, Eric Blore, Charles Laughton, Walter Catlett, Oliver Hardy, Spike Jones and Band in the act

Dormouse (Jim Macdonald) Stu Erwin, Franklin Pangborn, Charles Ruggles, Roland Young

Bill the Lizard (Larry Grey) Mortimer Snerd, Allen Jenkins

• Peering through a small door, Alice sees the Queen's garden, where the flowers sing "There's Gonna Be a Party."
• The talking "Drink Me" container, Dr. Bottle, warbles "It's All in the Diet," changing during the number from a bottle into a psychiatrist, a carnival medicine man, a chemist with fuming test tubes, a soda jerk, etc. (prefiguring the Genie from *Aladdin!*).
• In the flood, the Mouse and Dodo advise "Don't Drown in Your Own Tears."
• Alice and the Gryphon duet "Who's Dreaming of Whom."

Caterpillar (Richard Haydn) Sidney Greenstreet, Charles Coburn, Will Wright

Pigeon (Queenie Leonard) Cass Daley, Spring Byington, Una O'Connor, Bea Lillie

White Knight Victor Moore, Spencer Tracy, Walter Brennan, Kenny Baker

Tweedledee & Tweedledum (J. Pat O'Malley) Jack Benny & Fred Allen

Lion & Unicorn Jerry Colonna & Bob Hope, Jimmy Durante & Garry Moore

Humpty Dumpty Red Skelton, Cliff Nazzaro, John Carradine, Orson Welles

Frog Footman George Barbier, Billy Gilbert, Percy Kilbride

Duchess Bea Lillie, Charlotte Greenwood, Helen Broderick, Sophie Tucker, Billie Burke

Cook Cass Daley, Martha Raye, Betty Hutton

Pig Baby Fanny Brice as Baby Snooks

Rose Painting Gardeners Bob Hope & Bing Crosby

Card Soldiers (The Mellomen) Choral group, such as Kings' Men

Knave Reginald Gardiner, Phil Silvers, Ray Noble, Frank Sinatra, David Niven

Queen (Verna Felton) Elsa Lanchester, Betty Hutton, Agnes Moorehead, Marjorie Main

King (Dink Trout) Raymond Walburn

• The Mock Turtle sings "Once I Was a Real Turtle" or "The Soup Song."

• A "Lobster Quadrille" production number was planned to follow the Pool of Tears sequence (in the final film, lobsters do participate in the "Caucus-Race").

• In the forest, mushrooms pop out of the ground, with an instrumentalist on each. On the largest is their leader, a cute and friendly caterpillar, who doubles as a clarinet.

• Alice sings "I'm in the Middle of a Dream," "I'm All Mixed Up," or "Having My Ups and Downs."

• The White Rabbit sings "What's at the Bottom of It All?," "The Very Small Hello," "Remind Me to Remember," "I'm Always Rushing Madly to—I Can't Remember Where," or "Hurry, Hurry, Hurry (We've Got to Find the Queen)."

• The Mad Hatter, March Hare and Dormouse join in on "It's Always Tea Time in England," "All Tea Parties are Mad," "Riddle Song," or "Must It Make Sense?"

• The White Knight croons "Through the Looking Glass."

• Tweedledee and Tweedledum sing "Got to Pull Myself Together."

• The Cheshire Cat delivers "Why Is a Cheshire Grin."

• The Frog Footman sings "I Like to Sit."

• The Duchess provides a "Screwball Lullaby."

• Her Cook sings "Everybody Wants to Get into the Soup" or "Pepper Lullaby."

• The ensemble at the garden party sing "What Little Tarts Are Made Of."

• The Knave of Hearts (considered—as was the White Knight—as a love interest for Alice) serenades her with "In Love with Love" or "Rose Song."

• The Queen sings "Every Little Miss Is Alice" or "Off with Their Heads."

In 1947, in-house composers such as Oliver Wallace and Frank Churchill began writing songs for the picture, churning out one syrupy ballad after another. Walt quickly realized that Alice needed not love songs but "novelty songs," and he now knew where to look. Once again he called on Tin Pan Alley's Mack David, Jerry Livingston and Al Hoffman, Bob Hilliard and Sammy Fain, and

Gene De Paul and Don Raye. In all, by 1949, nearly 40 different songs had been penned for the picture, many with lyrics lifted directly from Carroll's text. Among the nearly two-thirds that were deleted: "Will You Join the Dance" (in place of the "Caucus-Race"); "Mock Turtle Soup;" "Beautiful Soup," similarly extolling the virtues of soup but set to the "Blue Danube" waltz; two different versions of "The Walrus and the Carpenter;" an instrumental "Entrance of the Walrus and the Carpenter;" "The Carpenter Is Sleeping;" "The Lion and the Unicorn;" the Unicorn's "If You'll Believe in Me;" "Everything Has a Useness;" "Humpty Dumpty" (the nursery rhyme set to music); "The Jabberwocky Song;" the jazzier "Beware the Jabberwocky" (the Jabberwock's lines were later used as lyrics for the Cheshire Cat's song, "Twas Brillig"); "Alice and the Cheshire Cat," with Alice singing operatically on how wondrous is the Cheshire Cat; "So They Say," another Alice song about the Cat; "Dream Caravan," a hypnotic number for the caterpillar; "When the Wind Is in the East," a ballad by the Mad Hatter, who has no business singing a ballad; the Duchess' "Speak Roughly to Your Little Boy;" "Gavotte of the Cards," as the King, Queen and Knave dance on the green; "Entrance of the Executioner," bemoaning the Executioner's task of being asked to cut off a head without a body, and "Beyond the Laughing Sky," as Alice daydreams on the meadow. Lyricist Sammy Cahn took composer Sammy Fain's music for the latter number (possibly intended for a storyboarded scene in which the clouds take animal shapes and the trees dance) and gave it new lyrics to produce "Second Star to the Right" for *Peter Pan*.

Plot Holes

• In *Alice in Wonderland*, the inconsistent parts should be any that make sense, since the whole idea of Wonderland is to be as nonsensical and illogical as possible.

Bloopers

• During "The Walrus and the Carpenter" sequence, the Walrus has one finger poking out of a hole in each of his white gloves. But in at least a half-dozen shots at least one glove is miraculously whole.

• When Alice arrives at the White Rabbit's house, she heads for the upstairs bedroom where there's a canopy bed covered by a multi-colored, multi-patterned quilt. When Alice begins to grow, her leg pushes the bed across the room but it now has an orange/pink bedspread. When Alice shrinks back down, the bed has the quilt on it again.

• During Alice's solo at the end of "Golden Afternoon," the pansies continue to mouth the song, but only Alice's voice is heard. Most likely animation on the sequence was completed before it was decided to let Alice solo, since on the demo recording of the song, the flower chorus sings until the end.

Strange Reactions

As if producing the film hadn't been troublesome enough, a month before it was set to open, Disney heard a domestic film distributor had acquired the rights to another *Alice in Wonderland*, made in Paris two years earlier by puppeteer Louis Bunin, and planned to release it in the U.S. on the same day as Disney's. Contending that the distributor was trying to ride on his publicity and confuse moviegoers, Disney fought to have the Bunin version barred from exhibition in the U.S. until eighteen months after his opened. But the courts ruled that the property was public domain and that anyone could make a movie out of it. The films opened the same day, but were easy to differentiate. The French version, featuring a human Alice mingling with stop-motion-animated puppets, garnered abominable reviews.

Yet even Disney's version received some of the worst reviews ever for an animated Disney film. It fared so poorly at the box office that Disney aired it in 1954 as the second episode of his *Disneyland* television show. Walt vowed he would never rerelease it in theaters because it was "filled with weird characters. It had an appeal to the intellect without anything to appeal to the emotions."

"*Alice* was an overload," admitted Joe Grant. "There was just too much material. And it became just a visual after a while, a little vaudeville show. Walt was very dissatisfied with it. He liked a complete story; (the lack of one) always bothered him."

Long afterwards, fans continued to ask the animators if they were "on something" when they made the movie. It's not such an odd question, considering all the things in the book and movie that suggest drugs: Alice ingests potions, wafers and mushrooms that change her size or alter her consciousness, her perspective constantly changes, she loses track of time, space and her own identity. There's the hookah-smoking caterpillar. In fact, the entire story, a dream framed by the "real world," might be seen as a hallucination or trip.

So, it wasn't surprising that in 1971 *Alice in Wonderland* was the top renting 16mm film in every college town across the country, playing to capacity crowds in heavy smoke-filled fraternity houses, university theaters, discos and private homes, where it sometimes ran over and over again for an entire weekend.

After the smash cult revival of *Fantasia*, Disney withdrew the 16mm prints of *Alice* and targeted a 1974 theater rerelease. The studio prepared ads with copy such as "Down the rabbit hole and through the talking door lies a world where vibrant colors merge into shapes of fantasy, and music radiates from flowers," "Nine out of ten Dormice recommend Walt Disney's *Alice in Wonderland* for visual euphoria and good, clean nonsense," and "Should you see it? Go ask Alice," a reference to Jefferson Airplane's song "White Rabbit" ("One pill makes you larger/And one pill makes you smaller/And the ones that mother gives you don't do anything at all/Go ask Alice when she's ten feet tall."). The swirling pink-red-yellow-blue-purple poster featured Alice sitting sedately on the caterpillar's mushroom, although there was no sign of the caterpillar or hookah. The experiment was so successful, the film was rereleased again seven years later.

Attraction Offspring

At Disneyland, *Alice in Wonderland* inspired both a dark ride and a Tilt-a-Whirl-type teacup attraction. Early designs for the Mad Tea Party called for a giant table in the center with animated figures of the Mad Hatter and March Hare in furious debate. The ticket booth would be a giant mushroom with a gigantic caterpillar on top. The Cheshire Cat would sit atop a second mushroom.

The mushroom ticket booth, topped with an oversized storybook, was used three years later when the dark ride opened. After

Disneyland went from A through E ticket books to an all-rides-for-one-price pass in the early 1980s, the mushroom was turned into a little storage office. Always trying to add little details to keep things fresh and interesting, Imagineer John Hench added sets of slippers on top of the booth, suggesting the caterpillar's transformation into a butterfly (although there's no sign of his gloves).

One thing Imagineers addressed during the 1983 remodeling of Fantasyland was Alice's reputation as a sissy ride. "I'd always thought it was a female ride," Imagineer Tony Baxter said. "So we added trees to mushy it up and explosives and weird sounds to make it more a male ride. I figured maybe a teenage guy wouldn't want to ride in a caterpillar."

- 9 -

Peter Pan

The Original Tale

Sir James Barrie's *Peter Pan* premiered on the London stage in 1904 and appeared in book form seven years later. In this fantasy, Peter Pan is a boy, a sprite, really, who can fly and doesn't want to grow up. One night, he pays a visit to the nursery of Wendy, John and Michael. After being detected by Mrs. Darling, Peter tries to escape, but Nana, the canine nursemaid, catches his shadow. Mrs. Darling rolls up the shadow and stows it in a drawer.

Peter returns with fairy Tinker Bell one night when the parents are out and invites Wendy to fly back with him to his home, Neverland, so she can tell stories to the motherless Lost Boys. All three children sign up for the flight. But Tinker Bell, jealous of Wendy, flies ahead and tells the six bearskin-wearing Lost Boys that Peter wants them to kill the incoming "Wendy bird." Wendy is downed by an arrow but survives, and Peter banishes Tink for a week.

Wendy plays mother to the boys and they share many adventures. Pan is constantly pursued by the ruthless Captain Hook, so named after Peter cut off one of his hands and tossed it to a crocodile. The croc, who ticks because he's also swallowed a clock, pursues the remainder of Hook.

One day, Peter and Wendy go to the mermaid lagoon where two pirates in a rowboat are holding Tiger Lily, the Indian Princess. Peter, imitating Hook's voice, has them release her. In return, the grateful Indians vow to watch over the Lost Boys' underground home.

Although John and Michael begin to forget their parents, Wendy realizes that mother and father must be very worried. She invites everyone to return with her, and only Peter refuses. But the pirates sneak up and slaughter the Indians on watch and capture everyone who leaves the underground home. Hook goes down into the house, where Peter lies sleeping, and puts poison in his medicine.

Soon after, Tinker Bell awakens Peter and tells of the capture. Peter wants to drink his medicine first, but Tink bravely gets in the way, drinks from the cup and keels over. She is revived by the clapping of children everywhere who believe in fairies.

Just before the boys are made to walk the plank, Peter arrives to save the day and send Hook tumbling over the side of the ship and into the mouth of the crocodile.

The group, sans Pan, finally returns to London, and a repentant Mr. Darling adopts all the Lost Boys. Wendy promises she will return to Neverland with Peter once a year, but Peter grows forgetful. He returns sporadically, eventually taking Wendy's daughter, then her daughter's daughter.

The Disney Version

Walt first proposed an animated *Peter Pan* in 1935 and acquired the rights four years later. The studio began story development and character design in the early 1940s as a follow-up to *Bambi*, but World War II forced a postponement.

After the exasperating *Alice in Wonderland*, Disney knew better than to fiddle too much with a literary source that had so many details familiar to so many people. His *Peter Pan* would stick fairly close to the original, although the benefits of animation allowed certain changes, such as making Tinker Bell's "death" more dramatic by changing the poison into a bomb. The expectations of a Disney audience forced other alterations, notably deleting all the bloodshed. Peter would still be cocky but more likable.

Some things that worked on stage just wouldn't work in animation. On stage, Peter was played by a girl, Nana by an actor, Tinker Bell by a beam of light, and the crocodile by offstage ticking. Tinker Bell was also revived by the audience clapping, but the ploy wouldn't play in a movie theater without live actors to egg on the audience. Disney did keep one stage tradition, that Captain Hook and Mr. Darling be played by the same actor. Disney had Hans Conried voice and model for both roles.

Plot Holes

- Wendy is rather unusual for a girl who looks to be about a teenager. Why is she so upset when she's given her own room instead of sharing the nursery with two little brothers? And even if it is her last night sleeping in the nursery, why can't she read John and Michael any more stories? Just how far away is this new room of hers?

- As Disney heroes go, Peter is a questionable role model. Maurice Rapf tried to put him in his place when assigned to write an early screenplay. "They were never gonna do mine. I made Peter Pan a villain," he explained. "He doesn't want anybody to grow up and that's dangerous, the temptation not to grow up. So I had Wendy tell him off."

Bloopers

- The opening shot shows the Darling house, with the second story windows to the parents' room opening out and the top story windows to the nursery closed. But once inside, we see the nursery window is now open—and it opens *in*!

- The pillow on a bench inside the nursery window is round. In a later shot, it's square. The chair to the right of the window has a red seat, which temporarily turns blue.

- Hook sits down for a shave from his sidekick, Smee, well away from the side of the ship. In the next shot, he leans back in his chair, against the side of the ship. He bolts from his chair when the crocodile approaches and then when he finally returns to the chair, it's inexplicably near the opposite side of the ship.

Attraction Offspring

It's easy to see why Peter Pan's Flight is the most effective and most popular of all the Fantasyland dark rides. Guests travel in flying boats, soaring above London, believably entering another world.

At Disneyland, the movie also inspired a Skull Rock Cove fronted by a Chicken of the Sea restaurant set in a pirate ship, where today sits the Dumbo ride. When Fantasyland was remodeled, the pirate boat was to be relocated to the end of the Storybook Land ride, and placed in the current boat storage/break area then known as Never Neverland (where they "never, never take you"). The Storybook Land canal boats would turn left at the end of skull rock cove and, before docking, pass the pirate ship featuring a restaurant with a show on board and an animated crocodile in the water.

Unfortunately, the detour was easy to cut off when the remodeling project went over budget. Workers carefully disassembled the pirate ship and gingerly loaded the pieces onto a truck to transport them to a location where they could be safely stored. But en route to the warehouse, the truck hit a bump, the plaster ship fell and shattered. The Imagineers were able to salvage some of the riggings and lamps and install them in the remodeled Peter Pan dark ride, to stand as a tribute to cost saving ingenuity and a dearly departed tuna boat.

- 10 -
Lady and the Tramp

The Disney Version

For inspiration for his animated features, Disney had looked to classic fairy tales, storybooks, short stories and novels. With *Lady and the Tramp*, for the first time he would create an original work which itself would inspire a book.

According to legend (better known as the Disney Studio Publicity Department), the idea had its roots in 1925 when Walt, as a peace offering for forgetting a dinner engagement, brought his bride a puppy in a hat box. The story department at first thought to incorporate the vignette into a short, but by 1943 Joe Grant and Dick Huemer were expanding it into a feature, a comedy about the romance between a well-bred house dog and a stray.

The same year, Walt came across a short story in *Cosmopolitan*, "Happy Dan the Whistling Dog." He liked the depiction of the carefree mutt and contacted the author, Ward Greene, general manager of King Features Syndicate. He persuaded Greene to write a book combining their dogs, *Happy Dan, the Whistling Dog and Miss Patsy, the Beautiful Spaniel*. "(Greene) was brought in after we were already finished with the story," said Joe Grant. "Walt said, 'Let's make a book out of it, for the prestige.' But there were a lot of refinements even after that."

The novel told the "amazing adventures" of the mismatched canines, but had minimal influence on the movie version. Grant and Huemer renamed the stray Rags and then Bozo. Then, in 1944, Walt heard a radio play based on another *Cosmopolitan* story, "Imperfect Lady," liked the romantic comedy approach, and hired its author, Cap Palmer, to develop a script for *Lady and the Tramp*.

In his screenplay, Palmer fleshed out the main story points and suggested ideas for musical numbers. "The Barking Song" would play over the credits, leading to an opening number built around

"It's a dog's life—but I love it." In the chorus, each couplet is tagged by barks, like the claps in "Deep in the Heart of Texas." Prim and proper Lady, deeply devoted to her family, is romantically pursued by next door neighbor Hubert, a stuffy, pompous, Ralph Bellamy-type canine. One of Lady's duties is to chase off rascally Herman the Rat whenever the brash comedy gangster character tries to sneak into the house.

We meet Tramp after a shotgun blast, as he scrambles out of a chicken coop, his face full of feathers. He seeks refuge in Lady's doghouse and persuades her to hide him. The street-smart stray gives her his views on people, explaining the difference between "good shoes" and "bad shoes." Hubert comes on the scene just as Tramp is walking out of Lady's doghouse.

Tramp joins Lady on the porch swing and sings "I Wear No Man's Collar," but Lady appears unimpressed. Tramp pokes his nose into the mistress' knitting basket and pulls out a small blue knitted object. "I'll tug you for it," he offers, then realizes it's a baby bootie. "I guess you're about washed up here," he says, but Lady refuses to believe him and is offended when Tramp suggests her owners will shove her aside for a "baby." Obviously, he says, she hasn't been around much.

That evening, Lady has a "Parade of the Shoes" nightmare (reminiscent of Dumbo's "Elephants on Parade" nightmare) in which the bootie splits into two and continues to multiply. The dream shoes fade into real shoes running down the stairs, their wearer exclaiming that the baby has been born. It becomes Lady's job to protect the newborn.

One day, Tramp stops by while Lady is on the porch guarding the baby carriage. She gives him the cold shoulder, but he notices her tail is wagging. "So they did buy a baby!" he says. "Oh, oh, that's bad. That's very bad." The rat wants to take a look in the carriage, but the dogs chase him off.

The master goes away on a business trip, and the mistress needs rest, so Auntie comes to stay. Out of her wicker basket emerge a pair of Siamese cats, Nip and Tuck. Lady spots one and, since cats aren't allowed in the house, lunges at it. It vanishes just before the other cat appears across the room. The cats torment Lady with "twin pranks," in a sequence built on music. She sees one's head behind one end of a divan and its partner's tail behind the other end, as if it's a nine-foot-long cat. Thinking there's only one cat, Lady goes crazy trying to catch "it," wrecking the house in the process. Auntie hears a crash and runs downstairs to see Lady's rubber ball at the foot of the stairs and her cats cowering as if terrified by the dog. Auntie immediately sets out to buy a muzzle for Lady from a Franklin Pangborn-type clerk.

That night, Tramp chews off Lady's muzzle and they take off for a night on the town, to a song with the suggested title "That's What I Call Living" or "On the Town Tonight." He teaches her how to mooch a candy apple, and the two "tug" for the sticky, stretchy candy. Flirtatious female dogs greet Tramp as he passes by, each one calling him by a different name. At the park, Lady and Tramp engage in a "Dog's World" fantasy, to the song "The World Is Going to the Dogs." Oversized dogs walk small humans on leashes, bathe them, comb, feed, play fetch with them, and separate them when they fight.

In the morning, Tramp takes her to chase chickens. At the sound of a shotgun, he flees, but Lady freezes. She is taken to the pound, where the collared and collarless are separated. She returns home disgraced and looked down upon by Hubert. Tramp shows up and wants to know what happened to her. She sings "I've Got a Bone to Pick With You," Tramp and Hubert argue, and Lady tells Tramp to go.

Lady is chained in the cellar. The rat scampers by and taunts her. She barks, seemingly in vain. The rat nears the crib. Tramp breaks through the grating to the cellar, nuzzles Lady and dashes upstairs. He argues with the rat, then lunges for it. The rat escapes into the closet, the bassinet tips and knocks the closet door shut. A second later, Auntie runs in, screams, "Mad dog!" and calls the pound. Tramp is taken away by the dog catcher.

Soon after, the master of the house returns. He frees Lady, and she runs upstairs. She sniffs around and yelps at the closet door. Meanwhile, Tramp is walking the Last Mile. At home, the vet arrives to tend to a disconsolate Lady. His diagnosis: she's not ill, just heartbroken. The master calls the pound, and Tramp gets a reprieve at the last minute.

We close on a Christmas group photo session, with Lady, Tramp (reluctantly wearing a collar), five prim sweet pups, and Scamp, a mini-Tramp, who glances at Pop, then turns to the camera and winks, just as it flashes a picture.

Although Palmer's script contained the main elements of the story, it would take Disney ten more years to produce the picture. The comedy was made less broad and the charm increased. The suitor next door became two older dogs, Jock and Trusty, who are protective of Lady and eventually propose to her only to help her save face. To add real drama, the comic rat became a nameless, more realistic threat. And the collarless dogs at the pound were given personalities, led by a broken-down showgirl of a dog who would sing "He's a Tramp."

"The dog was originally called Mame," remembered Peggy Lee, who wrote the songs with Sonny Burke, "but because Eisenhower's wife was Mame, they didn't wish to risk any kind of comment that wouldn't be befitting a president's wife. So Walt asked me if I would mind if they changed her name to Peg. I said, 'Of course not. I would consider it an honor.'"

The character was not only endowed with Lee's first name, but her looks and hip-swinging stage walk as well. Lee also provided the voice for Peg, as well as the movie's other singing females, the mother and the Siamese cats.

But perhaps her biggest contribution meant the difference between life and death. As originally planned, in running for help, Trusty would get hit by the dog catcher's wagon and killed. When the animators showed Lee the storyboards, she recalled, "I was like a little child. The rat scared me. And when Trusty was killed, I was so upset. I'm very sentimental about animals. It made me cry. I said, 'Oh, Walt, you can't do this,' and he said, 'You have to have some tension in the story. It would change everything if he's not killed.' I said, 'But if you kill him the children will cry too much, like with *Bambi*'—although I'd never seen *Bambi*. So he said, finally, 'Well, all right. Old Trusty can live... but the rat stays.'"

The five songs Lee and Burke wrote were enough to fill up the movie, but not the soundtrack album. So, they had to come up with two more, "Jim Dear" and, not surprisingly, "Old Trusty."

Plot Holes

• Fortunately, when Lady is introduced as a Christmas present, she doesn't fall limply out of the giftbox in need of resuscitation. The giftbox has no air holes.

• Is it common for the biggest area in a zoo to be reserved for a beaver? The area is billed as Beaver Dam, but until Lady and Tramp arrive, the dam has not yet been constructed. And when it finally is finished, it's quite a distance down a hill, likely to be out of sight from the zoo visitors beyond the fence.

• When Tramp takes Lady to an Italian restaurant, proprietor Tony takes the dog's dinner order. He calls out that "Butch" wants two Spaghettis Especial. For some reason, the chef just brings one plate of pasta. I also wonder what all of Tony's customers are doing while he and his staff are feeding and serenading two dogs in the alley. Perhaps they're trying to digest his pasta, which is evidently cooked with the noodles and meatballs simultaneously in the same pot.

• At the dog pound, the Chihuahua is so small he can easily fit between the bars of his cell. Why doesn't he make a break for it?

Bloopers

• Whatever you do, don't set your schedule by the strange calendars used to show the passage of time in *Lady and the Tramp*. The first shows December 31 as a Thursday, then segues into January 1, also a Thursday. The next calendar shows November 30 as a Friday, but December 1 as a Tuesday. On the third calendar, January 31 is a Sunday, as is February 1.

• In the first shot in front of a zoo, the leash hangs to Lady's right. In the next shot, the leash hangs to her left. Later, when Lady is tied in her doghouse, she looks out as Tramp leaves and her chain is entirely in the doghouse. We cut to the rat and then back to see part of her chain is looped out of the doghouse.

• In early scenes, the rat appears to be much smaller than Lady, who is, of course, smaller than Tramp. Yet in the climatic battle in the baby's room, the rat appears to be nearly as large as Tramp.

- The lovers at Makeout Point appear to be in a horsedrawn carriage—with no horse.

- As the shotgun-toting farmer chases the dogs off his farm, his first gun blast tears a hole through the wire fence but misses the building behind it and to the left. Strangely, his next shot tears a hole through the fence even further to the right, but takes a chunk out of the building to the left.

- One minute Aunt Sarah has the baby in her hands and the next she's swinging a broom at the dog with the baby nowhere in sight and the crib still tipped over. She locks Tramp in the closet and drags Lady to the cellar. Where's the baby all this time?

Strange Reactions

When *Lady and the Tramp* was released in 1955, no one could have foreseen the advent of home video. But a few resourceful producers, such as Hal Roach, did specify in their performers' contracts that rights would be withheld for "formats to be invented in the future." Disney was not so fortuitous. So, in 1990, Mary Costa, the voice of Princess Aurora, sued the studio for a share of the profits from the video release of *Sleeping Beauty*. The performers in *Cinderella* and the orchestra from *Fantasia* followed suit. In 1991, after *Lady and the Tramp* was released on video, Peggy Lee filed suit. The case would take years to resolve and weigh a heavy toll on Lee's health. She finally was awarded $2.3 million.

Attraction Offspring

Although *Lady and the Tramp* doesn't lend itself to reproduction as a theme park attraction, it did inspire several Italian restaurants at various Disney parks. And, if you ever get the chance, take a close look at the Italian chipped tile wall of the Bella Notte Pizzeria at Disneyland Paris. As a sentimental gesture, the wall was covered with broken tiles from an old mural, which artist Mary Blair had painted at Disneyland's Tomorrowland. Sections had chipped off when contractors were covering it up with a new Star Tours mural.

- 11 -

Sleeping Beauty

The Original Tale

Perrault's "The Sleeping Beauty" begins with the King and Queen inviting all the fairies in the land to be godmothers of their newborn daughter. After the christening, they hold a great banquet, but an elder fairy whom everyone thought was dead crashes the festivities. Each fairy blesses the princess with a gift: an angelic mind, beauty, grace, singing voice, dancing ability, command of all instruments, and, from the scornful old fairy, that she'll pierce her hand with a spindle and die. Fortunately, the youngest fairy had been hiding behind a tapestry and is the last to bestow a gift: the princess won't die of the wound, but will sleep for 100 years and then be awakened by a prince. The king, underwhelmed by this addendum, promptly outlaws spindles.

Sixteen years later, the princess wanders into a nook in the castle where sits a woman spinning, unaware of the proclamation. Curious, the princess asks if she can try; she pierces her hand and faints. She is laid upon a silver and gold bed in a beautiful room. The youngest fairy casts a spell on everyone, except the king and queen, so all will sleep as long as the princess. The king and queen forbid anyone from approaching the castle and, fifteen minutes after they leave, trees and bushes overgrow the palace.

A hundred years later, the son of the current king approaches the entangled castle and the branches part for him. He bypasses the snoring guards, finds the princess, and kneels down beside her, awakening the princess as well as her famished attendants. After dinner, the prince and princess wed.

The next morning, the prince returns to his simpleton father and suspicious ogress mother and explains he had gotten lost while hunting. The prince "goes hunting" almost every day and, after two years, he and the princess have a daughter, Aurora, and a son, Day. Two years later, the king dies. The prince publicly reveals his family and moves them into the palace.

He later goes to war, leaving his mother in charge of the kingdom and his family. Immediately, she sends her daughter-in-law and grandchildren to a cottage in the woods, planning to eat them and then tell her son they were gobbled by wolves. But her cook hides the family and serves the ogress animal meat.

One evening, the Queen Mother hears her grandchildren crying and commands that her daughter-in-law, the kids, the cook, his wife and their maidservant be thrown into a cauldron filled with snakes. But her son the king arrives just in time and the enraged ogress throws herself head first into the cauldron. Although the king is grieved at the loss of his mother, he "quickly consoles himself with his beautiful wife and children."

The Disney Version

With *Sleeping Beauty*, the studio returned to the familiar ground of a classic fairy tale. Because the original's second act is so bizarre and the wake-up kiss such a climactic moment, Disney concentrated on only the first half of the tale.

The story crew quickly realized that the strength of the story lay in its romance, but saw little romance in a stranger kissing a coma victim. The prince and princess, as in *Snow White*, would have to meet before the life-saving smooch. The question was how. The prince needed an excuse to go foraging deep into the woods, so the writers and storyboard artists worked out an elaborate sequence in which the king organizes a treasure hunt. But the scenario became so drawn out and started drifting so far from the story, the whole idea was dropped; the prince and princess would just meet by chance as she frolicked in the forest with her furry friends.

Another problem was that if the prince was going to meet the princess before she nodded off, she couldn't very well sleep for 100 years. Instead, she would end up sleeping just a few hours, as the prince battled goons, obstacles and the wicked Maleficent herself, transformed into a fire-breathing dragon.

And, for the final fadeout, Walt finally used the oft-deleted "dancing on the clouds" idea.

Plot Holes

- The fairies waited sixteen long years to return the princess to the palace. Couldn't they have waited one more day, until her birthday safely had passed?

- Why were the fairies in such a hurry to get back to their cottage after putting the kingdom to sleep? They had no way of knowing that the young man who was supposed to meet the princess there was the prince or that Maleficent would be lying in wait for him, let alone that Maleficent, who hadn't disturbed them for sixteen years, even knew where their cottage was. Yet when they arrive home and pick up a cap from the floor, one fairy says, "Maleficent," while another adds, "She's got Prince Phillip."

- The fairies arm the prince with a shield and sword because there are "many more dangers which you *alone* will have to face." That doesn't stop them from helping him at every turn. They unchain his horse and change falling boulders into bubbles, arrows into flowers, boiling oil into a rainbow, and a raven into stone. Leading him on, the fairies help the prince jump safely from the closing drawbridge, unsnag his cloak from the thorny briars, and command the sword to fly into the dragon's chest.

Bloopers

- In the first scene in the castle, when the three fairies fly towards the crib, Fauna, the green fairy, has her wand in her right hand. As she arrives at the crib, she holds the wand in her left hand.

Attraction Offspring

As advance publicity for the movie upon which he had only recently begun work, when Walt opened Disneyland in 1955 he called its centerpiece Sleeping Beauty Castle. This gateway to Fantasyland has become one of the most photographed landmarks in the world. It adorns a record 80 different postcards, even though the attraction inside is nothing to write home about. Maybe the Imagineers who designed Snow White's Scary Adventure to scare guests thought a Sleeping Beauty attraction should put them to sleep. As originally designed, miniature scenes from the movie were on display for visitors limber enough to wriggle through a seemingly miniature corridor. As a reward to the pliable, the attraction did feature some interesting Haunted Mansion-style visual effects.

Time has not been kind to Disney's dollhouse. Today, some of the characters in the first scene appear to be bad Christmas tree ornaments, while in other scenes the prince and princess look like Ken and Barbie dolls. Overall, the figures and effects can't even compete with the temporary mini-dioramas displayed in the Emporium's storefront windows to plug the latest feature.

One of the best scenes had even been completely boarded up. Guests peered through keyholes to see Maleficent's goons and their eyes reflected back in such a way that no matter where you stared it seemed the eyes were staring back at you. But the line through the ride could only move as fast as it took every guest to look through the keyholes, so management, with an eye to improving capacity, boarded up the bottleneck. Thirty years later, a maintenance worker discovered that the set was still intact and the scene was reopened.

In the early Nineties, the attraction was almost permanently closed, but it received a reprieve and a slight remodel, giving non-hunchbacked guests a little breathing room. To add some excitement, the Sleeping Beauty Castle at Euro Disney includes a Dragon's Lair. The castle sits on a bluff, allowing space for a dragon in the basement. For Disneyland, plans were devised to create a building for a Dragon's Lair at the back of Tinker Bell's Toy Shop, but the project fell through.

Strange Reactions

Disney registered the title *Sleeping Beauty* in January 1950, began production in July 1953, and released the film in December 1958 at a cost of $6 million. The film was greeted by generally hostile reviews and barely broke even at the box office. The problem was that, for the first time, the animators were starting to fall in love with their work. Dick Huemer remembers animator Marc Davis "pointing out that they had a whole new concept of design on these characters... notice the crispness or designy quality of her hair or of the drapery. How it falls and curls this way, all very carefully worked out. They thought this was important, which in its own way it was. But what was more important was that they didn't have a good story. I mean they didn't have one with the guts that it should have, or heart appeal or novelty or comedy."

Disney audiences wanted warm and fuzzy, but the new stylized animation made images look more like stained glass windows than cartoons, beautiful yet cold. Everything else suffered; the characters were not as memorable, the Tchaikovsky-inspired songs not as catchy. Even Walt was unable to warm up to the picture. He would never again have his staff spend nearly five years animating one feature. The second Golden Age was over.

Top 10 Disney Oddities

1. **Prince Charming Disease**. For some reason, the prince is always the blandest character in any Disney movie. Snow White's Prince Charming was so boring, his previously-planned action scenes were cut out, and after a brief hello, he disappears until the closing scene. Cinderella's, Aurora's and Ariel's princes aren't much more exciting. As a result, while you're sure to see lots of little girls in princess dresses like Snow White's, you won't see too many boys sporting Prince Charming's tights. Nor do you see too many actors at the theme parks in prince costumes.

Perhaps they're simply overshadowed by the marvelous Disney villains who typically steal the show. Or maybe it extends back to the archetypal Disney nice guy, Mickey Mouse, who became so popular in the 1930s that writers and artists grew increasingly restricted in what the public would allow them to do with their hero. So, while Donald and Goofy were getting into all types of incredible adventures, Mickey was content to sit on the porch and read the evening paper.

Makes you wonder if Aladdin lost his edge once he married Jasmine.

2. **The Pluto Syndrome**. It all started with Pluto, Mickey's faithful pet and the first major Disney character who couldn't speak! Talking animals are common in the animated features, but those same pictures also include other animals who can't speak. Like Pluto, they invariably end up as pets, servants or beasts (e.g., Max the sheepdog in *Little Mermaid*, Toby the dog in *Great Mouse Detective*, the alligators in *The Rescuers*, the bear in *Fox and the Hound*), while the talking animals assume more humanized-type roles and typically wear clothes.

You have to pity poor Pluto, unable to speak and therefore banished to a role of domesticated servitude, when even his annoying nemeses Chip and Dale could talk. Then again, maybe he could speak but after hearing the ridiculous intonations of Donald and Goofy, thought better of it.

3. **The Curse of Cats**. Legend has it that Walt Disney hated cats. Or maybe it's because his most famous characters are mice (cute, harmless) and dogs (man's best friend), the mortal enemies of cats (mysterious, sharp teeth, claws). For whatever reason, cats traditionally have been given a bad rap in Disney movies. Beginning with Mickey's *Steamboat Willie* nemesis, Pegleg Pete, if they're not downright evil (Lucifer of *Cinderella*), they're villainous (Gideon of *Pinocchio*), devilish (the Cheshire Cat of *Alice in Wonderland*, Si and Am of *Lady and the Tramp*), scrawny (Sergeant Tibs of *101 Dalmatians*) or at least tormented (Figaro of *Pinocchio*). In the meantime, entire movies were devoted to how wonderful dogs and mice are. It wasn't until after Walt died that cats started receiving a few decent roles in the features.

4. **The Clonus Factor**. Maybe it's because there are only so many ways to draw a hound dog or because all big tigers appear pretty much the same, but a lot of the Disney animated characters sure look alike. As proof, have you ever seen Prince John and *Bedknobs and Broomsticks'* King Leonidas in the same room at the same time? Tramp and *Oliver & Co.'s* Dodger? Baloo, Little John and *Bedknobs and Broomsticks'* Fisherman Bear? Disney's big bears look so similar that the same mold is used to produce their respective costumes for the theme parks.

Perhaps it's the claim that some of the similar looking characters were separated at birth which has led recent movies to feature more exotic players, such as a meerkat, warthog and frilled-neck lizard.

5. The Superwoman Complex. For years, critics assailed Disney for its heroines, that they were all passive, helpless characters whose only concern was finding a man to marry, and that the only dynamic females were the villains. In direct response, beginning with *Beauty and the Beast's* Belle, Disney purposely set out to turn that convention on its ear. From Belle to Jasmine to Pocahontas to Esmerelda, each heroine has become more aggressive, independent and heroic (and, curiously, has been endowed with a larger chest). Could you picture any of these women doing housework? Now the hero just stands back in awe watching her perform feats of derring-do. The age of the fair princess is over. Get ready for misunderstood mud wrestlers and biker chicks.

6. Problems of Perspective. A mouse as big as a duck as big as a dog? Mickey may be a mouse but he nevertheless is drawn of comparable size to Donald Duck and the rest of his co-stars, no matter what type of animal they are. The animals are designed in more believable sizes in the feature films; it's their features that are altered. Early on, Disney discovered that to instill innocence and sympathy into his characters, he could make them look more like babies, whose heads are much larger in proportion to their bodies than are those of adults. Sympathetic characters were drawn with big heads and especially huge, E.T.-sized eyes. The bigger the eyes, the cuter and more vulnerable the character. The smaller and beadier the eyes, the more evil. Critics noted that one reason why Pocahontas was more realistic was that she was the first Disney heroine whose eyes didn't take up half of her head.

All perspective is thrown out the window when it comes to the costumed characters at the theme parks, mostly due to the limited size of the available midget workforce. Abu as tall as Jasmine? Jiminy Cricket the same height as Pinocchio? The mice brushing shoulders with Cinderella? Redesigned costumes now team Snow White with the Seven Men of Average Height.

7. **Near Death Experiences.** The Disney wizards have many other sure-fire tricks to gain sympathy for their characters and few are more effective than pretending to kill them off. Although sometimes "knocked off" early on (the runt Dalmatian, *Fox and the Hound's* Chief), for maximum dramatic impact most almost die just before the end of the picture. If the victim can't be the star (Snow White, Pinocchio, *Oliver & Co.'s* Oliver), the best buddy will do just as well (Tinker Bell, Baloo, *The Black Cauldron's* Gurgi).

Do not fear. Nice Disney characters are immortal. No matter how hermetically sealed their fate may appear, they will quickly be revived by natural means (John Smith shakes it off, Esmerelda was only resting) or supernatural (Ariel, the Beast). Or, after everyone has given up hope, they just show up at the finale unscathed (*Lady and the Tramp's* Trusty, Robin Hood, Basil).

8. **The Parent Trap**. It's the toughest gig in show business: the Disney mom. From Snow White to Pocahontas, most of our animated heroes were brought to life on the big screen without a natural mother. And even the few cartoon stars who have mothers usually lose them, either being quickly orphaned or at least separated from mom for the bulk of the picture (see chart on page 158).

Disney dads typically don't get much meatier roles. Despite often being powerful figures who should have more to do (like running a kingdom), fathers spend most of their screen time doting on their restless offspring. Yet the overprotective Disney dads are hopelessly out of touch with the younger generation—and often out of touch with reality.

Even worse are the step-parents or guardians. Whereas in real life the goal of Child Services is to place the parentless with the best possible parents, Disney orphans are invariably adopted by the most overbearing, degenerate psychopath in town. Mowgli fared better than most; he was taken in by wolves.

Maybe it's because orphans instantly have our sympathy, or perhaps it's because if animated youngsters really had parents that were intelligent, practical and breathing, the youths could be quickly rescued or at least assisted through their problems—thereby severely cutting short the adventure and the movie. According to feature animation executive Tom Schumacher, in the idealized concept of the single unit nuclear family, if you have a mom and a dad, all the questions of security should be answered for you. That being damaged causes you to take on more independence. An orphan has to mature more quickly. If Belle had a mother who could sit her down and explain that even though Gaston looks good, he's bad, and although the Beast isn't such a treat to look at, he's a pretty nice guy inside, she wouldn't have to find out for herself.

9. **Family Breakups**. Disney's genius was in crafting high quality family entertainment, appealing to "kids of all ages." Specifically, when Walt dreamed up Disneyland he said his desire was to create an amusement park where adults and children could play together. Consequently, every attraction on opening day accommodated every age in the family. But, increasingly, new attractions are being introduced with age and height requirements. The Indiana Jones Adventure, Alien Encounter, the Twilight Zone Tower of Terror and others don't allow small children, while many of the Toontown offerings outlaw adults. Wasn't the whole idea to create attractions that wouldn't separate parents from their children?

The movie division seems headed in a similar direction, as each successive kid movie seems more juvenile and each adult movie seems more adult. Lines of separation are drawn even within the animated features. The central characters grow older, the themes more mature, but there are still a handful of precocious sidekicks to entertain children and connect them to the storyline. In the past, from the Seven Dwarfs and Jiminy Cricket to Abu, Magic Carpet, Timon and Pumbaa, although they may have played comparatively minor roles, they were active participants in the story. Kids still love Meeko, Flit and

Percy in *Pocahontas* and the gargoyles in *The Hunchback of Notre Dame*, but these characters cavort on the sidelines, operating separately from the plot, making it easier for children to lose interest in what's really going on.

10. **Synergytis.** Cross-promotion makes business sense, with different divisions promoting each other's products. It doesn't always make for good entertainment. It started inconspicuously enough, with notations to visit Disneyland at the bottom of newspaper ads for Disney movies and posters for the movies outside the parks, but now it's out of control. During a Disney Afternoon Live promotion, Disneyland was dressed up gaudily with cut-outs of characters from the company's syndicated afternoon television lineup.

"Synergy is very important for Disney," explained Imagineer Tony Baxter. "Divisions have to promote each other. So Disneyland Afternoon Live and Gadget's Go-Coaster were to please that division. Unfortunately, as soon as the shows are off the air, no one may remember them. In fact, Chip and Dale (Nut House) aren't there for the cartoons you and I know them for—they're only for *Chip and Dale's Rescue Rangers.*"

It's come to overkill. While the initial 1990 video release of *The Little Mermaid* features only the film, the video version of *Pocahontas*, released in 1996, contains a full eight minutes of commercials for Walt Disney World, upcoming movies, videos and an interactive CD-ROM storybook. For movie theaters, Disney puts so many key sequences in its previews of coming attractions that you feel as if you've seen the whole movie months before it's released. Even the fuzzy little animated characters seem increasingly designed with "plush toy" in mind and the big caravan sequences with an eye toward "theme park parade."

And as the Disney Company continues to grow and acquire other types of business, who knows what scary pairings may await us, further diluting the Disney name: A rap album by Winnie the Pooh? At Disneyland, the ABC-TV's *Roseanne* Dark Ride? The direct-to-video *Bambi Joins the Mighty Ducks*?

V

Disney Distracted
Microwave Magic
1960-1967

"I've been eating cold toast for eight years. Now... I kinda like it."

– W.C. Fields,
The Man on the Flying Trapeze (1935)

After the disappointing reception afforded *Sleeping Beauty*, Disney laid off hundreds of animators—the majority of his staff. The end of the era was official. But Walt had begun to lose interest in the film—and the medium itself—long before the final cel was photographed. Full animation was getting too expensive, too laborious. Walt was interested in making advancements, and economics prohibited him from even maintaining his former standards. And as animation in general became less ambitious and more restricted, the public also began to lose interest.

Disney would release just three animated features in the Sixties. "Walt felt that's all he could market," says Vance Gerry, who joined the studio in 1955. "All the market could take was one animated feature about every four years. They never made a great deal of money. My feeling was he wanted to keep the studio going for the loyal guys who had been with him all those years, to make sure they had work. Basically nobody was hired from 1960 to 1972."

Everything would be streamlined. Instead of beginning with months of meetings and dozens of storyboards, Walt would assign a single writer to work up a complete screenplay that he could read over before the expensive work began.

Although loath to limited animation, Disney animators did begin to take shortcuts. "(Director) Wooley Reitherman was always reusing animation. He repeated scenes not to save money but because he knew he had something that worked," Gerry remembers. "One scene Milt Kahl did in *Sword in the Stone* has a character pointing and saying, 'You're not going into that forest.' Wooley used it for another scene with new dialogue. Milt Kahl was watching in the sweat box (projection room), he didn't know they'd stolen his scene and when he saw it, he blew his top. The guy behind him leaned over and whispered, 'It worked better in the second scene.'"

Walt's attention and energies turned to newer, rawer outlets: television shows, live action films, live entertainment. He seemed most preoccupied with Disneyland. Here was a whole new canvas, an added third dimension to work in, to experiment in. Walt put many of his top animators and storymen to work designing attractions, but the technical nature of the new medium also required engineers. Walt recruited the most innovative, such as pioneering Imagineer Bob Gurr, whose motto became: "If it hasn't been done, then I'm very interested in doing it."

To amusement parks, Walt brought that same attention to detail, same quest for perfection, same striving to do something new and different, and same sense of what entertains the general public. As he had transformed the senseless, slapstick antics of primitive cartoons into believable, fluid animation, he turned the base thrills of primitive amusement parks into *theme* parks. He realized that a movie filled with non-stop action would be instantly forgotten without a good story, sympathetic characters, an interesting setting and proper staging. So, Walt gave a theme to every area in his park, to connect and give context to each ride, restaurant and shop. For Fantasyland, he built on the foundation of his animated characters and movies, for Frontierland Davy Crockett and the mystique of the Old West. Guests weren't just visiting a park and riding rides, they were active participants in their favorite stories. And, as in Disney movies, which always end with good winning out over evil, park visitors could experience exhilarating adventures and then, assuming they "sientate por favor" and "keep their hands and arms inside the vehicle at all times," return to civilization safe and victorious.

Feature animation took years to produce and was too expensive, once completed, to seriously change. With theme parks, Walt could see the progress immediately and change the components continuously. But what most excited him was starting something new, something that still had no formula.

- 12 -

101 Dalmatians

The Original Tale

Originally serialized in Woman's Day as "The Great Dog Robbery," Dodie Smith's 1956 book *The One Hundred and One Dalmatians* features canine Pongo and his wife, Missis, who live in London with their "pets," the financially secure Mr. and Mrs. Dearly, and two nannies who double as cook and butler. While out one day for a walk, the six run into Mrs. Dearly's old classmate Cruella de Vil, a deVilish woman with black hair on one side and white on the other. She worships furs, so much so she married a timid furrier, and shows an immediate interest in the dogs, especially upon hearing Missis is expecting. Cruella invites the Dearlys to dinner, after which they are followed home by her white Persian cat, whose kittens Cruella has drowned because they're not pedigree.

Obliged to reciprocate the invitation, the Dearlys make dinner for the de Vils—on the night Missis gives birth to fifteen puppies. After barely saving the runt, Cadpig, Mr. Dearly infuriates Cruella by refusing to sell any of the pups. Still, fifteen is too many for one mother to feed. The Dearlys happen upon a starving Dalmatian, Perdita, separated from her husband on her wedding day and from her eight pups soon after. The Dearlys bring her home to help nurse Missis' pups.

As soon as the puppies are old enough for their spots to start showing, Cruella returns, waiting for the Dearlys and adult dogs to go for a walk. She distracts the cook while her henchmen, Saul and Jasper Baddun, steal the fifteen pups. Distraught, the Dearlys contact Scotland Yard and take out front-page newspaper ads. During their walk the next evening, Pongo drags the group up a hill so, employing the Twilight Barking canine communication system, he can report the crime across England. The following evening, a Great Dane has a return message: puppies have been spotted in a remote Suffolk village.

Pongo and Missis set out for Suffolk in the middle of the night, leaving Perdita behind to watch their pets. After two days, they meet up with an elderly English sheepdog (the military-minded Colonel, slow yet seasoned) and tabby cat Pussy Willow (AKA Lieutenant Tib). They take Pongo and Missis to gloomy Hell Hall, where the Badduns are watching not fifteen but 97 puppies. The group resolves to save them all before the Badduns wake up in the morning, but must sneak out sooner after Cruella arrives and tells the Badduns the heat is on so they must slaughter and skin the puppies that night. After watching *What's My Crime?* on television, the Badduns discover the puppies missing and set out in pursuit.

As on the trek to Suffolk, various dogs provide meals and shelter for the caravan during the perilous journey home. The group rolls in soot to disguise themselves as black dogs. They finally hitch a ride to London in the back of a van. As they pass Cruella's house, her cat urges the dogs to tear up all her furs, bankrupting the de Vils, forcing them to flee the country and making London safe for Dalmatians. The Dearlys take in all 99 soot-covered dogs, and Cruella's cat. Perdita recognizes eight of the pups as her own. The Dearlys buy and fix up Hell Hall to house what become 101 Dalmatians when Perdita's husband shows up.

The Disney Version

One would think that, as far as appropriate subject matter for a Disney classic, "butchering puppies" would rate somewhere between "baby torture" and "liposuction." Yet, starting with a solitary screenwriter, *101 Dalmatians* would go pretty much by the book. Bill Peet did condense some of the characters, eliminating Cruella's husband and cat, as well as the surrogate mother dog, Perdita. He liked the dog's name, though, and gave it to Missis.

Peet also retained a scene in which the dogs, in unison with their masters, exchange wedding vows outside a chapel window. However, the censor board warned that it might offend certain audiences if the animals repeated the exact words of a solemn religious ceremony, particularly if the liturgy was identifiable. So, everything about the wedding became as generic as possible. So much so the ceremony looks like a Las Vegas special; there seem to be no guests in attendance, the bride is adorned in a simple dark blouse and skirt, and the groom wears a dark suit.

To work music into the picture, Peet relied on an old theater trick: make the lead, instead of a well-to-do professional, a down-and-out songwriter. But, quite unusual for a Disney picture, the actual songs used would not be written by a team. Mel Leven wrote both music and lyrics. His first assignment was to write a song called "Cruella de Vil," and he came up with three versions. "The first, 'The Creation of Cruella de Vil,' was about her being created out of a graveyard. It was dark and spooky," Leven said. "The second, 'Cruella de Vil (You Wicked Ole Thing),' was a nonsense version... 'Nobody loves you, everybody hates you. You are a monster, nothing but a monster.' And just before I was about to leave the house to play the songs for Disney, as I was waiting to leave, I had the idea to do it as a bluesy number. In 45 minutes, I wrote the song that was used in the picture."

The villain would also have to be done away with in a more visual manner than shipping her out of town (that could be saved for a less inventive picture like *The Aristocats*). Peet thought of four different ways to destroy her flashy roadster: she could drive it into a snowbank, over a cliff, into the back of a truck, or into a tree so it flies into a million parts. The ideas were so hard to choose from, he used them all.

Peet originally intended to close with newly rich Roger selling his song and buying the old De Vil place. Pongo and Perdita would settle down to a wonderful life on the Dalmatian Plantation, looking forward to another litter. Instead, he cut it short, with the reunion inspiring Roger to write a new song. Peet asked Leven to include "a lot of Dalmatian-ation rhymes," Leven remembered. "Bill Peet was the type of writer who thought every line in every song should rhyme. So I wrote 'Dalmatian Plantation,' but I didn't like it."

Leven wrote three additional songs for the picture, the dog food commercial ditty "Canine Crunchies" and two others that weren't used. "Don't Buy a Parrot from a Sailor" (because "all those birds know dirty words") was a drinking song sung by Horace and Jasper Badun [sic]. In the book, the Colonel offers to teach the puppies how to march and obey orders. So Leven composed "Cheerio,

Goodbye, Tootle-oo, Hip Hip," a marching song as the dogs tramp back to London.

Plot Holes

• "She's been investigated by Scotland Yard—what more do you want?" Anita asks Roger regarding Cruella the morning after the dognapping. But Cruella says she called because she just read about it in the paper—shouldn't this tip off Anita if Cruella was really investigated the night before? And Scotland Yard's investigative skills haven't improved any since the 1940s films in which Sherlock Holmes immediately knows that anyone suspected by Inspector Lestrade must be innocent. Hell Hall is the first place I would have checked.

Bloopers

• In the opening scene, as Roger lights his pipe at the piano, his watch momentarily vanishes from his left wrist. At the park, he evidently loses his watch in the pond because it's missing from his wrist when he removes his coat to put it on the drenched Anita.

• The first couple Roger and Pongo pass in the park—the short woman with the short dog—were walking in the opposite direction of the park when Pongo spied them from the apartment window a few minutes earlier.

• To encourage a meeting between Roger and Anita, Pongo puts Roger's hat on the park bench beside Anita. Instead, Roger tackles Pongo and snaps a leash onto his collar. Pongo, noticing Anita and Perdita have left, starts pulling Roger in pursuit, leaving the hat still on the bench. But when they get about ten to 20 feet away from the bench, the hat has somehow gotten back on Roger's head.

• Walking down the sidewalk on her way to the park, Anita wears a pale tan outfit. Later in the park, her clothes are a much darker brown. Also, she carries only a book. Yet after tumbling into the pond with Roger, she forgets about her book and instead fishes someone's purse from the bottom of the pond.

- Reaching for a second sandwich, which a pup has sneakily stripped of its innards, Horace says a few words, his speech garbled by the food in his mouth. He then takes a big bite out of the two bare slices of bread and speaks—but now he sounds as if there's nothing in his mouth.

- In the stable, Captain the horse rears up his left hind leg to kick the Baduns but from the back we see him kick with his right leg. And he kicks Jasper first, who had been lined up behind his left leg.

- Television-fixated puppy Lucky is identifiable throughout the movie by his two black ears. But in one shot where, slipping on ice, he complains he wants to walk on snow, his ears are white. Perhaps they were momentarily frozen.

Hidden Images

They're not exactly hidden, but note the dogs in the pet shop during the Twilight Bark. In addition to Peg and the bulldog from *Lady and the Tramp* are seven unspotted pups who were first drawn as Dalmatians barking at the TV for an earlier scene.

Strange Reactions

Before 1960 it would have been impossible to animate one spotted dog let alone 101. The development of the Xerox photocopying system made it not only possible, but led to a revolutionary, more abstract style of animation devoid of sharp lines. The animators, whose original drawings always had been inked in and painted over, loved it because it allowed more of their actual work to show up on screen. Walt didn't like it. "There had always been a disparity between characters and backgrounds because characters always had a line around them," layout artist Vance Gerry said. "When they said, 'Let's go to Xerox,' Ken Anderson was afraid everything would blend together. Plus, we all loved to draw with pen and ink, so we really overdrew. In the end, Walt felt the backgrounds were much too competitive with the characters with lines around them."

- 13 -

The Sword in the Stone

The Original Tale

In *The Sword in the Stone* (1939), T.H. White retells the legend of King Arthur, peppered with other figures from literature, legend and Greek mythology for good measure. It begins in a town where lives Sir Ector and his son, Kay. Ector is the foster father of another boy, two years younger, called the Wart because it almost rhymes with his given name, Art. The boys are friends. Young Wart is smarter and Kay a bit brutish, but destined one day to be knighted and become master of the estate. One afternoon, while hawking, their bird flies off into the dangerous forest at the edge of Sir Ector's land. Wart heads in after the bird, stumbling upon the magician Merlyn's cottage. The grizzled wizard, aware of the future since he lives backwards through time, has been expecting the boy and introduces him to his temperamental old talking owl, Archimedes.

Merlyn returns with the boy to serve as his and Kay's tutor. But the wizard gives Wart some extra-special lessons: turning him into a perch to learn from a pike, king of the moat; into an owl to learn from Archimedes, and into a hawk, snake and badger to learn from the like. Merlyn and Wart also turn invisible to help free some prisoners from an ogre's castle.

Practicing archery one day, Wart shoots an arrow into the woods. He and Kay go in to retrieve it and happen upon the cottage of Madame Mim. The sorceress imprisons them and plans to eat them, until Merlyn arrives. During their wizards' duel, Merlyn and Mim turn themselves into various beasts, ending with Merlyn becoming a germ that infects and kills Mim.

Other adventures include a joust, a boar hunt, and a rescue mission with Robin Hood and his Merry Men.

Six years pass and Kay, nearing knighthood, has become more proud, difficult and sarcastic, and spends less time with Wart. But the day before Kay is to be knighted, all learn that King Uther has died and a sword in an anvil and stone have magically appeared in a church courtyard. The sword carries the inscription "Whoso pulleth out this sword of this stone and anvil, is rightwise king born of all England." Everyone is invited to a tournament to see if anyone can free the stubborn blade. Merlyn, though, says it is time for him to leave, since his one pupil is to be knighted and his other student will become his squire.

After the knighting, the family sets out for London, but once there Kay realizes he has forgotten his sword. He tells his squire to fetch one, and Wart reluctantly consents. He sees a sword in a stone and is unable to pull it out. On the third try, encouraged by advice from a nearby pike, badger, owl and snake, he easily slides the sword out. He takes the weapon to Kay, who tries to take credit for it. But after the sword is replaced in the stone, no one can remove it but Wart. He is crowned and identified as King Arthur, Uther's son whom Merlyn took to Ector as a baby.

The Disney Version

The Sword in the Stone was the feature the animators made against their will. They wanted to follow up *101 Dalmatians* with *Chanticleer*, based on Edmond Rostand's 1910 psychological drama about a rooster who thinks his crowing makes the sun rise. For 25 years, the studio had tried unsuccessfully to make the story work, and writer Bill Peet finally told the animators to give it up. The story wouldn't come off, he explained, because it was too weird, and no matter how well you can draw a rooster, you can't make him sympathetic.

The veteran animators were furious at Peet, who had already been given the go-ahead by Walt to write a screenplay from T.H. White's novel. The artists wanted to develop their own project, the old way. Walt's preoccupations had left everyone in the department with more freedom but less direction.

Left to their own devices, Marc Davis, Ken Anderson, Wooley Reitherman, Milt Kahl, Frank Thomas and Ollie Johnston spent about six months meeting at night, developing a manuscript for *Chanticleer*, elaborate storyboards, giant pastel paintings, even musical numbers. Finally came the big presentation to Walt. He hated it. Walt then led the sulking animators down the hall to find out what Peet had been up to. The writer showed them his more modest storyboards and a few gags with Merlin [sic] and Archimedes. Walt liked it, and the humiliated mob nodded with forced smiles and gritted teeth. This movie would not be animated by loving hands.

Peet's first task had been uncomplicating White's narrative. To get a tighter, more direct storyline, he had to extricate the Arthurian legend from all the mythical tangents. Peet deleted most every character who wasn't crucial to the story. Pellinore, an eccentric king eternally hunting the elusive Questing Beast, was cut down to not much more than a messenger. Hobs, Sir Ector's hawk trainer, became Kay's substitute squire who is never seen on film. The palace's nineteen hounds became two.

The one nonessential holdover was Mim since the wizards' duel leant itself so well to animation. When Walt saw Mim drawn as a frowzy old lady, he suggested a darker villain, "a big, tall dame with black hair." "Walt," Peet responded, "we always do that. She has to be a counterpart to Merlin. He's an old eccentric, and so she has to be, too. They have to match."

Peet's scenario also stressed the angle of brains versus brawn. While Wart remained the sympathetic pre-teen of the first part of the book, Kay would be the more boorish near-20-year-old of the end of the story. Foster father Ector similarly became less understanding and more oafish. Wart's transformations took the shape of vulnerable animals under attack by stronger foes, a small fish, squirrel and sparrow. Instead of talky lessons, the scenes became excuses for action, comedy business and musical numbers. A Wile E. Coyote-type wolf was also thrown in for added slapstick.

A sticking point for Peet was the idea of predestination, that Wart was born to be king, so he omitted any mention that the boy might really be Uther's son. He thought making the boy out to be a waif who earned the throne was a better message. Besides, Walt hadn't read the book and would never know the difference.

Another thing Walt would never know was that *he* was Peet's model for the crusty old Merlin. Peet saw them both as argumentative and cantankerous, playful at times and extremely intelligent. In his drawings he even borrowed Walt's nose.

By this time, even the songwriting process had become more streamlined. Instead of looking for outside help, Walt had hired two full-time staff songwriters, Richard and Robert Sherman. After writing "Tall Paul" and other rock and roll songs for Annette Funicello, the Sherman Brothers joined Disney in 1960 to write a number for Annette in *The Horsemasters*. They would write about 200 more songs for Disney movies, television shows and theme park attractions over the next eleven years. "For *The Sword in the Stone*, we were given the storyline by Bill Peet and told which sequences needed songs, and we wrote songs for those sequences, 'Higgitus Figgitus,' 'That's What Makes the World Go Round' and 'The Most Befuddling Thing,'" Richard Sherman recalled, "all except for 'Mad Madam Mim.' That one was a concept without a song, and we thought it'd be fun to have a song there."

It was also a little easier, since Peet's dialogue became the lyrics.

Plot Holes

• If Merlin is really "the world's most powerful magician," why can't he magically fish a bucket of water out of the well in the opening scene or fix the leaky roof of the guest room during his first rainy night there?

• "He's alive—and he talks!" exclaims Wart upon discovering that Merlin's owl is not stuffed, obviously having never before met a talking animal. Yet a second later the boy's serving the bird tea.

• Merlin at one point is looking for his "flying machine model," and Wart points out a miniature biplane above his head. Wart then asks, in wonder: "You mean man will fly in one of those someday?" Never before having seen anything like this craft in any size, where did Wart get the idea a man would be in it?

Bloopers

• The dancing sugar bowl isn't the only "animated" object on Merlin's kitchen table. We first see the bowl of cookies in the middle of table, but in subsequent angles it is closer to Wart's side of table, then closer to Merlin's side, then back in the middle. The creamer gradually edges from near the middle of the table to Merlin's side and then back again. A spoon suddenly appears alongside Wart's cup, disappears and returns again. After Merlin pours tea into the cup in front of him and has Wart hand it to the owl, yet another cup now assumes its place on the table. Merlin pours tea into a mini-locomotive, which chugs across the table passing a spoon that wasn't there before. It also passes by the teapot, which should still be in Merlin's hand, but not by the creamer, which has vanished. There are no other spoons on the table until Merlin asks Wart if he would like some sugar at which point a spoon suddenly is sticking out of the creamer. Another spoon is lying next to the sugar bowl. As the sugar bowl tramps across the table towards Wart, it passes a saucer that wasn't there before.

• To look up a magic spell, Merlin brings four books to the table. But when the books begin filing into Merlin's bag, there are five of them.

• Kay is wearing a brown shirt while sparring with his father, but when he runs downstairs to battle the dirty dishes he has on a green shirt. Then, in the middle of his sword fight with the brooms, Kay's sword suddenly vanishes. He gets his sword back in the next shot, but is now fighting with his left hand instead of his right. Finally, after Merlin arrives to deactivate the dishes, Kay's sword now hangs from his side in a sheath that wasn't there before.

• That's an awful weird deck Mim is playing solitaire with. It contains *two* cards reading Three of Hearts.

• When Wart runs into Merlin's room to tell him he's going to be Kay's squire, Merlin is sitting with his chair facing the fireplace and his pipe on a stand to his right. In the next shot, his chair is turned away from the fire, and the pipe and stand have vanished.

- 14 -

Mary Poppins

The Original Tale

In 1934, mysticist Pamela Lyndon Travers introduced a most extraordinary nanny in the first of a series of four *Mary Poppins* books. Mary first blows into town upon hearing of an opening at the Banks home to watch Jane, Michael and infant twins John and Barbara. The children are immediately intrigued by the nanny whose attitude is no-nonsense but whose actions are quite magical, such as when she unpacks a variety of items from an empty carpet bag and gives the children medicine that tastes like the sweet of their choice.

The nanny tells the children bizarre stories and takes them on many strange adventures. They meet her uncle, Mr. Wigg, who has laughing gas that's contagious and makes them all float. They find a compass that takes them to wherever they spin it, and meet a polar bear in the North, a macaw in the jungle of the South, a panda bear in the East and dolphins in the West. On the way to visit their father at the bank, the kids buy some birdseed from the Bird Woman, who sits on the cathedral steps shrieking, "Feed the birds! Tuppence a bag!" In the middle of the night, Jane and Michael join Mary Poppins at a strange zoo where the people are in cages and the animals throw Mary a birthday party.

On her day off, Mary visits Bert the Match-Man, who sells matches on rainy days when he can't draw pictures on the pavement. After entering one of his sidewalk sketches of a countryside, he and Mary are served tea, then take a quick trip on merry-go-round horses.

When the wind changes, Mary opens her umbrella, catches up with the breeze, and flies away. Mrs. Banks is furious that she has left. The children are heartbroken, but relieved to find she has left Michael the magic compass and Jane a picture of herself drawn by Bert and signed "Au revoir," suggesting they will meet again.

A polite waiter serves Mary Poppins and Bert tea in Mary Shepard's original illustration to Pamela Travers' book.

The Disney Version

For twenty years, Walt tried to purchase the rights to *Mary Poppins*, but Travers stubbornly refused, convinced no one could do justice to her adventures or characters. Disney finally turned to the Sherman Brothers. "Since I wasted so much time with this," he said, holding the book, "why don't you take it home with you and tell me what you think of it."

Richard Sherman remembered, "He handed us the book and that changed our entire lives. We realized that this was our chance, that it would make us or break us."

"In about two weeks we brought in copious notes and we had a half-hour meeting with Walt that turned into two-and-a-half hours," Robert Sherman added. "By coincidence, we'd selected seven chapters that we thought would be good, and he pulled out his notes and he had selected the same seven chapters."

The Shermans began without a screenplay, simply writing songs for the sequences they thought would work best. Over the next two years, the team wrote 35 songs (of which fourteen were included in the final film) and helped convince Travers that Walt would take good care of her nanny. For the magic compass scene, the Shermans transported Mary and the children to different lands, each with its own musical number. They wrote the "Chinese Festival Song" for China, "South Sea Islands Symphony" and "Tiki Town" for the jungle, "The North Pole Polka" for the icy north, "The Land of Sand" for the Sahara Desert, "The Beautiful Briny Sea" for the bottom of the ocean, and "The Chimpanzoo" for the relocated sequence with monkeys walking around the zoo and people inside the cages. Walt, finally realizing the extraneousness of a series of intercontinental sidetrips, dropped the whole idea of a magic compass.

Fortunately, the Shermans were able to resurrect some of the sliced songs for later projects, "using the trunk," as they call it. They reworked "The West Wind Song" into the wispy French ballad "Mon Amor Perdu" for *Big Red*. "Strengthen the Dwelling" was meant to be used by the first nanny to teach the children Bible verses, but was quickly discarded. It was salvaged verbatim as an exercise song for the Biddle Bible Class in *The Happiest Millionaire*.

Walt's first choice to play Mrs. Banks was Glynis Johns, but when she arrived for the audition she thought she was reading for the role of Mary Poppins. Walt convinced her the Shermans had written a wonderful song for her and, after she left, he broke them the news. In four days, they rewrote a previously discarded number for Mary, "Practically Perfect," into "Sister Suffragette." Johns loved the song and agreed to the role.

For Andrews' first song, the Sherman Brothers wrote the lullaby "The Eyes of Love." But, said Richard Sherman, "Julie Andrews wanted a bright song there for her keynote number. So it was replaced by 'A Spoonful of Sugar,' which, of course, was a big hit, so we couldn't complain."

Also going unused was another song in the children's bedroom, "A Name's a Name" ("you're a Michael, you're a Jane and I'm a Mary Poppins"), for Mary to sing as she measured the children's height.

Then, for a scene before Mary, Bert and the kids jump into the chalk drawing on the pavement, the Shermans wrote a short "ball of fluff song." In its place, the director decided it was a better opportunity to let Dick Van Dyke do some physical comedy, such

Doo Wop Disney

Walt always liked "nonsense songs" because they were so catchy. For songwriters, make-believe words make for easy lyrics, such as in a magic spell, because they can sound like, rhyme with or mean anything the lyricist wants them to. Coincidentally enough, one of Walt's proudest achievements, *Mary Poppins*, contained two such numbers ("Chim Chim Cher-ee" and, that pinnacle of patter, that summit of mumbo jumbo, that high tower of babble, "Supercalifragilisticexpialidocious").

Can you match the gibberish title to its respective movie?

(1) "Bibbidi Bobbidi Boo"

(2) "Biddle-dee-dee"

(3) "Bye-Yum Pum Pum"

(4) "Hi Diddle Dee Dee"

(5) "Higgitus Figitus"

(6) "La La Lu"

(7) "Oo-De-Lally"

(8) "Passamaschloddy"

(9) "Substiuiary Locomotion"

(10) "Tee-Dum Tee-Dee"

(11) "Twitterpated"

(12) "Zip-a-Dee Doo-Dah"

(a) *Bambi*

(b) *Bedknobs & Broomsticks*

(c) *Cinderella*

(d) *Lady and the Tramp*

(e) *Peter Pan*

(f) *Pete's Dragon*

(g) *Pinocchio*

(h) *Robin Hood*

(i) *Song of the South*

(j) *The Happiest Millionaire*

(k) *The Sword in the Stone*

(l) *Toby Tyler*

Answers:
(1) c. (2) l. (3) j. (4) g. (5) k. (6) d. (7) h. (8) f. (9) b. (10) e. (11) a. (12) i.

as a pantomime balancing act. Van Dyke, though, does recite the opening lyrics to the song ("You think, you wink, you do a double blink...") before bounding into the sidewalk sketch.

The "Jolly Holiday" sequence that follows was first conceived using all live actors and only backgrounds drawn. Walt suggested that the four waiters be penguins, which led to animating everything except the principal actors.

The closing number was first titled "Sticks and Paper and Strings," after its opening line ("With sticks and paper and strings, you can have your own set of wings..."). But when the first line was changed to "With tuppence for paper and strings," the title had to be changed as well, and became "Let's Go Fly a Kite."

The story slowly took shape. "We changed the period," Richard Sherman said. "There's no romance in 1934. So we set it in Edwardian England at the turn of the century. With all the costumes and everything, it was a whole different world. You could make believe in a flying nanny."

Walt eventually assigned storyman and artist Don da Gradi to work with the Shermans. The main problem with the book was that it had no story. So Disney looked to its surest formula: children separated from love. Since Mr. Banks in the book seemed a bit too preoccupied with his bank, Disney put his job between him and his children. Mrs. Banks became an air-headed suffragette. The infant twins were discarded, and Mary Poppins, toned down a bit from the book's ever-in-a-foul-mood heroine, became the conduit to bring the children and parents back together again.

Unfortunately, Travers contractually had the last word on the screenplay and songs, and she proved even testier than her fictional heroine. "Everything was subject to the approval of Miss Travers and she didn't like any of our ideas," Richard Sherman recalled. "After two years of work, we had two weeks of solid meetings with her making copious, ridiculous notes and tape recording everything. We fought like crazy to get some semblance of a storyline, since her book was just incidents, but she didn't like the idea of a storyline. She didn't like the color red and didn't want it used anywhere in the picture, until Don da Gradi pointed out, 'But the postboxes and telephone boxes are all red in England.' She complained the songs were for women not for men; she couldn't visualize that although we were singing them for her, women would sing them in the picture. In the end, it came down to she just wanted to make herself heard. Walt finally convinced her to let us make our version. We finally got the go-ahead to do it. But she was weird and tried to make the whole thing miserable."

Plot Holes

• Although the movie's Mary is markedly less rude than Travers', it's bewildering that the Banks family should be so loyal to her. For someone "practically perfect in every way," Poppins can be quite a pill. A sampling of her attitude, spoken to her employer: "I don't explain anything."

• Dick Van Dyke occasionally loses his cockney accent. In particular, check out the opening one-man-band scene when, after drifting off, he says, "I'm sorry where was I..."

Cutting Room Floor

Walt was confident he had a great picture in *Mary Poppins*; he just worried that maybe he had too much picture. It clocked in at 139 minutes plus an intermission, an eternity for a child to spend in a movie theater seat. Walt considered cutting the lullaby "Stay Awake" and the laughing sequence with Ed Wynn, but, fortunately, thought better of it.

Strange Reactions

Mary Poppins proved tremendously successful, made tons of money, won five of the astounding thirteen Academy Awards for which it was nominated, and further popularized Travers' series. Yet, according to Richard Sherman, "even after its tremendous success, (Travers) said she never liked it and cursed it, but it sold more books for her than she could have ever imagined. She didn't like that it was *Walt Disney's* Mary Poppins."

Attraction Offspring

It is such a natural that Disney has long considered a Mary Poppins attraction. "In fact, plans for a Mary Poppins ride were part of my portfolio when I first applied to WDI (Walt Disney Imagineering)," said Tony Baxter. "I thought it was so original, but it got tossed on a shelf with 50 others, and they were all umbrellas or carousel horses. I did horses."

The closest it ever got was for the grand opening of Florida's Magic Kingdom. The Disneyland dark rides are classified by mood: Snow White is scary, Peter Pan beautiful and Mr. Toad fun and crazy. In designing Disney World, the Imagineers intended to substitute Sleeping Beauty for the scary ride, Mary Poppins for beautiful and Ichabod and the Headless Horseman for fun and crazy. But Roy Disney, Sr., said, "No, I think it should be exactly the same as Disneyland." Ironically, the rides would be changed completely anyway. Poppins was finally included as a scene in the Disney-MGM Studios' Great Movie Ride.

- 15 -

The Jungle Book

The Original Tale

The Jungle Book was based on *The Jungle Books* (1894-1895), Rudyard Kipling's two volumes of tales of life in the Indian wild. The first book's first three chapters feature Mowgli, a baby whose parents are scared off by the menacing tiger Shere Khan. Before the beast can kill the boy, Mowgli is taken in by a family of wolves. Bagheera, the sly, bold and reckless black panther, instructs the boy to hunt, while Baloo, the sleepy old brown bear, teaches him the Law of the Jungle.

During one lesson, the lawless gray apes abduct Mowgli in hopes of learning from the man-cub. Swinging the boy from tree to tree, the monkeys take him to a lost city, where they dance about and sing foolish songs. Bagheera and Baloo finally arrive, but are badly outnumbered. But when Kaa the 30-foot-long rock python shows up, the monkeys begin to flee. Kaa commands them to freeze, then orders the transfixed apes to step closer until they walk right down his throat.

When Mowgli is about 12, Bagheera tells him that Shere Khan has been plotting with some of the younger wolves to overthrow the pack's leader, Akela, who maintains the Law. Mowgli goes to the man village to get a basket filled with red hot coals, for all animals are afraid of the Red Flower. Confronting Shere Khan and the wolves, the man-cub thrusts a branch into the fire and waves it menacingly at the mutinous gang. Akela is reestablished as leader, but Mowgli realizes he no longer belongs in the jungle.

He returns to the village and is taken in by a couple whose infant son was carried off by a tiger about the time baby Mowgli was. For three months, the boy tries to adapt, learning the ways and language of man. He doesn't ingratiate himself to a hunter named Buldeo, for as the great outdoorsman regales the village with tall tales of the jungle, Mowgli corrects him.

One day, while tending the cattle and buffalo, the man-cub learns from one of his wolf brothers that Shere Khan is lying in wait in a ravine. So Mowgli has the wolf and Akela drive the cattle into one side of the ravine and the buffalo into the other side, trampling the tiger to death. Having promised he would one day mount Khan's hide on Council Rock, Mowgli begins to skin the beast. But Buldeo arrives, intending to take credit for the kill. Mowgli commands Akela to scare away the hunter. Buldeo convinces the villagers Mowgli is a sorcerer, and they cast the boy back into the jungle.

In Book Two, Buldeo leads the villagers into the jungle to hunt for the bewitched boy. They then plan to execute Mowgli's foster parents, so, while his animal friends hold the hunters' attention, the boy sneaks into the village and frees the prisoners. Hathi and the other elephants then level the village. About five years later, during a particularly lonesome mating season, Mowgli again realizes his place is with other people and rejoins his mother.

The Disney Version

In 1962, Disney purchased all thirteen *Jungle Book* stories, but decided to concentrate on the Mowgli tales. Bill Peet was again assigned to the story, Terry Gilkyson to the music. Walt was looking for something both naturalistic and fantastic, suggestive of the compelling stag fight in *Bambi*. "It was Walt's wish to be closer to the Kipling version, a little more serious," Gilkyson recalled. "Wooley Reitherman took me to see parts of *Bambi* that had a *Fantasia* look to them, quite beautiful, quite ethereal, pretty heavy stuff."

Instructed "to write with Kipling in mind," Gilkyson's opening number, "Brothers All," would begin with a book, its cover illustrated by Mowgli and a wolf, echoing the book's theme that "whether we swim or crawl, we are of one blood." Next, the wolf pack performs a barbershop quartet, "The Song of the Seeonee," punctuated by howls.

When Peet suggested "Bare Necessities" as the title of a song for Baloo, Gilkyson wrote a bouncy jazz number. The animators, however, were looking for a different tempo to match the smoother movement of the character they had designed, so Gilkyson slowed down the beat and revised the lyrics.

Next, the vain monkeys, after capturing Mowgli and swinging him through the trees, would sing the Gilbert and Sullivan-influenced "Monkey See, Monkey Do." In the solemn "Hate Song," Shere Khan and Buldeo alternately boast of their vicious plans for the other ("It isn't fair to hate me when you know me very slightly/When you know me better then you can judge me rightly/And all who know me very well/Hate me, hate me, hate me..."). Bagheera and Baloo sing the perky "In a Day's Work," reminding Mowgli that the early bird catches the worm.

Finally, Mowgli, after briefly returning to his mother's village, sings to Bagheera the sentimental "I Knew I Belonged to Her," recalling a dream of a place and a face that he had once known.

Peet kept the story fairly faithful to Kipling. His main departure would not only be from Kipling, but from Disney, as well. Peet, according to Vance Gerry, "wanted to take it in an entirely different direction. He wanted to base the characters on the actors, instead of creating characters whom the actors become. It was like radio voices. And when you get somebody like Phil Harris, it's hard to swallow. At first, Phil Harris didn't like it either. He was reluctant. But after the success he had (as Baloo) in *Jungle Book*, he loved it."

But by the mid-1960s, Peet was growing increasingly successful writing children's books on the side, as well as increasingly disgruntled with Walt's sometimes tyrannical rule. After a fight over the preliminary recording for Bagheera's voice, Peet walked out.

Walt took another look at the completed script and score, and realized the mistake. Peet's version "was closer to the authentic Kipling, a morose story, a real downer, spooky, mysterious, with all these bad things happening to this kid. Walt said, 'This is a total disaster. I don't care how artistically correct it is,'" according to Richard Sherman.

Walt handed the screenplay back to the story department to transform it from a "jungle fantasy" into a "jungle farce." Kipling's serious old brown bear became a tutor by chance who wasn't serious, old or brown. The aged, well-respected lords of the jungle, Hathi and Kaa, became buffoons, the elephant a blustery British Colonel, the snake a hissing comic villain.

Cut were the two most pathetic characters, Buldeo the hunter and Ishtar, a buzzard who preyed off other beasts' kill and furnished information on the movements of the hunter and the mancub. The conniving carrion was replaced by four smart-talking vultures patterned after the Beatles who, like the crows in *Dumbo*, prove to be unlikely encouragers to Mowgli. The boy's mother gave way to a little village girl, whom lovestruck Mowgli can follow with his wide eyes the only explanation necessary.

The story's new direction forced out Gilkyson's songs, except for the original jazz version of "Bare Necessities," which was already in animation as test footage. Walt turned to the Sherman Brothers. "Have you read the book?" he asked them. "Well, don't. We have one good song. We need a few more."

The Shermans crafted a march for Hathi, a new barbershop quartet number for the vultures ("That's What Friends Are For"), a scat song for lead ape Louis Prima ("I Wan'na Be Like You"), and a gentle melody for the village girl ("My Own Home"). Lastly, for Kaa's hypnotic number, the brothers revived the mysterious "Land of Sand," written for the discarded Around the World sequence from *Mary Poppins*, and simply wrote new lyrics to produce "Trust in Me."

Bloopers

• During the elephant inspection as Colonel Hathi retells his Victoria Cross story, a gray elephant appears among the troops at the front of the lineup who hadn't been there before. Then, when Hathi leans on his pointer, it seems to snap near the center. But when he holds it up to his eye for a closer look, we see it has actually broken just a couple of inches from the end. Miraculously, in the next shot of the Colonel swatting a fly off one elephant and cropping the hair of another, the stick has healed itself. A second later, as Hathi turns to Mowgli, it is again broken and, a second later, re-mended when he uses it to poke Mowgli in the nose.

• At night, after the King Louie battle, Baloo speaks with Bagheera as Mowgli sleeps. Baloo has a shiner around his left eye. But when he looks down at the water, his reflection, which should present a mirror image and show the black eye on the opposite side, has the black eye on the same side. Do not despair. Through the miracle of modern medicine, by the end of Baloo's brief conversation with Bagheera, not only does the shiner completely clear up, but the sun completely rises, as well.

• When Bagheera approaches Colonel Hathi to enlist his help finding the runaway Mowgli before Khan does, Hathi stuffs his pointer behind his right ear. In the next shot, the pointer is behind his left ear.

• As the girl from the village arrives at the waterside and begins playing with her hair, she has bows in each ponytail. But in her reflection, there are no bows. She is playing with her hair over her right shoulder, and her reflection, which should mirror her hair over the opposite shoulder, shows her hair over the same shoulder. Fortunately, in the next shot she has her bows back.

Strange Reactions

When Walt died on December 16, 1966, *Jungle Book* was well into production. It opened ten months later to favorable reviews and record-setting box office, briefly quieting talk of shutting down the animation department. The film was so successful, the studio reportedly considered something else Walt wound never have approved: a sequel. Terry Gilkyson, Floyd Huddleston, the Sherman Brothers and others wrote a batch of songs, Phil Harris and Louis Prima recorded them, and they were released on the album *More Jungle Book*, to see if audiences really wanted more of the characters. The record sold poorly, quashing any hope for a movie sequel. More significantly, Walt hadn't been gone a year and already his successors were trying to repeat themselves.

VI

Disney Duplicated

Reheated Leftovers

1968-1984

"Recipes without the author, without the cuisine to which they were once a living, seamless part, die."

– John Thorne,
Simple Cooking (1987)

In Salten's novel, Bambi's mother would leave him alone in the forest so when the inevitable day arrived that she wasn't around anymore, he would be ready to fend for himself. So after Walt died, it wasn't that everyone was incompetent and didn't know what to do and let the company fall apart. It was that most everyone was *competent* but didn't know what to do and let the company fall apart.

Walt had spent a lifetime retaining control and final say over everything. He kept all his talented writers, animators and designers as suppressed and anonymous as possible to make the Disney name synonymous with quality family entertainment, and now there was no one ready to take charge.

What Walt had instilled in everyone was that the hallmark of Disney entertainment was consistency of vision, *his* vision. Mistakenly, his successors saw that vision as a paint-by-numbers kit, instead of a living blueprint that was more than beautiful art, an uplifting moral, some catchy Sherman Brothers songs and a happy ending. Walt's movies had a pulse and his pulse was the audience's. His successors, too busy looking at him, lost sight of the audience. In a sense, Walt continued to run the company, from the grave. Every decision wasn't second-guessed with "Is this the absolute best idea?" but with "What would Walt say?"

"About the time Walt died, the power was 'The Committee of Indecision' and everything was done by committee," recalls Richard Sherman. "They'd hang things up, twit, worry, suffer. Good songs were sliced out of pictures, pictures were put on the shelf. They couldn't make up their minds."

The powers that be grew so afraid of doing something that Walt wouldn't, that it resigned itself, in animation, live action, television and theme parks, to repeat what it had done before. Try dipping the same tea bag for the seventh time and sample how fresh and watered down the results are. The once innovative idea men were growing older and losing touch with their audience, but refusing to let go. "I think what probably hurt Disney in the early years was the lack of competition for animation. For 30 years, they just had the same people doing the same thing the same way, serviceable but pretty creaky," suggests animator Will Finn. "There was a diminishing circle of people, which led to a diminishing product, which led to a diminishing audience, which led to a diminishing infusion of new blood. This self-defeating cycle of events almost torpedoed an art form."

Animator Tom Sito agrees: "If in the early Sixties you said you wanted to be an animator, they'd say you were out of your mind. It was a shrinking business where everyone was clinging tenuously to their jobs and nobody moved up till somebody left. I had to grow up on sweetened cereal and Saturday morning TV."

"I got the impression that the old-timers kind of wanted the classic animation to die with them, that they felt it couldn't—or shouldn't—go on without them," notes writer Fred Lucky, one of the younger generation finally recruited in the early Seventies.

Walt's brother, Roy, died in 1971. The same year, Walt's son-in-law, Ron Miller, realized that Walt's animators must also be mortal. If Disney animation was to continue, the Nine Old Men would have to give way to young men. Just before his death, Walt had broken ground in Valencia, California, on a private arts college, the California Institute of the Arts. The school opened an animation department in 1972. Certain students, once recruited by the studio, would work side by side with the old-timers, apprentices learning at the knee of the master. The veterans were proud to share techniques and secrets they had not only learned but created. Still, there's one thing about sharing something; you can't take hold of it until the giver lets go.

Meanwhile, things weren't any more inventive at Disney's theme park division. Walt Disney World's Magic Kingdom, which opened in Florida in 1971, was Disneyland photocopied with the Enlarge button jammed. Over the next decade, few original attractions were added to either park. For one thing, there were no classic movies to inspire them. Rides were designed after *Robin Hood, Island at the Top of the World, The Black Hole, Tron* and others, but the movies proved financial and critical disappointments, and were quickly forgotten. Unlike a film, which can quickly disappear from movie theaters and live a life of quiet anonymity bridging used car commercials on late night TV, themed attractions remain on stage month after month, year after year, for people to ask, "The *Watcher in the Woods* ride? What's *that*?" The subject must endure or be reconfigured to appeal to current audiences.

The Imagineers were able to keep somewhat busy resurrecting old ideas that never came to life when Walt was alive (Country Bear Jamboree, Haunted Mansion), or creating themed roller coasters (Space Mountain, Big Thunder Mountain), then the craze at competing amusement parks. Among the most aggressive ideas was a log flume ride, but even it would be themed to a 40-year-old film and, in fact, "languished for years," Tony Baxter says. "Ron Miller was on his way out. It was a sad state of affairs because he hadn't created any viable movies to turn into attractions. We couldn't build a *Black Hole* ride because Disneyland is where the greatest American myths reside. After a decade, parents might remember (such a movie), but I didn't want the kids to not know. I didn't want Disneyland to become Lawrence Welk Village."

- 16 -

The Aristocats

The Disney Version

The plot of *The Aristocats* sounds vaguely familiar: a pampered cat and her three kittens are kidnapped, she is romanced by a smooth-talking stray and, after the villain is bested by a motley collection of animals, reunited with her master, who also takes in her suitor and the rest of the strays. Déjà vu! A feline *Lady and the Tramp* meet *101 Dalmatians*—right down to the photo pose finale!

Actually, it was first planned as a two-part live action show for NBC's *Wonderful World of Disney*. In 1962, Tom McGowan and Tom Rowe wrote a 106-page story, then, joined by Harry Tytle, they penned two screenplays, with Boris Karloff in mind for the role of the kidnapping butler and Francoise Rosay as the victimized matron.

Walt eventually decided that it would make a better animated feature, and postponed work on it until after *The Jungle Book*. By that time, *Jungle Book* would also heavily influence the project. Again, the animators patterned the characters after the actors, O'Malley the alley cat after happy-go-lucky Phil Harris, the refined Duchess after Eva Gabor and the trumpeting swinger Scat Cat after Louis Armstrong, although Disney had to settle for the voice of Scatman Crothers.

Pat Buttram and George "Goober" Lindsey were cast as two farm dogs who interfere with the butler's kidnapping attempt. The characters proved so popular that the story was rewritten so the butler returned to the farm to retrieve his lost hat and umbrella just to work in another scene with the dogs.

The Aristocats would be the last Disney picture the Sherman Brothers would work on as staff songwriters, growing increasingly frustrated by the direction the studio was taking after Walt's death. They wrote a long list of songs, but only two ("The Aristocats," "Scales and Arpeggios") and a half ("She Never Felt Alone") survived. The latter was first titled "Pourquoi (and Why)," and then "I Never Feel Alone," since originally Madame sang, "The reason why I never feel alone...," her cat purred, "Pourquoi," and Madame continued, because she has her cat. Later, in the snippet that made it to film, Duchess would reprise the song as "she never felt alone..."

For the musical band of strays, the Shermans wrote a big production number called "Le Jazz Hot." Disney, looking for something a little more raucous, a little more like *Jungle Book's* frantic "I Wan'na Be Like You," enlisted Floyd Huddleston and Al Rinker to come up with "Ev'rybody Wants To Be a Cat."

Another Sherman Brothers song didn't make it because neither did one of the characters who sang it. Originally, the devious butler Edgar had a love interest and partner in crime, Elvira the maid, and they were to sing a romantic duet in counterpoint, "How Much You Mean to Me (and Court Me Slowly)."

Also cut was a song for O'Malley, "My Way's the Highway." In its place, the filmmakers had Terry Gilkyson write the more autobiographical "Thomas O'Malley Cat," which, in a show of further indecision, they recorded in two versions. "It was the same song, but they orchestrated it twice," Gilkyson explained. "They used the simpler one, because they may have thought the other too elaborate or too hot. It was a jazz version with a full orchestra."

Plot Holes

- Anachronisms abound. There are the two dogs from the Old South—in the middle of France. There's a jazz band in 1910, although "Le jazz hot" was a post-World War I phenomenon. And Scat Cat's party is more Sixties than Dixie, featuring a long-haired, beaded hippie cat and a psychedelic light show produced by a spinning Tiffany lamp.

Bloopers

- Thirty seconds after the dog Napoleon bites the seat out of the butler's pants while he drives the motorcycle, the pants miraculously patch themselves up, because as the butler hangs from the windmill, the dog again bites the seat out of his pants.

• During the climactic battle, after the cats dump the butler into a chest, the lid falls shut and the horse kicks it across the floor of the stable. As it slides to a stop outside the door, the chest suddenly has a padlock on it.

Strange Reaction

Although *The Aristocats* seems a bit like a taxicab driver in a tuxedo, overdressed with no place new to go, it is a pleasant little film. Maybe a little too pleasant. The butler is practically likeable, a trait never to be found in Walt's villains. "Disney characters, and I don't mean chromatically, are always black and white, drawn very sharply, no grays. You're a villain or you're not," Dick Huemer said. "That was his formula, anyway. As a matter of fact, it's characteristic of our medium—that's how cartoons have to be. Otherwise, they're wishy washy."

- 17 -

Bedknobs and Broomsticks

The Original Tale

In Mary Norton's fanciful children's story *The Magic Bed-Knob* (1943), Carey, Charles and Paul are staying with their aunt in Bedfordshire, next door to Eglantine Price, a witch in training. One day, Miss Price falls from her broom and hurts her ankle, and the children discover her secret. She demonstrates her powers by turning Paul temporarily into a yellow frog. To retain her privacy, she gives the children a spell which will expire if they tell anyone she is a witch. If Paul twists the knob on his bed next door, he will be taken anywhere he wants, even back in time.

For their inaugural journey, Paul wants to visit their mother in London. The bed magically transports the children there, but mom's not home. A policeman discovers the children in the bed on the sidewalk and takes them to the station. Fortunately, the bed is later confiscated, allowing the kids to escape when no one is looking.

The children convince Miss Price to join them on their next adventure. They travel to the South Seas island of Ueepe for a picnic but are captured by cannibals. After a duel of magic between Miss Price and the local witch doctor, she turns him into a frog and escapes with the children. When the kids return filthy and wet, their aunt sends them back home to mother.

The sequel, *Bonfires and Broomsticks* (1957), takes place two years later. The children notice Miss Price has an ad in the paper to watch children for the summer. Although Miss Price has purchased Paul's old bed from their aunt, the kids are disheartened to learn she has given up magic. They finally convince her to let them use the bedknob one last time, to travel back to 1666 where they meet Emilius Jones, a phony magician. Dumbfounded at the sight of real magic, Jones returns with the children to meet the woman who did it and equally impresses Miss Price with the

In Erik Blegvad's original illustration to Mary Norton's book, Miss Price and the children narrowly escape cannibals.

smooth talk of a "professional."

After sending Emilius back, Miss Price begins to regret not saying a proper goodbye. She and the children go back in time to discover Emilius in prison awaiting execution for practicing witchcraft. The next day, as Emilius is about to be burned at the stake, a shrouded figure flies in on a broomstick and cuts him free with a sword. The townspeople open fire, and the shroud falls to the ground, revealing nothing but air; Miss Price had used "intrasubstantiary-locomotion," a spell to animate inanimate objects. Emilius escapes to the bed, and all return to the present. After a spell (but not a magic one), Miss Price decides to marry Emilius and accompany him back in time.

The Disney Version

When Walt first bought the rights to *Bedknob and Broomstick*, a double edition of Norton's two stories, he did it not so much out of interest in the project as for blackmail. Pamela Travers wouldn't let him do *Mary Poppins*, so he'd have her believe he'd be just as happy doing this other magical British children's story. "Walt had bought it in case Miss Travers said no to *Mary Poppins*," recalled Richard Sherman, "so he could say, 'I have another picture,' as a backup plan."

When the *Poppins* negotiations got rocky, the Sherman Brothers went to work on the insurance policy. After Travers finally relented, *Bedknob and Broomstick* was put on the back burner. Then, because *Mary Poppins* turned out to be such a big hit, the Shermans resumed work on it, under the working title *The Magic Bedpost*. Then, after Walt died, it was again sidetracked. Four years later, the Shermans returned to the studio to finish it, with *Poppins* producer Bill Walsh, director Robert Stevenson and writer Don da Gradi.

Their wish list to play Eglantine included Julie Andrews, Lynn Redgrave, Leslie Caron and Judy Carne, but as soon as Angela Lansbury's name was suggested, everyone knew she was perfect for the role. Ron Moody initially agreed to star as Emilius, but the part ended up going to David Tomlinson, Mr. Banks of *Poppins*.

While no one admits wanting to do a sequel or a remake, Tomlinson wasn't the only holdover from *Mary Poppins*. *Bedknobs and Broomsticks* was recast during World War II, but both movies featured stubborn yet sweet children, a stern yet sweet guardian who can secretly fly, scenes in which she gives life to clothing and other inanimate objects, a beguiling street performer, a short animated sequence showing a sporting event and our heroine winning a prize, plus the same producer, director, screenwriters and songwriters. The bedknob is so similar to the function of the magic compass deleted from *Mary Poppins,* it's not surprising that one number, "Beautiful Briny," was written for the deleted Around the World sequence. The Sherman Brothers suggested that as long as the group was going to an island, maybe the bed could "short-shoot it and end up at the bottom of the ocean."

Cutting Room Floor

Although Roddy McDowall received third billing, he makes but two brief, inconsequential appearances. Before the editor got his hands on him, McDowall had a much expanded role, as a suitor for Eglantine, though she didn't show much interest in him.

Less conspicuous but far more important was the omission of

three songs written by the Sherman Brothers, recorded and filmed, but deleted at the last minute to keep down the film's running length. Eglantine sang "A Step in the Right Direction" to her cat as she prepared for her maiden voyage on her broom. Huckster magician Professor Brown explained to the crowd that it doesn't matter what you do, as long as you do it "With a Flair." And, when all hope of love looks lost, the children and then Eglantine sing "Nobody's Problems," a roundabout betraying their loneliness. (The Shermans wrote another song about Eglantine's loneliness, "Two Cups of Tea," which wasn't shot.)

"They had to cut twenty minutes so it could play at Radio City Music Hall, so they sliced three numbers," said Richard Sherman. "They didn't like ballads. But could you imagine *Mary Poppins* without 'Feed the Birds' or 'Stay Awake'? The heartbeat of the movie was all cut out."

"They also wanted to get it down to two hours for the airlines," added brother Robert.

The cuts were made so late that the last two songs remained on the soundtrack album and their melodies were incorporated as part of the background score.

Plot Holes

• Even though the movie's plural name sounds better than the book's singular title, there aren't multiple magic bedknobs.

• Let me get this straight. Professor Brown discontinues his correspondence course scam because he runs out of spells which he not only rewrote but thought nonsense. And the book, *Spells of Astoroth*, omitting the magic words for Astoroth's most spectacular spell is akin to a cookbook explaining its featured recipe without the ingredients.

• When the group returns from Naboombu and discovers it no longer has the pendant, Eglantine says, "I should have realized that it would be quite impossible to take an object from one world into another." Yet they had no problem taking themselves, their clothes, the bed, the blankets and pillows from one world into another. And, come to think of it, don't they ever have to make this bed?

- A panoramic shot of the hills shows hundreds and hundreds—if not thousands—of animated suits of armor. How did it all fit in that museum? And, after it fell lifeless to the ground, who cleaned it all up?

- Only in a Disney movie would an entire brigade of Nazis be thwarted without any of them getting hurt.

Strange Reactions

Critics decried *Bedknobs and Broomsticks* as a poor man's—or orphan's—*Mary Poppins*. What was missing was Walt. "It wasn't that we didn't have the technique, a good story or the material. We didn't have a producer," said Richard Sherman, "although Bill Walsh tried to do what he could. We didn't have any champion in our corner among the seven or eight twits, the Board of Indecision."

- 18 -

Robin Hood

The Original Tale

The Twelfth Century legend of "Robin Hood" told of Sherwood Forest's finest bowman, who with his band of merry men robbed from the rich and gave to the poor, opposing the tyrannical, over-taxing Prince John, who assumed the throne while his brother, King Richard, was away.

The Disney Version

Disney's *Robin Hood* grew out of the studio's unsuccessful attempts to create an animated "Reynard the Fox." Since 1937, writers and artists such as Ken Anderson had grappled with trying to turn the latter tale's title swindler into a sympathetic character. Finally, in the character of Robin Hood, Anderson found a fox who was a cunning thief and master of disguise, yet a brave, altruistic hero whom audiences could feel for and cheer.

"What sold (the studio) on *Robin Hood* was all these beautiful drawings Ken did of the characters," Vance Gerry recalled. "The story itself wasn't really that important. They'd go for sequences with entertainment possibilities, and then they'd start to tie them together. Ideally you made the visual first or you'd end up with talking heads."

For a change, there would be no hint of humans, but the charac-ters again would be heavily influenced by their respective voice actors, especially Phil Harris as a Baloo-type-bear Little John. Anderson drew Robin Hood and Maid Marian as clever foxes, and Prince John as a cowardly lion. The Sheriff of Nottingham, first pictured as a stupid, bossy goat, became a wolf to create a stronger villain. Friar Tuck was originally drawn as a pig, but, to avoid offending religious sensibilities, was later changed to a badger.

Anderson also had big plans for Robin's band, but director Reitherman wanted a buddy picture instead. "Ken Anderson had to throw out all character development on the merry men because Wooley wanted to make it like *Butch Cassidy and the Sundance Kid*," explained storyman Steven Hulett.

Some minor characters were also deleted, including a messenger pigeon who was so overweight he had to be shot into the air by a crossbow.

Plot Holes

• Maid Marian's companion is a chicken, rather an odd choice to accompany a fox.

• Overall, *Robin Hood* really has no plot to have holes in; the whole movie is more of a situation.

Bloopers

• To elude the Sheriff's men, Robin Hood and Little John swing into a tree before being struck by any arrows. The posse, without shooting any more arrows, gives up. Yet up in the tree, Robin suddenly has an arrow in his hat and Little John an arrow in his shirt. When Robin pulls the arrow out of his hat, it doesn't seem to have made a hole, yet he then puts a finger through to show there actually is a hole. He then flicks the arrow at Little John, who says, "Watch it, Rob. That's the only hat I've got." Little John really has nothing to worry about since as soon as you pull the arrows out, the holes disappear.

• After Robin and Little John, disguised as fortunetellers, enter Prince John's coach, the curtains somehow become tied back open, as well as change color from purple to white. Then, while Little John "kisses" the stones off the rings on Prince John's left hand, Robin slips the entire ring off his right hand. A minute later, Prince John has a stoneless ring back on his right hand.

• Robin gives his yellow hat to the small rabbit, Skippy, and in the next scene the hat is brown. During the escape from the castle, the cap is green.

• When the kids trespass into the castle courtyard, Skippy has a bow and arrow. Midway through the visit, the bow and arrow vanish and Skippy pulls a previously-unseen sword from his belt.

- Keep your eyes on the Sheriff's magical belt. He has a pouch on the belt that appears and disappears during the archery contest, his robbing of the poor box, and in every other shot during his first trip to tax the peasants. While keeping watch at the castle before the big rescue, the Sheriff's pouch, sword and ring of keys keep appearing and disappearing and changing places on the belt. And right after he unbuckles his belt before leaving the peasants and after Robin unbuckles it to slip off the ring of keys, his belt somehow gets refastened.

- Before the archery contest, Little John attempts to kiss Prince John's right hand, which has one ring on it. When the Prince pulls his hand away, there are three rings on the hand. Later in the scene, all the rings are gone.

- During Robin's heist, Prince John is sleeping with two bags of gold, then turns on his side and there's just one bag. Back on his back, there are two bags again. He returns to his side and there's just one bag. After taking all the other bags of gold, Robin discovers one last bag stashed behind Prince John's pillow that wasn't there before. A second later, another last bag of gold appears under the Prince's arm.

- Four little raccoons are taken in chains to the dungeon and are later freed, but as they flee to safety across the courtyard, there are five raccoons.

Hidden Images

"The Phony King of England" scene is not much more than a thinly disguised "Best of Disney" music video. As a shortcut, the animators copied drawings from earlier movies, making small changes to accommodate the new characters' anatomies. They even patterned some forest musicians after characters from earlier movies to make the tracing easier.

The animators turned Snow White dancing with the Dwarfs into Maid Marian dancing with her forest friends, Baloo swinging with King Louie into Little John swinging with Lady Cluck, and Duchess grooving by herself and with O'Malley into Marian grooving by herself and with Robin. Also from *The Aristocats*, the

Chinese drummer cat became a Chinese drummer rabbit, Scat Cat became a horn-blowing cat, and the hippie cat became a shaggy, sunglasses-wearing dog playing the guitar.

As a result, the scene is filled with ill-matched styles of dance and Maid Marian momentarily ends up looking unusually Snow White-tall.

Strange Reactions

Robin Hood is the type of film that's so mediocre, most everyone involved probably wishes they hadn't been. But Louis Prima was furious because he *wasn't*. "Louis Prima was really PO'ed there was no part for him in *Robin Hood*, since Disney was using his other friends," said Huston Huddleston, son of songwriter Floyd Huddleston. "So he said, 'Floyd, write me some songs, and let's get Disney off their a—! We'll do it ourselves, even if they don't buy it.' So he paid for the whole (recording) session and sold it to Disney."

The subsequent album, *Let's Hear It for Robin Hood*, features eight songs, including "King Louie and Robin Hood" about what inseparable pals the scat-singing King of the Jungle and Sherwood Forest's finest were.

Attraction Offspring

It was during the development of a never-built Robin Hood dark ride that Tony Baxter realized not only what makes a good attraction but more specifically what makes a bad one: "Whether it's a good movie or not is beside the point. It's a movie that's characters, there's no atmosphere in it. I call it 'sticks and stones and rocks and leaves.' First you have the stone walls outside the castle, then the stone walls inside the castle, then the leaves in the forest, that's it. There are no exotic environments, you just have all these scenes with Robin meeting Friar Tuck, then Robin meeting Little John, then Robin meeting Maid Marian. That's when I figured it out: the rides are about exotic places not characters. The best attractions are where you suddenly find yourself in a jewel mine or flying over London."

- 19 -

The Rescuers

The Original Tale

Margery Sharp's children's book *The Rescuers* (1959) opens at a meeting of the Prisoners' Aid Society, a worldwide organization of mice devoted to cheering lonesome inmates. When the group hears of a Norwegian poet held at the dreaded Black Castle, they realize the poor prisoner will likely die unless they rescue him. They first need a Norwegian mouse who can communicate with the prisoner. Fortunately, the beautiful, cultured white mouse Miss Bianca belongs to the son of an Ambassador, who has just been transferred to Norway.

Stocky, rough but decent Bernard, who works in the pantry at the Embassy, is volunteered to ask Miss Bianca to secure a translator. She agrees to go because she, too, is a poet. In Norway, she enlists Nils, a sailormouse, and they steal aboard a cargo ship, then find a model speedboat to make the rest of the journey to rejoin the Society. There, to impress Miss Bianca, Bernard offers to join Nils on the rescue mission. Miss Bianca, intrigued by this adventurous new lifestyle, volunteers as well.

They ride in the back of a wagon and finally arrive at the Black Castle. There, the three set up a little home in the castle's only mousehole. So heavily is the castle watched by the Head Jailer, his guards and his enormous, ferocious cat, Mamelouk, the dungeon seems impossible to reach or escape from. Luckily, every New Year's Eve all the jailers, including the Head Jailer and Mamelouk, gorge themselves on a marathon midnight feast and spend the next day incapacitated from indigestion. The mice take the opportunity to filch the keys to the prisoner's cell and help him escape.

In the sequel, *Miss Bianca* (1962), the title mouse has become chairwoman and Bernard secretary of the Prisoners' Aid Society. Learning a little girl is being held captive in the Diamond Palace by the cruel, abusive Grand Duchess, Bianca incites the other

153

ladymice to join her in frightening the Duchess' ladies-in waiting and running off with the child. But upon reaching the palace, they discover the servants are mechanical and, consequently, unafraid of mice. As the mice scatter, Miss Bianca resolves to stay. The Duchess forcibly keeps young Patience to help her dress, and majordomo Mandrake for cooking and keeping the doors locked.

The only hope for escape is when the clock-maker visits to tend to the robots. So Bianca tampers with their gears, causing them to break down. But instead of waiting for the clock-maker, the Duchess heads for her hunting lodge to be waited on by Patience and Mandrake. In the meantime, Bernard has set off in search of Miss Bianca disguised as a knife-grinder, pushing a cart filled with small swords, axes, knives and part of a lawnmower.

Although the lodge isn't bolted or barred as securely as the palace, it is guarded by the Chief Ranger and his two vicious bloodhounds, Tyrant and Torment. Nevertheless, Miss Bianca and Patience make a break for it and, after a perilous flight through the forest, arrive at Happy Valley. Unfortunately, the Ranger finds them hiding in a barn and is about to capture them when Bernard arrives. He throws one of his daggers at the Ranger, whose screams rouse the farmer's two big sons. They overtake the Ranger, and the farmer and his wife adopt Patience.

Additional books followed, including *Miss Bianca in the Antarctic* (1971), in which Miss Bianca and Bernard learn from Nils that the Norwegian poet has again been imprisoned, this time in the Antarctic. After rescuing him, Miss Bianca and Bernard find themselves captives of a well-meaning polar bear cub, and are finally freed by a bypassing brigade of little penguins. But the mice are separated in a storm, and Miss Bianca ends up being held in the underground ice palace of a 3-foot-6-inch Emporer Penguin, who plots to enslave the other penguins.

The Disney Version

The Rescuers was yet another idea that dated back to Walt. He had a treatment developed from the first book, complete with the poet being held captive by a totalitarian government in the Siberia-like stronghold. But as the story grew overly involved with international intrigue, Walt, disinterested in the politics, shelved the whole project.

It was revived in the early 1970s as a vehicle for the young animators, led by Don Bluth. As a cost-conscious way to train the newcomers, the studio would alternate between full-scale "A pictures" and smaller, scaled-back "B pictures" with simpler animation. The newcomers would also take a decidely lighter approach. They selected the most recent book, *Miss Bianca in the Antarctic*, as a starting point. "They gave me the Margery Sharp books and I started development, next to Ken Anderson," said writer Fred Lucky. "It was originally set in the Arctic. We had a demented King Penguin who lived in a massive, palatial schooner and had a captured polar bear that he made perform in shows like a freak. The polar bear was very unhappy and wanted to get away, so he put a note in a bottle that reaches the mice."

Louis Prima would play Louie, the cool polar bear who is lured away from his happy home in the zoo, and Floyd Huddleston wrote five songs: "(Sittin' in My Fav-o-rite Position Doin' Nothin' Is) Doin' What I Really Do Best," about Louie's life of leisure; "Peoplitis," as the bear wonders why people aren't the ones in the cages and leads the other animals in a scat sing-a-long; "I Never Had It So Good," a blues number about forsaking his friends and true happiness for fame; "All I Ever Do Is Think of You," sung by the girlfriend Louie left behind in the zoo, and the mice's anthem, "Rescuers Aid Society."

Meanwhile, the "A" crew had finished *Robin Hood* and begun work on an adaptation of Paul Gallico's Barbary ape story, *Scruffy*. When *Scruffy* was shelved and there were no other projects waiting, the old-timers went to work on *The Rescuers*, turning it into a more traditional, full-scale production. That made the Arctic setting a problem. "It was too stark a background for the animators," Lucky explained. "There was not enough to draw."

The writers reverted to a more conventional approach. They took the kidnapped orphan girl of *Miss Bianca* and recast the story in a much more colorful setting, the bayous of the South, where the vain old woman imprisons her because she is small enough to retrieve a lost diamond.

The villain's accomplices became a pair of crocodiles and Mr. Snoops, a caricature of journalist and animation historian John

Culhane, who was always snooping around the studio. But the primary ingredient missing was a lot more cute animals. For transportation to the bayou, the mice were to ride a pigeon, until veteran animator Frank Thomas recalled seeing some film shot for the True-Life Adventure series of albatrosses making clumsy takeoffs and crash landings. After Jim Jordan, radio's Fibber McGee, was persuaded out of retirement to do the albatross' voice, the part continued to grow.

For transportation through the bayou, the Disney artists created a pint-sized swampmobile for the mice—a leaf powered by a dragonfly. As they developed the comedy potential of having the character display his exhaustion in his buzzing, the dragonfly, too, grew from incidental to major character, forcing scenes of villainess Medusa and her crocodiles to be trimmed.

Bernard and Bianca would also need help battling the forces of evil. The local swamp creatures were organized into a dedicated home guard that drilled and marched incessantly. Slowly, they evolved into a volunteer group of helpful little bayou creatures. Their leader, a singing bullfrog voiced by Phil Harris, was cut entirely. And, although a sequence in which they marched and sang as they prepared for a rescue maneuver was scaled back in final production, each character retained a distinct personality that determined his role in the action.

The writers also considered making Miss Bianca and Bernard married professional detectives, but there seemed to be more romance in making them unmarried novices. Their organization evolved into a rodent version of the United Nations, headed by a chairmouse modeled after Robert Morley. Morley, though, declined to voice the character, so Bernard Fox agreed and did his best Robert Morley impression.

Sammy Fain wrote new songs, including "Swamp Volunteers March" and a new "The Rescue Aid Society." But after hearing neophytes Carol Connors and Ayn Robbins audition a musical they had written, the filmmakers pondered doing something a little more contemporary. While Walt had always modernized his tales, he sought timeless elements so they would endure for future generations. Ron Miller asked Artie Butler, who wrote *The Rescuers'* score and was familiar with Connors' and Robbins' work, "Do you think their songs will be contemporary twenty years from now?" Butler replied, "Do you think the Sistine Chapel needs a new coat of paint?"

Connors recalled: "We got a call from Wolfgang Reitherman's office, and we were shown storyboards on the scene with the mice flying on the bird. We wrote 'Tomorrow is Another Day' that night. I told my agent it was finished and he said, 'You have to wait two weeks.' I said, 'I can't.' I didn't, and Wooley said it was exactly what he wanted."

To play over the credits, Connors composed an emotional symphonic piece, "The Journey." Reitherman was so taken by the music, he sent an animator to the beach, who lived in a van for 24 hours and sketched to the demo tape.

The songwriters then went to work on a new version of "Rescue Aid Society," likewise instructed to turn the group's anthem into "a simple little ditty, like M-I-C-K-E-Y, that the children could go out of the theater singing."

Connors was also to write a melody for the villain, Medusa. "I remember dreaming it, but I never wrote it down and I never could remember it, even to this day. They never pushed it, so I never wrote such a song," Connors said.

Finally, came a song for when the little girl is at her lowest, "The Need to Be Loved." Reitherman, though, preferred one of Fain's melodies, and asked Connors and Robbins to write new lyrics to his song. The result, "Someone's Waiting For You," would be nominated for for an Academy Award, but presented a strange situation for the two fledgling songwriters. "I grew up a great admirer of Sammy Fain," said Connors, "but we suddenly found ourselves in competition with our own song!"

Cutting Room Floor

Phil Harris wasn't the only one to end up on the cutting room floor. Originally, Penny was supposed to be introduced in a happy scene as a cheerful, spunky child, so that the later sad sequences might have greater impact. A sequence was written, storyboarded and partially animated of Penny on a visit to the zoo. But the filmmakers wanted audiences to feel for her immediately, so her first scene is alone in the corner of a big bedroom at the orphanage.

Not showing Penny going to the zoo made obsolete another sequence in which Bernard and Bianca question the animals in the

---

Orphan-O-Meter

Using state-of-the-art computer analysis, the research staff of DWI (Disney Waif Institue) has been able to scentifically quantify the degree of orphanhood of various Disney characters. For each, they've calculated a Pity Quotient (PQ), accuracy ±4 percent, from 1 (totally unsympathetic) to 100 (totally pathetic), factoring in such variables as age, degree of helplessness, availability of parents, helpfulness of friends and guardians, and difficulty of hardships.

1 Penny (*The Rescuers*) Drawn for maximum pity (big doleful eyes, pouty lips, missing tooth, pig tails, baby voice, constantly on the verge of tears), she's the archetypal orphan: has no parents, is kidnapped from the orphanage, and finally has her teddy bear swiped. Bonus points awarded for Medusa's remark: "What makes you think anyone would want a homely little girl like you?" **PQ: 100**

2 Quasimodo (*Hunchback of Notre Dame*) Older but no less troubled—loses family, abused by foster parent, hated by everyone else except a few blocks of stone, ugly, albeit big-eyed, Disney ugly. **PQ: 92**

3 Bambi "Mother?" **PQ: 87**

4 Dumbo Heartrending separation from his mother second only to Bambi's, but at least Bambi had a father. You know what they say about circus women... **PQ: 83**

5 Snow White and **Cinderella** Young, attractive, overly trusting princesses-to-be with dead mothers, dead fathers, and stepmothers who, if they can't kill the girls, at least want to give them dish-pan hands. **PQ: 72**

6 Simba (*Lion King*) Precocious, lovable and has to nuzzle dad's carcass. Penalized for running out on his mother. **PQ: 71**

7 Tod (*Fox and the Hound*) and **Oliver** (*Oliver & Co.*) Cute, cuddly and, two minutes into the movie, abandoned. But quicker than you can say "soup kitchen," they've got fancy new homes and more friends than they have time for, leaving little time to pity them. **PQ: 53**

8 Wart (*Sword in the Stone*) and **Pete** (*Pete's Dragon*) Authentic biological orphans, abused by their guardians, but you stop caring about them as soon as you hear their whiny, annoying voices. **PQ: 37**

9 Pinocchio and **Ariel** (*Little Mermaid*) Likable, vulnerable and constantly in over their heads, due to their own selfishness and bad decision-making skills, despite caring papas and pesky consciences. **PQ: 34**

10 Mowgli (*Jungle Book*), **Cody** (*Rescuers Down Under*), **Belle** (*Beauty and the Beast*) and **Aladdin** All sympathetic, but get into trouble because of their bravery. Too fearless. They don't seem too worried, why should we be? **PQ: 9**

11 Jasmine (*Aladdin*) and **Pocahontas** Babes who have it all—great bodies, fame, fortune, a way with animals, everything except they're unlucky in love, which is their own fault for falling in love at first sight. Also too self-reliant to pity, but their predicaments are caused by stubbornness. **PQ: 7**

12 Peter Pan Fairly likable but always at an advantage and too brash to feel sorry for. The ultimate Disney brat. One suspects he may have done away with his parents himself. **PQ: 0**

zoo as to her whereabouts. It was revised so the mice decide to take a shortcut through the zoo, Bernard bravely offers to go on ahead, offscreen we hear a lion roar and Bernard comes running out of the zoo.

Plot Holes

• After arriving at the United Nations, the mice of the Rescue Aid Society begin jumping out of the briefcases and satchels of the various U.N. delegates. Even more amazing than the fact that no one at this top security facility seems to notice all the vermin scampering down the halls, is how the mice miraculously unzip the satchels and unsnap the briefcases—from inside of them.

• In trying to salvage the diamond, Bernard, Bianca and Penny are nearly drowned by the rising, tumultous tide, even though one animator pointed out that there's hardly any tide in the bayous.

• These truly are capable mice. Although the Rescue Aid Society headquarters is a hole in the wall where an old dresser's drawers have been fashioned into balcony seating, a book into a stage and a spool into a podium, for the final scene, this group of mice is able to secure and install a 19-inch color TV set.

Bloopers

• To retrieve Penny's note, Bernard leans a comb against the side of the bottle to use as a ladder. As he begins his climb, Bernard has rope slung around his left shoulder. In the following shot, he has the rope around his right shoulder. After rescuing the note from the bottle, Bernard now finds himself seemingly trapped inside. The rope he used to pull himself from the top of the comb to the top of the bottle is tied around the lip of the bottle and draped down its side. Yet, somehow, right before Bernard wants to climb out, the rope is hanging down *inside* the bottle.

• As Bernard and Bianca plummet from albatross Orville down into the swamp, they slow their fall by opening their umbrella. Unfortunately, the umbrella is pulled inside out, sending our heroes plunging toward the water. Yet the next time we see the mice, they are under the umbrella, which is no longer inside out.

• When Penny first meets Bernard and Bianca, she shows them that the alligators have torn the backside of her underwear. Likely story. There was no rip visible when she pulled her nightgown over her head a few minutes earlier.

Strange Reactions

The Rescuers was a gentle little film that fared surprisingly well at the box office. But its seeming innocuousness didn't prevent trouble overseas. The picture ran into censorship trouble in Denmark and Scandinavia for "suggested violence."

- 20 -

Pete's Dragon

The Disney Version

Pete's Dragon started as a short story Walt bought in 1962. It was worked into a seventeen-page treatment, "Pete's Dragon in the U.S.A.," centering on a mythical dragon who after various adventures arrives in Maine to help a young boy. But the story sat on a shelf until being rediscovered in 1975 by producer Jerome Courtland. He enlisted Malcolm Marmorstein to write the screenplay and Al Kasha and Joel Hirschhorn to compose the music.

The screenwriter set out to develop the idea into a traditional musical comedy with all the standard Disney elements. He changed the story from a contemporary to a period setting, and the dragon from a wholly imaginary creature to a real one. Pete became an orphan boy pursued by hillbillies who want to enslave him, by medicine man Doc Terminus who wants his dragon, and by an entire town who see the boy (but not his invisible, disaster-prone pet) as a jinx.

Marmorstein named the dragon "Elliott" after Elliott Gould, a mischievous friend since their theater days, and dubbed the town "Passamaquoddy" after a real Indian tribe in Maine. Still, in his early drafts, the dragon remained invisible except for a single brief sequence in which the Doc tried to butcher him into marketable portions.

As its creator, Ken Anderson lobbied for his animated dragon to appear in visible form more often. Though biased, his argument was a good one. With the dragon invisible, the other characters spent half the movie explaining what he was doing, and that was bad storytelling. (And bad marketing—you can't sell plush toys of an invisible character!)

Others who read the script also wanted to know where the dragon was, especially since he was supposed to be the star of the picture. "We tried a completely invisible dragon, but it was no fun. It was lacking," admitted Marmorstein. "It's a visual medium, and you're making a movie for kids."

With a fully animated dragon, the filmmakers could do anything, well, *about* anything. There was a limit: animation was more expensive and time consuming. Numerous ideas couldn't be used because they had to be animated.

Even the sequences that did get the go-ahead presented problems, as the live action crew battled the animators over technique. "On those scenes there was a struggle between animation and live action," Marmorstein said. "Animation believed that when this dragon landed on the lighthouse, the lighthouse should sway and bend like a branch. We wanted more a basis in reality."

Some scenes were cut to speed up the story, such as Doc Terminus' first attempt at capturing Elliott. To identify the invisible beast, the Doc has a brainstorm: covering him from head to tail with paint. But, questions his sidekick Hoagy, "you think you can just walk up to a dragon and start painting him?" Terminus explains they'll use the "saturation technique" and dump buckets of paint on him. They follow Pete and Nora, the kindly woman who has taken him in, to a dry goods store, convinced the dragon is walking just behind the boy. What they didn't see was Pete sending Elliott off to look for Nora's missing beau, Paul. Terminus and Hoagy steal several buckets of orange paint from a paint wagon, and stalk Nora and Pete. They start pitching paint behind the pair, but instead strike various townspeople. A giant paint fight erupts, with a baker tossing orange-stained pies, a fishmonger throwing orange fish and Hoagy being thrown through a barber shop window. Nora and Pete walk on, unscathed and oblivious.

Other scenes were rewritten to increase Elliott's role. Originally, the hillbilly Gogan clan was to confront Pete and Nora with their "Bill of Sale" for the boy when the family first rolls into the waterfront town and blocks the pair's path with their wagon. But Nora whacks their horse's rump with her hat, the animal takes off and swings the wagon (with mother Gogan at the reins) into the drink. The scene was reset in the water with everyone on boats, so Elliott could come to the rescue and throw all the Gogans overboard.

For the music, explained Al Kasha, "we have a saying in the theater: when you can't talk anymore, you have a musical number."

There would be plenty of numbers, since Disney signed a talented cast and each member required his or her own songs. Kasha and Hirschhorn had to write one or more songs each for Helen Reddy, Mickey Rooney, Jim Dale, Red Buttons, Shelley Winters, the actors who would play Pete and Elliott, as well as a big production number. "It's not often where almost everyone in the cast gets a chance to sing," Kasha said. "In an hour and 40 minute picture probably one hour and 20 minutes is music."

Their most memorable song was the Academy Award-winning "Candle on the Water," which combines the subjects of their two earlier Oscar-winning songs. "It might sound superstitious, but we won our first Academy Award for *The Poseidon Adventure*, which was about water, and our second for *The Towering Inferno*, which was about fire," Kasha said. "Plus, I love to do inspirational songs, and 'Candle on the Water' has just as much to do with my belief in God."

The team composed one song that they decided on their own not to use, a duet between Pete and Elliott called "Loyalty." They also wrote an unused finale number, "The Greatest Star in the World," an ensemble piece sung by the town paying tribute to Elliott for his heroics, although in the finished picture the dragon performs far fewer heroics for the benefit of the town.

Whereas Doc Terminus and his sidekick Hoagy are literally left hanging in the filmed version, originally they were to flee to their wagon, raise its sail and think they are making a speedy escape—until they realize they are traveling so fast because Elliott is pushing their cart. He pushes it through the streets of the town and lets it sail through a wall of the jail, catapulting the villains into a pair of cells. Elliott then hears Pete calling for help and sets out into the storm. Along the way, the roof of one house is blown off, exposing the occupants inside, but it blows in one piece into Elliott's hands and he replaces it. Another house is being ripped from its foundation, and the dragon stabilizes it. Strong winds are buffeting an outhouse, and Elliott sets the structure down safely in a yard. The outhouse door slowly opens, and a confused man sticks his head out. Elliott then catches a wall just before it collapses on the schoolteacher.

For the finale, instead of a whole new number, it was decided to substitute a medley of reprises. The townspeople would sing "We Saw a Dragon" ("we're proud to love a dragon"), Pete and the other village children would sing a chorus of "Elliott Did It" ("Elliott did it/Elliott did it/We're braggin'/'cause our dragon/Elliott did it"), and the mayor would lead a revised rendition of "Passamaschloddy," promising in the final line that a monument to Elliott would grace the shore of "Passa-mocka, Passa-quocka, Passa-flocka, massa-clocka, classa-bocka, classa-socka-ma..." Completing the running gag, the crowd, after a beat, would shout, "PassamaQUODDY!"

In the end, the filmmakers decided to close with a short reprise of "We Saw a Dragon" and a gag with the mayor. Elliott and Pete say their tearful goodbyes, and then Pete skips off with his new family to a reprise of "Brazzle Dazzle Day," itself edited down to abruptness.

Plot Holes

• While Dick Van Dyke struggled to sustain a British accent throughout *Mary Poppins*, Helen Reddy had the opposite problem in *Pete's Dragon*: she seems preoccupied with trying to lose her Australian accent. She plays her part with more diction than conviction, concentrating more on pronunciation than performance. Oh well, the part had originally been offered to Julie Andrews.

Strange Reactions

Pete's Dragon received generally harsh reviews upon its release. Yet, even if the movie wasn't an all-time classic, it did help to inspire one. Steven Spielberg reportedly said that if not for *Pete's Dragon*, he never would have made his own Elliott movie, *E.T.*

- 21 -

The Fox and the Hound

The Original Tale

More so than even *Bambi*, Daniel P. Mannix's *The Fox and the Hound* (1967) presents a realistic look at life through the eyes of a fox and a hound. The animals don't speak, think or act like humans. In fact, they pay dearly for acting on instinct and not being able to better communicate. While writing the novel, the author kept his own foxes and intensively studied their habits and abilities, then, through narrative, tried to make sense of their hunting, fighting and mating.

The fox, Tod, is rescued by a hunter who has killed his mother, brothers and sisters. After being taken home by the man, the cub soon discovers he doesn't like being cooped up in the house. Tod spends less and less time there, and makes the local area his domain.

The half-bloodhound, Copper, who, like Tod, lives by scents, is the finest tracker of the Master's many hunting dogs. He is the favorite, until the day the cockier Chief fights off a bear and saves the Master's life.

One night, Tod finds himself being hunted and, hearing a train in the distance, lures his pursuer, Chief, onto the tracks. The oncoming locomotive strikes and kills the dog. Jealous Copper is ecstatic, but the Master is furious and vows to find that fox.

The Master and Copper hunt Tod for years. Foxes are creatures of habit, so Copper tracks Tod's regular route, while hunters lie in wait further down the path. After Tod acquires a wife and then children, the hunter tracks down their burrow, runs a line from a car's exhaust pipe into their hole and gasses the cubs. The Master sets countless traps; one badly wounds Tod, another kills his vixen. Tod finds another mate and has more cubs, but his entire family is gunned down one by one after being lured out into the open by animal calls.

Still, Tod refuses to leave his territory, despite drastic changes in the landscape. Most of the other foxes have been poisoned to death. Trees, wildlife and farms have given way to housing developments, highways, factories and other scent-fouling sources of pollution. About the only old-timers left are Tod, Copper and the Master. Disconsolate, the hunter begins drinking. Men from town want to send him away to a place where dogs are not allowed.

One day, he takes his aging hound for one last hunt. After a torturous, daylong chase, Tod finally gives up, and the equally exhausted Copper collapses on top of him. The Master kills the fox and proudly hangs up the pelt. But the revelry does not last long. There are no more foxes to hunt, and the Master again grows despondent and resumes drinking. The men return to take him to the place where no dogs can go. But first, the Master, sobbing, must take old Copper out to the field with his shotgun, and closes the eyes of his hound, trusting to the end.

The Disney Version

Mannix's original seems better suited to a True-Life Adventure documentary rather than an animated children's feature. The author went to extraordinary lengths not to anthropomorphize the animals, to explain their motives through normal animal behavior. But as a consequence, there was no uplifting message, no moral and no happy ending. Disney would change all that.

The story of survival was changed to a fable of friendship. Copper and Tod, two lifelong enemies, would be childhood chums, torn apart by circumstance and expectations. Copper and Chief became buddies, although Chief would be the old pro who grows jealous of young Copper. The farmer who took in Tod after killing his family became a protective widow. The ferocious, older vixen whom Tod finds in the wild became a submissive lovebird. Birds, both a fox's prey and enemy (for divulging its position to trackers), became Tod's friends.

The filmmakers originally planned to change the title to *The Fox and the Hounds*, but dropped the plural as the story began focusing more and more on the two leads. And as everyone became friendlier, the characters lost their edge and the movie lost all semblance of realism. It also led to two no-nos in Disney animation: too much talk and no real villain.

But the serenity on screen masked increasing tension off screen. The biggest battle concerned whether or not to kill Chief. "Ollie Johnston did this sequence where Chief tries to get pity, and they thought it was such a good scene and he was such a good character, they didn't want to lose him," said writer Earl Kress. "So Chief just gets hurt. We see him lying in the water, and he immediately moves. They wouldn't even let you think for a second that he's dead. But that ruins the motivation for Copper to swear revenge. There's no reason for a great vendetta. It completely undercuts the motivation. Copper and Tod are best friends and then suddenly they're mortal enemies. Plus, he didn't even lead Chief onto the tracks on purpose."

Co-director Art Stevens, though, argued that they couldn't kill a major character. That had never been done, and certainly no one expected anything new or innovative in a Disney movie.

Another fight erupted over a planned sequence with Tod at the game preserve. Co-director Wooley Reitherman wanted Tod to meet a crazy crane played by Charo. She recorded a song and voice tracks, shot some live action reference footage, and the sequence was storyboarded. "But Art Stevens was dead set against it, and they fought tenaciously," writer Steve Hulett said. "Art didn't think it went with the tone of the picture. Wooley thought something needed to be in there. My feeling was that Wooley was right. The picture needed something there, although not necessarily that. The problem Wooley had was Ron Miller, the producer, kept telling him, 'Wooley, you're 70 years old, back off, leave it to the young guys.' There was a power struggle with Art Stevens, and if he didn't let some of the younger guys develop, there would be some problems. So Ron Miller had Wooley go develop *Catfish Bend*."

Don Bluth had already made up his mind. He and other new-comers felt Reitherman was too stern and out of touch. But even if all the old-timers retired, the "creative dry rot" seemed to have grown too widespread, too deep. Halfway through production, vowing to reinvigorate the field of animation, Bluth walked out to start his own studio and took half the animation staff with him. "Bluth and those guys were always talking about leaving.

Everybody knew they were going to leave," Vance Gerry said. "It was all these young people, who would say, 'Wooley made me cry.'"

Miller, who was partly responsible for bringing in the young animators, took the defection personally. Industry experts predicted Disney's ailing animation department might be permanently crippled. The remaining animators took on a heavier workload, and new artists were hired. The film's release date was pushed back from Christmas 1980 until the following summer. It didn't help. With *The Fox and the Hound*, Disney continued to fall into the trap that its imitators had, mistakenly targeting small children instead of families. Critics collectively yawned. Still, the film attracted big audiences starved for anything resembling traditional Disney animation. The best thing to come out of it was that the new generation of animators was allowed to exert itself for the first time. Animator Glen Keane, for one, stepped in and entirely reboarded the bear attack, turning it into the highlight of the picture.

Plot Holes

- Trapper Amos Slade leaves to go hunting for the entire winter, but evidently doesn't lock his front door, since a bird is able to push it open. Also, during this long trip, who's watching his prized chickens?

Bloopers

- From the owl's eye view, we see Tod's mother stashing the little fox in a tuft of high grass at the base of a fence post. On closer inspection, there's a large clearing at the base of the post with the tall grass a few feet back.

- In the opening scene, Boomer the woodpecker has five dark specks on his chest, then six, then five, then six again. In the next scene he has eight specks, in another seven.

- Amos Slade must shop at the same pet store where Mr. Darling bought his puppy in *Lady and the Tramp*. After getting his new puppy, Amos keeps him in a sack. But the trapper obviously trusts the pup because, although his trustworthy dog Chief is roped to his doghouse, Amos lets the mischievous pup run around unleashed.

• When Amos first arrives at the game preserve, he carries only a gun and wire clippers. During his walk, he stops and pulls two traps from behind his back. He then sets up at least five traps. Tod eventually springs about a half dozen traps, and there's still one more left for Amos to step into.

Strange Reactions

The Fox and the Hound would be the first Disney animated feature with which Walt had nothing to do and, as a result, would be the one most directed at small children. The film is so mild, so innocuous, it seems that it could offend no one. Wrong. The National Stuttering Project targeted the stammering woodpecker in protesting the film's release on video.

VII

Disney Disassembled
Cleansing the Palette
1985-1988

"Food is to eat, not to frame and hang on the wall."

– William Denton,
in the *New York Times* (1987)

Disney's separate divisions were all *worth* a lot of money, they just weren't *making* a lot of money. The company's stock, as a result, grew severely undervalued. Naturally, the situation caught the eye of Wall Street, sparking hostile takeover bids by ruthless corporate raiders who wanted to split the company up and sell it off in individual pieces at a huge profit. But, on their own, the segments would have benefited a few for a short time and, like dissecting Elliott the dragon, killed the whole thing in the process. It took big investors who realized that the portions fed and strengthened each other, providing each other content and marketing clout, and must be left together. The components merely had to be better cultivated.

In 1984, Disney's board ousted the hesitant Ron Miller and brought in Michael Eisner as chairman and Frank Wells as president. The new management, which soon added Jeffrey Katzenberg to head the studio, had no compunction about making major changes.

Feature animation was the company's sickest patient. Walt didn't care if a picture took a little longer or cost a little more, if it made the characters stronger, the songs more memorable, or the story tighter. *The Black Cauldron* (1985) took a lot longer (planning began in 1971), went way over budget (costing a then-unheard-of $25 million), and had no memorable characters or songs—but *did* boast enough overwrought plot to fill a half-dozen PBS mini-series.

Audiences stayed away in record numbers. Had feature animation become ancient history? "Part of the problem of Sixties animation was we were in love with our work and too concerned with preserving the science and study of animation," Tom Sito says. "We were dead set on preserving what was in the past and forgot the name of the game is entertainment. It's impact. Disney needed someone from the outside to come in and slap us around."

Disney characters made even the simplest movement as if they'd had way too much coffee. Look at the stylized, overexpressive gesticulations of, say, the attorney in *The Aristocats* who can't sit down or take off his jacket without a flourish of flying arms. "Who cares how they move?" Sito points out. "People don't move like that!"

172

One option was completely disbanding the department. But Roy Disney, Jr., Walt's nephew who was instrumental in recruiting Eisner and Wells, wanted to give it a little time. Then came Steven Spielberg's *An American Tail* (1986) to remind audiences why they liked animation in the first place: exciting stories, engaging characters, hilarious gags and other inventive elements which couldn't come together in any other medium. The film's success caught Disney off guard—and woke them up. "Wait a minute," the company stuttered. "This is what *we* do." Now that everyone realized animation could be successful, it was just a matter of making it so.

Attendance had also been stagnant, even declining at Disney's theme parks. New rides were few and far between. And, instead of new technology, original types of rides, or attractions distinctly Disney, the two biggest introductions were what everyone else was doing—roller coasters (albeit dressed up as a Space Mountain or a Big Thunder Railroad). By adding typical amusement park fare, Disneyland and Disney World became more like your typical amusement park, leveling the playing field with their competitors. Even the more ambitious EPCOT Center, which opened at Disney World in 1982, was an Experimental Prototype Community Of Tomorrow in acronym only.

The company's more aggressive new management would permit the theme parks to once again lay track, in innovative directions. After *The Black Cauldron* bombed, the Imagineers realized they would have to look outside their own company for inspiration. Blockbuster entertainment in the Eighties was Michael Jackson music videos and the *Star Wars* and Indiana Jones trilogies, so Imagineering brought in those movies' characters and producers to make theme park versions. Producer George Lucas and director Francis Ford Coppola put Jackson in outer space (now there's a thought...) for the 3-D Captain E-O. Utilizing additional letters (C3PO, R2D2) and flight simulator technology, Lucas helped produce Star Tours and begin work on an Indiana Jones Adventure.

Many Disney purists weren't happy with rides based on non-Disney properties, charging that the Imagineers were getting lazy and unimaginative. Walt, they cried, wouldn't have rented the Muppets; he would have created his own characters. "A lot of peo-

ple tell me it's sacrilege, but I tell them if they want to get technical, Walt Disney died in 1966, so movies made after that really
aren't Disney movies," Tony Baxter responds. "Kids growing up
in the Seventies and Eighties don't have great Disney movies, so
anybody who does a film for Disney now, like Robert Zemeckis,
it's just his film released with the Disney name. The spirit's more
important, the state of mind. Look at *E.T.*, *Star Wars*; the parent's
missing, there's the sense of something different, all the things that
endear you to the character are there and work for many of the
same reasons. *E.T.'s* truisms are the same as Disney's, and it was
sort of sad that we had no movies like that (at that time). But we
were committed that Disneyland be the place where the very best
of American myths reside. If you're a child now, it's an entirely
different situation. We now have a constant supply of excellent
animated films, and today's literature is film."

He adds: "You could have called (the Indiana Jones Adventure)
Kentucky Buck and the Temple of the Forbidden Eye, but you
wouldn't have had the best in that genre. And a kid doesn't know
the difference between Disney and Paramount. If we do it, that's
great. What's more important is that it's the best." Unfortunately,
Baxter laments, competition sometimes makes the best harder to
get, such as for future dinosaur attractions at Disney parks; the ultimate dinosaur movie, *Jurassic Park*, was produced by Universal,
which operates its own movie studio theme parks.

- 22 -

The Great Mouse Detective

The Original Tale

Basil of Baker Street (1958) is the first of Eve Titus' series of children's books recounting the exploits of the famed mouse detective, as told by his close rodent friend and associate, Dr. David Q. Dawson. Basil, well hidden, studies at the feet of Sherlock Holmes, listening intently as his hero explains to aide Watson how he solved his cases. Basil similarly gains a reputation as super sleuth to the mouse world and even persuades his neighbors to relocate their town to Holmes' cellar. They construct a row of cozy flats, shops, a school, library, town hall and other buildings in the basement, dubbing it Holmestead.

One day, a neighbor calls on Basil. Her young twins have vanished, and a reluctant messenger soon appears with a ransom note from the Terrible Three. They threaten that no one will ever see little Angela and Agatha again unless everyone clears out of town within 48 hours, so the Three can turn the Baker Street cellar into their headquarters.

Analyzing the messenger's footprints, the sleuth tracks the Terrible Three to the harbor town of Mousecliffe-on-Sea. There, disguised as sailors, he and Dawson question the locals to discover the criminals' whereabouts. They steal aboard the threesome's yacht, confiscate the typewriter that produced the ransom note and have the mousepolice nab the kidnappers. The frightened messenger then leads them to the twins.

Basil's nemesis Ratigan, leader of London's mouse underworld, first appeared in the next book, *Basil and the Lost Colony*, in which the arch villain constructs a golden hill of cheese, with a deadly mousetrap concealed inside.

The Disney Version

The idea for an animated *Basil of Baker Street* originated with Ron Clements, who got his first break as an artist because of a fifteen-minute Sherlock Holmes short he animated on Super 8 film as a teenager. In 1980, Clements and partner John Musker began working on storyboards between other projects.

Although the typical Holmes mystery is intricately plotted, Disney's story crew started from ground zero. Writer Steven Hulett explained, "The storyline originally went back to us stringing together a bunch of visuals: there should be a fight on Big Ben, something in the sewers, they should go in disguise to a bar near the wharf. We used them as 'tent poles' to pin scenes on."

"Clements took a whole different direction than what we ultimately ended up with," Hulett added. "It was Warner Bros.-Looney Tunes stuff, all gags. There were twelve storyboards and the story still hadn't started. It was an endless amount of shtick. Pete Young could see it was not going anywhere, so he called in Ron Miller, and Miller chose Pete's (approach)."

The first idea for a victim was a female mouse whom Dawson falls for, but Miller knew what seemed to work time and again. "You're nuts," he told the storymen. "Get a little girl, someone they can feel sorry for."

On their rescue mission, the mice were originally going to be pulled in a cart by a goat. Eventually, their transport became Toby, a dog trained by Basil but more receptive to the small girl's requests.

One of the last characters dropped was a stool pigeon who always hung around Buckingham Palace and tipped Basil off about the skullduggery. In the end, the writers decided to let Basil figure everything out for himself.

Production began in the fall of 1984. The artists first modeled Basil after Bing Crosby, but eventually patterned him after Leslie Howard. Ratigan would have a hulking form, a caricature of 6-foot-6-inch Ron Miller's, but would still be a debonair, Ronald Colman-type. Then, after Vincent Price agreed to do the voice, the character became a wilder, more comical villain based on Price's role in *Champagne for Caesar*, co-starring Colman.

For the voice of the silhouetted Sherlock Holmes, the filmmakers wanted to use a recording of Basil Rathbone, but the publisher wanted too much money. Reluctantly, they called in an actor and began taping in Rathbone's style. At the last minute, the publisher and studio came to an agreement and Rathbone's voice was used.

Cutting Room Floor

Although production was well underway by the time Katzenberg arrived, he made his presence felt. "There was a much longer ending, but Jeffrey didn't go for longer, cornball, old-fashioned stuff," said Vance Gerry. "He wanted to cut to a new scene, cut to a new scene, faster, faster."

His biggest change was a dancehall girl's number. A song by Henry Mancini was recorded and animated, but Katzenberg hated it so much he had Melissa Manchester write and record a new song, "Let Me Be Good to You," requiring the sequence to be partially reanimated. "Mancini had an old-fashioned feel," Gerry said. "(Katzenberg) probably thought it was too mild."

The last thing cut was the movie's title. After Steven Spielberg's *Young Sherlock Holmes* bombed, Disney's marketing staff figured *Basil of Baker Street* also might sound "too British for American kids." Marketing invited the animation department to suggest new titles, then threw out all their suggestions and renamed it *The Great Mouse Detective*. After the years of work they put into the picture, many animators couldn't believe it was being rechristened with such an overly unimaginative title. One prankster even posted a phony memo on the department bulletin board announcing the studio had renamed all its animated classics. The new titles:

- *Seven Little Men Help a Girl*
- *The Wooden Boy Who Became Real*
- *Color & Music*
- *The Wonderful Elephant Who Could Really Fly*
- *The Little Deer Who Grew Up*
- *The Girl with the See-Through Shoes*
- *The Girl in the Imaginary World*

- *The Amazing Flying Children*
- *Two Dogs Fall in Love*
- *The Girl Who Seemed to Die*
- *Puppies Taken Away*
- *The Boy Who Would Be King*
- *A Boy, a Bear and a Big Black Cat*

Management asked for an explanation from the department chief, who was innocent and unamused although his name appeared on the memo.

For the film's theatrical rerelease in 1992, it ingeniously was retitled once again, as *The Adventures of the Great Mouse Detective*.

Plot Holes

- How does Ratigan's sidekick Fidget the bat know he will find the girl at Basil's apartment? Ratigan couldn't have directed him there, since the archvillain was surprised to learn that Fidget ran into Basil while at the toy shop.

Bloopers

- In the saloon, part of Dawson's disguise is a gold earring in his right ear. But the ear is momentarily bare when he first takes a seat and in two separate shots after he gets drunk. After he's captured by Ratigan, the earring disappears completely, except for one brief shot while he lies pinned in a giant mousetrap.

Hidden Stuff

One of the toys at the toy shop is a bubble-blowing Dumbo.

- 23 -

Who Framed Roger Rabbit

The Original Tale

Science fiction/fantasy writer Gary Wolf's 1981 mystery novel *Who Censored Roger Rabbit?* presents a 1940s Los Angeles where humans uneasily live side by side with 'toons. One day, Roger Rabbit, the stooge in Baby Herman's comic strip, begs hard-boiled private eye Eddie Valiant to take his case. Another syndicate has been trying unsuccessfully to buy Roger's contract from Rocco and Dominick DeGreasy. The rabbit wants to know who wants to buy and why the DeGreasys won't sell. Eddie hates 'toons, but needs the money.

Rocco is soon murdered and, since he was living with Roger's estranged wife, Jessica, the rabbit becomes the prime suspect. Unfortunately, about an hour later, Roger is found dead. 'Toons, however, have the ability to conjure up "doppelgängers," temporary, mentally protected doubles that do their most dangerous stunts, like getting run over by a bulldozer or smashed by a safe. And just before he died, Roger created a doppel, who (before he disintegrates) wants Eddie to let him help find the murderer.

Their list of suspects includes Jessica Rabbit, a sexy humanoid 'toon who models for car and liquor ads and more than anything wants Roger's missing teakettle; Rocco's son, Little Rock, a comics art gallery proprietor who thinks Jessica's really in love with him; Carol Masters, Roger's photographer and an outspoken advocate of 'toon rights, and Sid Sleaze, an X-rated comics publisher who gave Jessica her first big exposure.

It turns out everyone, even Roger, has his own nasty secret. Eddie, slowly growing fond of his gradually crumbling partner, solves the mysteries of the nondescript teakettle, the humans who used to be 'toons, and who murdered Roger and Rocco.

The Disney Version

Director Darrell Van Citters immediately recognized the possibilities of mixing live action actors not with comic strip characters but with well-known cartoon characters, and convinced Disney to buy the rights to the novel before its release in 1981. Marc Stirdjvant was signed as producer; Jeffrey Price and Peter Seaman, who were trying to break into movies from the advertising business, were hired as screenwriters. Although the writing duo's career highlight thus far had been writing dialogue for Snap, Crackle and Pop in Rice Crispies commercials, they packed their scripts with tight storytelling (something long missing in Disney movies), biting humor (something *always* missing in Disney movies), and violent slapstick (something long missing in animated movies, period, thanks to a generation of overprotective parents paranoid that watching too many Bugs Bunny cartoons would turn their kids into serial killers). In fact, Price and Seaman's screenplays were so out of the ordinary for Disney at the time that one animator, after reading an early draft, asked, "This is *really* good. We're not actually gonna make it, are we?"

The studio initially approved fifteen minutes of interactive animation and a limited amount of full animation. Over the next year, Price and Seaman wrote two full scripts to fit those parameters, featuring a more sympathetic hero, who doesn't get plugged at the end of the first reel. "In the original drafts we switched some characters, who were villains and who were heroes. Baby Herman at one point was the evil mastermind," recalled Price. "We also had a big fight in a zeppelin over Los Angeles, with characters hanging by handcuffs from the zeppelin bay door. But we eventually wrote ten drafts, so there were countless characters."

Price and Seaman kept the shell of the plot: Because he's a Toon, nobody believes Roger when he says he didn't kill out of a jealous rage, and hard-boiled, Toon-hating Eddie is the only one who will help him. They replaced Wolf's fantasy gimmicks (doppelgängers, characters talking in word balloons, a genie) with clichés from dime store detective novels (a Toon killed Eddie's brother, Eddie unwittingly becomes handcuffed to Roger) and classic Warner Bros.-type cartoons (falling safes, props by Acme).

Their victims became gag factory owner/Toon advocate Marvin Acme and cartoon producer R.K. Maroon, their villains Judge Doom (an evil Toon disguised as a human) and a quintet of hench-toons modeled after the weasels from "The Wind in the Willows" (*Mr. Toad*).

Disney, to make the movie look like as if it were set in "Toontown" instead of their own backlot, would have to "rent" other studios' characters. The writers, never knowing how the negotiations were going, simply inserted whatever well-known cartoon character they thought best for each scene. Among those who couldn't or wouldn't be bought: Heckle and Jeckle, Krazy Kat, Screwy Squirrel, caricatures of Humphrey Bogart and Clark Gable, and, from the days of silent movies, a mute Felix the Cat.

Mired in the Disney indecision of the early 1980s, the project drifted in and out of limbo. The studio interviewed new directors, including Robert Zemeckis. It finally ended up with executive producer Steven Spielberg, who assigned his own writers. Then, in 1985, after teaming on *Back to the Future*, Spielberg and Zemeckis were looking for something else they could work on together, and Zemeckis noticed Spielberg had *Roger Rabbit* under development. But Zemeckis preferred the earlier drafts by Price and Seaman, so the writers returned to write a few more, now titled *Who Shot Roger Rabbit*.

By now, the heavier hands of Katzenberg and Eisner were at Disney's helm and Spielberg had his own production company, Amblin. Naturally, there was a tug of war. Disney wanted to make the movie in-house (cheaper and more control), and Amblin wanted to shoot it on the Paramount lot (more expensive and more control). Special effects specialists Industrial Light & Magic then stepped forward and said the movie should be made in the San Francisco Bay Area, but no top animators seemed eager to relocate for one movie. Finally, noted animator Richard Williams consented to offer the services of his London studio, with the remainder of the footage animated by Disney's staff. The rest of the workload was split right down the middle; for every Disney executive or production person, there would be one Amblin executive or production person.

Working in a more isolated manner (and having the film

released as a PG-rated Touchstone Picture) allowed a looser, zanier and more adult style. "During development Steven Spielberg and Robert Zemeckis protected us pretty much. We didn't have to work much with Disney," Seaman said. "Disney just didn't want us to use Mickey and their characters in a bad light. We had to be very careful about their own characters. Such as in Toontown where Eddie, Bugs (Bunny) and Mickey jump out of the airplane, they wanted Bugs to be the one to play the gag on Eddie."

Most of the sexual innuendo is spoken by or directed at Jessica, a dead-ringer (though more buxom) for the voluptuous nightclub sirens in Tex Avery cartoons such as *Red Hot Riding Hood* and *Uncle Tom's Cabana*. Among the deleted one-liners: After Jessica saves Eddie's life in a Toontown alley, he admits that he had her pegged wrong. "Don't worry," she replies. "I've been pegged before."

In the typical Avery cartoon, the nightclub singer performs to a debonair wolf who grows more excited as the performance goes on. His jaw drops to the ground, his eyes bug out, he smashes plates over his head. Price and Seaman originally planned to feature "an Avery-type Toon wolf" in the audience at Jessica's performance but, since the Ink and Paint Club allowed only human patrons, he would come disguised as a human. Then, during the sultry performance, unable to hide his true colors, he begins howling and finally rushes the stage. A gorilla bouncer grabs him by the suspenders and snaps him back against an anvil; the wolf slides to the floor, and the gorilla whisks his remains into a dustpan and carries him out.

Some scenes that mixed animation and live action had to be scaled back for budgetary reasons. Originally, Eddie was supposed to go to the bar to question Baby Herman, who would be slugging down martinis from his baby bottle. It was replaced with a simpler interrogation in his baby buggy.

When Doom captures Roger in the bar, Angelo was to speak up that even he got a trial... all three times. Whereupon, Doom opens a Weasel's briefcase and up pop twelve Toon kangaroos as if in a jury box. Baby kangaroos then pop out of their pouches, each holding a letter that together spell "Y-O-U A-R-E G-U-I-L-T-Y." A true kangaroo court.

The most elaborate scene that proved too expensive to film was a lavish Hollywood funeral attended by a Who's Who of cartoon celebrities. Marvin Acme's casket would be carried in by Droopy ("Tragic, isn't it?"), Elmer Fudd, Yosemite Sam, Goofy ("Gawrsh… pallbearin's sure hard work, a-hyuk!"), Popeye ("Paul, huh? I thought we was bearin' Acme, arg-arg-arg-arg") and Bluto ("You outta bury dat joke, Popeye"). After Foghorn Leghorn delivers a brief eulogy, Casper the Friendly Ghost rises from the open grave and breaks up the service. The writers hope to work the funeral scene back in if there is ever a sequel.

As production neared an end, Disney could see it had a winner on its hands, and thought maybe this might be a good time to bring back the beleaguered Walt Disney Pictures banner. Zemeckis protested, worried that the association would hurt box office. After all, he argued, people associated Walt Disney Pictures with movies like *Unidentified Flying Oddball*. The film was released as a Touchstone Picture in conjunction with Amblin. Being a Disney picture would remain a stigma a little while longer.

Plot Holes

• Although the film is set in 1947, it features some characters created later, such as the Road Runner (1948) and the penguin waiters from *Mary Poppins* (1964). Some footage from *Goofy Gymnastics* (1949) is playing at a movie theater where Roger and Eddie hide out. But, as Seaman explained, the aim was "entertainment, not animation history."

Cutting Room Floor

One sequence was filmed and then edited from the picture to "make the movie play faster." After Eddie saws off the handcuffs and leaves Roger with Dolores, he heads back to the theater dressing room to look for Acme's will. But the gorilla bouncer jumps the detective and roughs him up. Doom and the Weasels arrive and take Eddie out in their paddy wagon. They work him over and dump him out of the truck in a burlap sack. Eddie removes the sack to reveal the Weasels have given him a "Tooneroo," a painted-on Toon pig face. He's showering off the pig face at his office when Jessica arrives. To bridge the gap in the final film, the filmmakers dubbed in Eddie telling Dolores he's going back to the office and added a toilet flush as Eddie exits the bathroom to try to explain why he greets Jessica with his pants unzipped and his shirt off (must have been hot in there).

As originally scripted, Jessica was going to surprise Eddie as he first steps from the shower, explaining that she rang the doorbell but he must not have heard it. He didn't hear it, he answers, because he doesn't *have* a doorbell. Caught in a lie, Jessica flutters her eyelashes nervously and says that she just had to see him. "Okay, you've seen me," Eddie answers. "Now give me a towel." As Jessica hands him a towel, she stares down at his anatomy and asks, "What's that thing?" Looking down, Eddie responds that he can't believe she's never seen a mole before. Jessica replies that Toons aren't given imperfections, which prompts Eddie to suppose that lying, stealing and murder must not count.

Hidden Images

Liberated by the wilder, more adult tone of the picture and the detachment from the usual Disney scrutiny, the animators added a number of hidden, fleeting extras. In the final scene, a train crashes into the Dipmobile and whizzes by, with Winnie the Pooh's pal Piglet dangling off the end of the caboose. Less noticeable is that in every window of the train there's a murder scene—characters get knifed, shot, strangled, poisoned, hanged, clubbed, even caned.

Graffiti on the wall of a Toontown restroom reads, "For a good time, Call Allyson Wonderland," and scrawled beneath it: "The Best Is Yet To Be." When the film was first released, in a single frame the second line was replaced by Michael Eisner's home phone number.

And the additions got spicier. In the opening scene, as Baby Herman storms off the set of *Somethin's Cookin'* (originally titled *The Bunnysitter*), he playfully "exits under the dress of a script girl who jumps as if goosed," according to the script. On closer inspection, the dirty old infant extends a middle finger upward under the dress and seems to reemerge with a spot of drool on his upper lip.

As first animated, Betty Boop as a cigarette girl at the Ink and Paint Club dropped her top in one frame, supposedly done as an homage to her creator, Max Fleischer, who was notorious for sneaking X-rated shots into some Betty Boop cartoons. But at the last minute, the filmmakers reportedly decided to airbrush Boop's boobs since they didn't own her image and didn't want to get sued.

Most sensational was the sequence in which Jessica is thrown from a cab. During a twirl, her skirt hikes up, revealing for three frames that she's not wearing any underwear. Although there's not much to see (the shot is not a close-up and you don't see defined genitalia), news of the previously undetected frames started a run on the laser disc version, with late shoppers offering $250 a copy at Los Angeles-area video stores. The Hidden Image Craze was born.

After the film proved hugely popular, Disney anticipated doing a full-length sequel, actually a prequel tentatively titled *Who Discovered Roger Rabbit*. But such films are so expensive, the writers figure, "the time for one kind of came and went. The technology is not novel anymore." Still, the studio has produced three animated Roger Rabbit shorts, each with its own share of hidden images. Among the extras:

In *Tummy Trouble* (1989), when Roger first visits Baby Herman in the hospital, Mickey Mouse's familiar red shorts are draped over a dressing screen with his yellow shoes sitting nearby. A weight scale has a bag of money on it, and later has a fish hanging from it. Among the hospital floors that Roger crashes though are a laboratory with a lava lamp and a profits chart, and a restroom with shoes that look like Mickey's poking out from under a stall.

In *Roller Coaster Rabbit* (1990), Roger pushes Baby Herman's buggy past posters for *The Little Mermaid*, *The Wooden Boy* (in memory of the brouhaha over the renaming of *The Great Mouse Detective*), and a roller coaster that promises you'll "have fun til you puke." Roger tosses various items out of the buggy, including a pair of mouse ears and a "Disney Look" training manual. Three stuffed Mickeys are among the prizes offered at the darts booth. As Roger and Baby Herman are about to take the second big plunge on the roller coaster, the track in front of them spells "Jeepers."

In *Trail Mix-Up* (1993), the can of bug spray is labeled "Mink Off," a nod to co-executive producer Rob Minkoff. When Roger spits out bees, they include Mickey as a bee and a brunette Tinker

Bell. In a sawmill, as Roger chases Baby Herman and a Beaver across the tops of the timbers on a conveyor belt, he passes a poster reading "Rigid Tools" that depicts a buxom, bikini-clad woman straddling a bandsaw. As they ride down a flume, there's a bumper sticker on the back of their log that reads "We visited Splash Mountain."

Evidently, Disney had no idea how prevalent or bawdy the extras were and immediately recalled the *Best of Roger Rabbit* laser disc, claiming there was some sort of "glue" problem.

Strange Reactions

Sadly, many have mistaken mischief on the part of a few animators for some satanic conspiracy by the Disney Co. to brainwash the impressionable, unsuspecting youth of America. Watchdog groups began going frame by frame through Disney movies in search of subliminal messages and, at the first sign of anything vaguely resembling anything objectionable, would hold press conferences to demand massive recalls and formal apologies.

A favorite target has been Donald Duck. What protesters may be forgetting is that, to do Donald's voice, the actor must blow air through his gritted teeth, meaning he can't fully open his mouth when speaking. This ensures that every word will be less than clear. Consequently, the temperamental duck has been accused of shouting, "F— you" in the 1937 short *The Clock Cleaners* (he actually says, "*Sez* you") and of calling Daffy Duck a n——r in *Who Framed Roger Rabbit* (he really says, "You doggone stubborn *little* –"). Ironically, immediately before the questionable comment, Daffy asks, "Does anybody understand what this duck is saying?"

Attraction Offspring

The inspiration for the Roger Rabbit-influenced Mickey's Toontown traces back to Mickey's Starland at Walt Disney World, itself engendered by two interrelated problems at the theme parks. Here was Mickey Mouse, Disney's most famous, most beloved character, and in 30 years of theme parks, he didn't have his own attraction. Neither did his pals, Minnie, Donald, Pluto and Goofy. Furthermore, for small children the highlight of a trip to Disneyland or Disney World is getting the chance to meet the characters, especially Mickey, yet there was no place to reliably find him. Mickey's Starland was developed as a collection of cartoon-style homes and shops where guests could meet the costumed characters. It was always planned as a temporary area since the concept was so limited. About all there was to do was shake a few furry hands and snap a few photos.

Something more active had to be added. The Imagineers thought back to the wildly popular promotions of celebrating the characters' birthdays. So, for Disneyland, the concept was changed to Mickey's Birthdayland, where there would always be a party for Mickey. Tony Baxter was against it. "I always thought it was sort of incongruous to celebrate Mickey's 60th birthday," he said. "The last thing you want to do is celebrate antiquity. There was even a portrait done of a graying Mickey."

Fortunately, *Who Framed Roger Rabbit* became a hit. It seemed perfect for balancing the new land: the character village for little kids and Toontown for teenagers. During a trip to Tivoli Gardens in Copenhagen, Baxter had seen an attraction with a spinning bucket and was determined to find a way to use it. Imagineers first took a spinning cup from the Mad Tea Party ride and rode it through the Haunted Mansion. The low clearance made the journey difficult and dangerous. You'd be spinning along and then scream, "Duck or we'll die!" Next, they tried it out, more successfully, on Pinocchio's Daring Journey.

They then decided to use it in an all-new Winnie the Pooh dark ride as part of the "Mickey" land. The vehicles became spinning honey pots, traveling past the greatest scenes from the top three Pooh films. But after the success of *Who Framed Roger Rabbit,* the vehicles became cabs spinning through wild cartoon effects.

Roger Rabbit's Cartoon Spin was ready soon after the opening of the rest of Toontown, but was left padlocked for six months. The marketing department figured it could milk extra business by opening it separately after the first of the year, but few people were fooled. Instead, now everyone thinks Toontown is solely for kids.

Another fully designed blacklight attraction for the Disney-MGM Studios which remains on the shelf is Baby Herman's Runaway Buggy Ride in which guests would careen in buggies through a hospital, a la *Tummy Trouble.*

Hide & Squeak

What began as innocent inside jokes by the Imagineers have become some guests' sole purpose for visiting Disneyland and Disney World. Hidden Mickeys are images of the character, often Disney's three-circled mouse head trademark, inconspicuously incorporated into park attractions, restaurants, shops, hotels, even films and television commercials.

One common technique is painting Mickey into park murals. In Disneyland's Frontierland, a mural next to the Stage Door Cafe depicts the Mark Twain sailing around the Rivers of America. Three passengers stand on the lower deck: a man, a woman and a certain mouse. At EPCOT Center's Wonders of Life pavilion, a mural above the entrance to Body Wars and the Well & Goods store features assorted clumps of broccoli, one shaped into Mickey's profile. On a mural behind the loading area for Norway's Maelstrom ride, one boatman aboard a small Viking ship sports mouse ears.

Another method is mixing the three-circled logo with other symbols, such as the icons on the large power coil in front of the Magic Kingdom's Alien Encounter. On Disney-MGM Studios' Great Movie Ride, the Raiders of the Lost Ark scene features several blocks of stone with hieroglyphics on them. One block includes Mickey having lunch with Donald Duck, another has a small icon with mouse ears.

Other Mickeys were added after the fact. In the Magic Kingdom's Village Haus restaurant, a painter transformed a blue sparkle above the banner on a mural of the Blue Fairy into a mouse head. In the mural in front of Snow White's Adventure, a Dwarf's heart-spotted boxer shorts hung from a clothesline near the cottage. A painter changed one and finally all of the hearts into mouse ears.

Even park employees have tried to get into the act. Soon after the opening of the Indiana Jones Adventure, a ride operator put on one of the show's skeletons a mouse ears hat enscribed with the name "Bones."

Intensely devoted visitors who, after countless pilgramages to the parks, thought they had seen all there was to see, now had something new to look for and a new way to pass the time spent waiting in lines. Each visit became an undercover mission. Mickey Head hunting has become so popular that when checking in to Disney World's Wilderness Lodge, children are given a list of hints on how to find some of the silhouettes in the hotel. All day long you'll find kids—and not a few adults—combing the property.

In 1994, Tom Shaw, who has been visiting Disney World every few months since the park opened in 1971, created a Web site on the Internet to chart the existence of subliminal Mickeys and separate the bogus sightings from the authentic.

According to Shaw, two criteria must be met to gain official Hidden Mickey Status. First, is the image *Hidden*? Novices often think they've spotted a "Hidden Mickey," when it's actually a "Decor Mickey" (or "Decorative Mickey") that was not meant to be concealed. Three purposely shaded rocks on a Splash Mountain wall, Hidden. A bush or a pad of butter not-so-subtly carved into three circles, a picture of Mickey on a T-shirt, most of the Mickey-shaped decorations in Toontown, Decorative.

Some tread the fine line between Hidden and Decorative. At Disneyland's Candy Palace on Main Street, lollipops are often displayed in distinctly arranged sets of three.

The second criteria: Is it *Mickey*? Is the similarity intentional or coincidental? The distinct, circular scrollwork above the entrance to the Disney-MGM Studios' Cover Story shop was probably on purpose. Others are more questionable. The sign at the entrance to the Magic Kingdom's Jungle Cruise is dotted with barnacles. Under the letter "C" in the word "EXOTIC," three of the barnacles, separated from the other clusters, vaguely suggest the trademark.

According to the Imagineers, most of what guests see are not Mickeys. "It's such an easy pattern, it's a club, a common Victorian pattern," says Tony Baxter. "But now they've made us so conscious of it, they've influenced us. We consciously put a *Life* magazine with Mickey Mouse on the cover in (the Indiana Jones Adventure), but also because it's dated 1938 and that's when we wanted to place the attraction."

Hidden Mickey Mania, though, can cause hallucinations. "I get a lot of wishful thinking reports," Shaw says. "They aren't formal Hidden Mickeys nor are they informal Hidden Mickeys. They're simply not there. I even got 25 reports of a Hidden

Mickey on the *ID4* (*Independence Day*) movie poster! I think it is that they want so bad to find one and don't that they convince themselves that they have."

One overly imaginative fan saw secret configurations among the dozens and dozens of round tables and chairs at EPCOT's lower-level Land Grill. "Enter and go straight to the railing and look down," he directed. "The table and stools are arranged to be Hidden Mickeys. During the day the stools are moved around a lot so it may not be that way for long."

How Not To Spot A Hidden Mickey

If during some future theme park expedition, you happen upon a Hidden Mickey, feel free to take its picture, just don't try to publish it. The Walt Disney Co., you see, has trademarked "the configuration of a round head with round mouse ears attached" (Registration No. 1760110), and any reproduction of said mark "falsely implies endorsement or sponsorship," "is likely to cause public confusion," and "constitutes unfair competition."

So, while we are legally prohibited by state and federal laws from reproducing an actual Hidden Mickey, instead we'll assist Mickey Head hunters by presenting images that are absolutely not Hidden Mickeys but commonly mistaken for them:

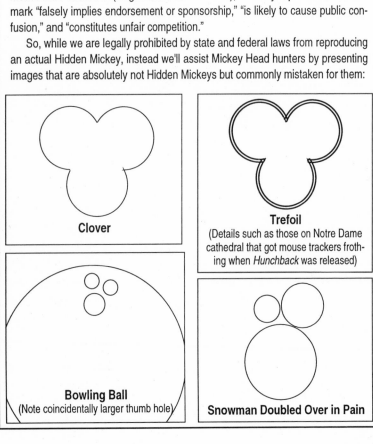

Clover

Trefoil
(Details such as those on Notre Dame cathedral that got mouse trackers frothing when *Hunchback* was released)

Bowling Ball
(Note coincidentally larger thumb hole)

Snowman Doubled Over in Pain

- 24 -
Oliver & Co.

The Original Tale

The title character of Charles Dickens' grim social commentary *Oliver Twist* (1838) is orphaned after birth and at age nine finds himself imprisoned and abused in a workhouse. He runs away and on the way to London meets Jack Dawkins, the Artful Dodger, who takes him to the pickpocketers' hideout and introduces him to the gang's cruel, old leader, Fagin. Fagin encourages Oliver to take up the illegal trade and sends him to watch the Dodger and another youth in action. The gang members pick an old gentleman's pocket and flee, but the man nabs Oliver and takes him into his home.

Fagin, fearing Oliver will turn them in, looks to Bill Sikes, a hulking, volatile ruffian who, with his hideous dog Bull's-eye and girlfriend Nancy, captures Oliver and returns him to the open, abusive arms of Fagin. Determined to get Oliver fully in his power by implicating him in a crime, Fagin has Sikes take the boy on a burglary, which goes awry, and Oliver is again taken in by the intended victims.

Angriest at the lad's good fortune is Monks, secretly Oliver's half-brother, who had paid Fagin to trick Oliver into a lawless life so he could keep their inheritance. Nancy overhears them and secretly goes to warn Oliver's new guardians. But Fagin has a gang member spy on Nancy, and the old man informs Sikes, who kills her. Sikes flees; while being pursued, he falls to his death from a house top, as does his dog. Fagin is arrested and sentenced to death, the gang is broken up, Monks confesses and Oliver is adopted.

The Disney Version

Like *Robin Hood*, *Oliver & Co.* started with a simple premise: "Let's do *Oliver Twist* with animals." It was storyman Pete Young's wife who first noticed the similarities between the novel

192 • "Mouse Under Glass"

and street animals, and had her husband pitch the idea: a rat, a pigeon and various other creatures living by their wiles to survive on the streets of New York. Eisner and Katzenberg liked it.

Young and director George Scribner soon turned Oliver into a naive kitten, Dodger and the rest of the gang into dogs, and Fagin into a human. Almost everything else—Dickens' 53 chapters and nearly 40 major characters—was up for grabs. "At one point, we put up an outline of the novel, and early on watched various versions of the movie, but (Dickens) wasn't a constant source of direction, just a jumping off point," admitted Scribner.

Like Dickens' book, the tone of the film at first was dark and gritty, the gang members tough, Fagin mean-spirited. Proposed at one point was opening with a "Dickensian coincidence": Sykes' [sic] two Dobermans kill the kitten's parents, setting the story in motion and leading to Oliver ultimately exacting his revenge. Although that proved too dark an opening, Scribner was determined to make the film street smart.

The real resistance came when the old-timers started joining the project after finishing *The Black Cauldron*. "It was a difficult first year," Scribner said. "There were producers, directors and storymen who thought they weren't particularly welcome, some who were unhappy with the direction the studio was going in, who thought it had lost some of its contemporary edge. I wanted to bring a more hip, contemporary sensibility, something more of the period. Humor changes; it's such a transient thing. Some things won't play at all in another period. (Earlier films) had a literal quality, more simple-minded, more charm. They lacked another level; subtext wasn't an issue. I tried to do things on different levels, to be less obvious with the material, with more sarcasm, more wit, more bite."

The music would also be harder. "There were different camps that thought rock music would date the film quickly," he recalled. "But we had to commit, to start fresh. We wanted to tell audiences we had moved beyond a certain period, and hopefully the characters would be strong enough and sincere enough that (audiences) could move beyond it, as well."

To find just the right sound, various songwriters submitted tunes in a range of musical styles. Many of their songs didn't work. A gospel/blues number to open the movie was too dark; a song by Herbie Hancock, "It's a Jungle Out There," intended for a scene where a little girl celebrates finding the kitten by putting on a light show with fantasy animals on her bedroom walls, was extraneous.

Except for Roy Disney, Jr., who would sit in on daily story sessions, the executives weren't taking animation too seriously and were happy to shake things up. Veterans quit, retired or got fired. New writers came and went. Pete Young died. Roy Disney stopped coming by every day.

Said storyman Steven Hulett, who left Disney during preproduction: "*Oliver & Co.* started out as a whole different picture, with a panda in a zoo. We kept trying to make it work. They had an expensive Chinese panda that Fagin steals for ransom that the cat is instrumental in getting back, but we could never get the panda heist to work. Then, the director, George Scribner, said, 'Why don't we make the cat valuable, but you can't tell because it's dirty, then it rains on the cat?'"

The focus slowly shifted to Oliver's adopted family, a little rich girl named Jenny. The kitten would be torn between his safe, new home with Jenny and his friends in the gang. And the story began to bridge the Disney theme of the past (a hero who longs for domestic security) with the Disney theme of the future (a hero who yearns to be part of an exciting new world).

At first, Jenny was to live with her mother. The story crew later changed the mother into a maid and finally into a butler. Oliver's jealous rival became Georgette, Jenny's prissy poodle.

One character who didn't make the final cut was Kaminski, a policeman's horse who's always asking Dodger if he's staying out of trouble. In his first scene, the police horse, tied to a post while his rider is shoving a pretzel down his throat, greets his "good friend and his usual entourage of delinquents" and, noticing Dodger is accompanied by a kitten, asks him if he's corrupting other species now. The dog introduces Oliver as his cousin from Jersey.

Oliver then was to watch the gang in action, picking pockets, pilfering purses, snatching a hunk of meat from the butcher shop, as Afghan hound Rita sings "The Art of Street Survival." Dodger tries to get Oliver into the act by planting him on a park bench near a wealthy businessman. As the gentleman turns to pet the cat, Dodger lifts his wallet, but Oliver twists to watch Dodger, causing the man to catch him and Dodger to sheepishly return the billfold.

Chihuahua Tito and bulldog Francis offer to show them how it's done, using the old Good Dog/Bad Dog scam. Tito begins barking at a woman and Francis arrives to chase him off. When the woman bends down to pat Francis on the head, Oliver opens her purse and steals, to Dodger's amusement, a comb.

Kaminski was supposed to make a repeat appearance when the gang raids Jenny's limo. To distract the policeman, horse, a K-9 agent and his policedog, Rita gets the policedog to chase her, thereby entangling the horse with its leash.

Interestingly, in working scripts titled "Oliver and the *Dodger*," Dodger has less to do than he would in the final film version. For sympathy, the writers had intended for Fagin to go to loan shark Sykes' office with the older dog, Einstein, who is attacked by the Dobermans and carried out, bloodied and lifeless, by Fagin. During the climactic escape, after Sykes' car smashes into the back of Fagin's trike, Jenny is thrown onto the hood of his car and the Dobermans leap after her. Originally, Einstein was going to shake off his bandages, leap at the dogs, and then brutally fling them back into the car. In the final film, Dodger took over Einstein's two big scenes.

The writers intended to wrap things up with a birthday party for Georgette in Jenny's backyard. The entire gang would help howl "Happy Birthday, Georgette" (with Jenny's the only human voice), before eating birthday cake from their own personalized bowls. Fagin and the butler are nearby playing cards, wearing deadly serious expressions and kiddie party hats. Fagin asks, "Got any... Jacks?" "Go fish," the butler replies. After Fagin wins the hand, he stretches out his arms to sweep in his winnings, and several cards drop from his sleeve. "Time to go," he announces nervously. Jenny reminds Georgette not to forget to thank everyone for her presents. The poodle smiles wanly and eyes her pile of gifts: the gang's usual assortment of stolen garbage. As his gift, Tito will give Georgette a kiss. He puckers up, we hear an offscreen slap and Tito comes stumbling out of the gate. "She's really startin' to cave in, man," he smiles, dazed. Fagin and the gang drive off on his trike, all except Dodger who, he tells Oliver, "knows how to get home." He suddenly steps into the middle of fast-moving traffic, reemerging in a convertible next to a beautiful woman, then leaps from car to car on his way to the trike, accompanied by a group rendition of "Why Should I Worry?"

For the final film, the writers made it Jenny's birthday, moved Tito's slap to an earlier scene in the movie, and gave the running gag of his infatuation a new topper: Georgette comes around and Tito flees.

Hidden Images

It's no coincidence that one group of dogs shown during the first rendition of "Why Should I Worry?" look suspiciously like Peg, Trusty and Jock from *Lady and the Tramp*. Then, later, Fagin visits a skeptical pawnbroker who is a dead-ringer for feature animation president Peter Schneider.

But the staff's favorite in-joke was, in the scene where Oliver strikes out on his own, effects animator Kelvin Yasuda drew himself as a toddler who takes a liking to the kitten. Every time the scene was screened in the sweat box, as soon as Yasuda's character appeared, his fellow animators would drone, "Kel-l-l-l-l-vin..."

Less subtle are the plugs. The movie features at least 30 shots of company logos and brand names, including Ryder truck, Yamaha piano, Coca Cola, Kodak, Dr. Scholl's and *USA Today*. Yet it wasn't a typical case of product placement to make a few extra bucks, according to Scribner, but "a story need first. There were product tie-ins, but it began when we started to put up the backgrounds and they were all neutral gray. (The logos) brought an immediacy and if that looked like advertising, so be it."

Bloopers

• When Oliver lashes out at one Doberman, he leaves three bloody scratches on the dog's nose. The scratches clear up in the next shots, but reappear before the dog leaves.

• When Tito first meets Georgette, the two notches that had been on his left ear are now on his right ear.

- In Sykes' warehouse, Jenny, while tied to a chair, falls from a cable. But when she lands, the chair is gone.

- As the Dobermans chase the escaping trike, instead of fading into the distance, first the dog on the left and then the dog on the right suddenly vanish into thin air.

- After Sykes' death, when Dodger returns Oliver to Jenny, the cat's collar is missing. It's absent as well when Jenny is holding Oliver in front of her house as the dogs leave her birthday party.

VIII

Disney Distinguished
Icing on the Cake
1989-1994

"I remember thinking as a child that if these pictures are so enjoyable to watch, they must be even more enjoyable to make. That turned out to be 200 percent true. Nothing compares to making them. The process is so fascinating, the time flies by so quickly. Three years is as little as I would want to create an entirely synthetic film one frame at a time. It's a series of incredible creative challenges, looking for solutions. The challenge is getting it right. Energy comes out of that. It's the greatest satisfaction, the greatest fulfillment. The fact that we're making something that people will enjoy is icing on the cake."

– Will Finn, animator (1996)

Noone of Disney's new leaders had any prior background or
interest in animation, but they did know entertainment.
Katzenberg would quickly become the strong-willed leader, the
lightning rod which had been needed since Walt's death. Finally,
efforts could be refocused on a unified vision. "Walt was an idea
man," Joe Grant says. "Jeffrey Katzenberg was more or less of a
coordinator. He has a very good audience sense, and he provided a
stern father figure."

Like Walt, Katzenberg knew what worked. He'd listen to ideas
or look at storyboards and immediately respond, "Yes. No. I like
this. I don't like this." On *The Little Mermaid*, he'd say, "I don't
believe she's in love with that prince, and if I don't believe that,
who cares about the rest of the movie?" He gauged everything for
maximum impact, second-guessed every decision and third-
guessed every second guess, like Walt, sensing that every idea
could be improved.

Things really came together about a third of the way through
making *The Little Mermaid*. Katzenberg, caught up in the powerful story, the catchy songs, the wild exchange of ideas, in the entire
unique process of creating an animated feature, fell in love with it.
At first, he thought the animation department was just a bunch of
old men who took five years to make a movie. Animators had
grumbled that he had no respect for the medium. Now Katzenberg
was saying *they* had no respect for the medium.

Gradually, the new generation of animators found their stride.
They were able to take what worked from the studio's heritage and
make it their own. By the late Eighties, they were ready for quin-
tessential Disney, the classic fairy tale. Everything—characters,
story, music—would come together in a mature film. Best of all,
Disney would rediscover its audience. After Walt's death, the company began to make the same mistake made to this day by studios
trying to emulate Disney's magic: confusing *kiddie* movie with
family movie. "The problem with films like *Thumbelina* and *Swan
Princess* is the filmmakers are not sure who their audience is,"
explains Tom Sito. "Disney never limits its audiences. If you can
read, you're too old for *Care Bears*, whereas *Beauty and the Beast*
turned out to be a date movie."

Disney animation again provided something for everyone, and

the moviegoing public showed its appreciation in big numbers, such as $500 million (profits, to date, of *Beauty and the Beast*), $650 million (*Aladdin*), and $1 billion (*The Lion King*).

- 25 -

The Little Mermaid

The Original Tale

Over his lifetime, Danish storyteller Hans Christian Andersen wrote 156 fairy tales, the first five compiled in *Fairy Tales Told for Children* (1835). Two years later, for a second edition, he added four more, including "The Little Mermaid." Earlier folk stories told of a water urchin who yearned for a soul so she could marry the human she loved, but Andersen turned it into a story of self-sacrifice. The tale begins at the ocean bottom, home of the Sea-Folk and site of the Sea-King's palace. He has been a widower for many years, so his aged mother keeps house and watches over his six sea-princesses. Each princess has her own garden, which she adorns with strange objects found in wrecked ships. The youngest and loveliest decorates her garden with only a salvaged marble statue of a handsome boy.

The mermaids are fascinated with humans and love to hear grandma tell tales of life above the surface, where each could venture once she turned 15. After reaching 15, each girl returns from the top with tales of her own, but soon grows indifferent to such trips. When the youngest finally turns 15, she swims up to see a ship filled with music and singing. Through a cabin window, she watches the sixteenth birthday party of a handsome prince, who looks like her statue. Unfortunately, a storm hits and smashes the ship to pieces. The little mermaid rescues the prince and lays his unconscious body on the shore. Upon hearing girls approaching, she swims behind some rocks. The girls wake him and help him off.

The mermaid returns to the shore often but never spots the prince and grows increasingly sorrowful. Her only consolation is to fling her arms around her statue. She finally locates the prince's kingdom and spies on him constantly, as her love grows. Grandma explains the difference between men and mermaids: men have eternal souls that rise to the sky; mermaids live to be about 300, but when they die they turn into sea foam. The only way for them to gain a soul is to have a man fall in love with and marry them—a longshot since men prefer legs over tails.

To cheer her up, grandma decides to throw a big undersea ball. The little mermaid sings beautifully at the party, but, growing sad, she sneaks away to see the dreaded Sea-Witch. The witch's home is surrounded by bushes and trees of polypi—half-animal, half-vegetable creatures that grab out with their slimy, snake-like fingers. The Sea-Witch, covered by fat, slithering water-snakes, offers to brew a potion that would turn the mermaid's tail fin into legs. Walking would feel as she were stepping on knives, she could never again be a mermaid and unless a prince falls in love with and marries her, she wouldn't get a soul. If he marries another, she would become foam the morning after. And as payment, the witch requires a lovely voice, so she cuts out the mermaid's tongue.

The little mermaid swims to the shore and drinks the witch's potion. The pain of her tail fin splitting into legs causes her to pass out. In the morning the prince discovers her—naked, so she must wrap herself in her long, thick hair—and takes her to his palace. The sweet mute dances as gracefully as she used to swim, and captivates everyone. Yet at night she sneaks out to soak her burning feet in the cold sea water. The prince loves her dearly, but feels he could only wed a similar-looking girl—the youngest of those who discovered him on the seashore and, he thinks, rescued him.

One day the prince's parents ask him to marry a neighboring king's daughter, but he says he'll only have the girl who rescued him. It turns out the neighboring king's daughter *is* that girl. They wed, with the little mermaid serving as little bridesmaid. Following a festive reception on the prince's ship, the mermaid gazes out to sea, realizing she'll be foam come morning. Just then, her now-bald sisters rise up from the water. They have traded their hair to the Sea-Witch for a knife. If the little mermaid plunges it into the prince's heart before sunrise, his warm blood could sprinkle on her feet and change them back into a tail so she could regain her 300 years as a mermaid.

But as the knife-wielding mermaid draws the curtains to the honeymoon couple's chambers, with the sun about to rise, she realizes she can't go through with it. She tosses the blade into the waves and dives into the sea, as her body begins to dissolve. Suddenly she realizes she's rising out of the foam into the air amid hundreds of beautiful, transparent shapes. She also now has a body like these hovering Daughters of the Air, who have no immortal soul, but can earn one by performing good deeds over their 300 years.

The Disney Version

Disney first explored the possibility of using "The Little Mermaid" as part of a Hans Christian Andersen biography or a compilation of his tales in the early 1940s, but Samuel Goldwyn's *Hans Christian Andersen* (1952) with Danny Kaye beat him to it.

Years later, as Ron Clements was wrapping up work on *The Great Mouse Detective*, he wanted his next project to be *The Little Mermaid*. The studio turned him down. After all, they explained, they'd just released *Splash*. Why did they need another mermaid picture?

Clements kept pushing and finally got the go-ahead. In 1985, he wrote a two-page treatment, adding a few characters such as the bespectacled crab Clarence, "a stuffy, English conductor" who leads the mermaids at an undersea concert. Lyricist Howard Ashman, who had done some work on *Oliver & Co.*, suggested that Clarence become a Jamaican crab. That allowed Ashman and his partner, Alan Menken, to incorporate a range of calypso and reggae styles, which they hoped would give the film a bouncier, more contemporary feel.

Similarly, Clements and partner John Musker tried to make the story more contemporary, identifying with the dreamy, misunderstood teenager instead of the father who thinks he knows best. Unlike Pinocchio, who is punished for his wanderlust and rewarded for returning to his family, mermaid Ariel runs away from home, never comes back and lives happily ever after. From now on, Disney would leave the helpless kidnapped waifs to Don Bluth.

Clements and Musker wrote a twenty-page treatment, making the unnamed Sea-Witch more of a villain and shaping the personalities of the prince, the out-of-touch father Triton, Sebastian the crab, Flounder the fish, and Scuttle the seagull.

Musker first modeled Ursula the Sea-Witch after Joan Collins' nasty character on *Dynasty*, but changed his mind after seeing a Rob Minkoff drawing of the drag queen Divine with a Mohawk haircut.

The one song Ashman and Menken wrote that wasn't used, "Silence Is Golden," was intended for Ursula to sing as she took away the mermaid's voice. They reworked the number into "Poor Unfortunate Souls," stressing the fate that might befall Ariel: being turned, like others who struck unsuccessful deals with the witch, into the pitiful polypi.

The biggest change was that Clements and Musker wanted a happy ending. So, instead of the prince falling in love with another woman, they had Ursula the Sea-Witch disguise herself as the other woman and hypnotize the prince into marrying her. After snapping out of it, he takes a cue from *Sleeping Beauty* and impales the villainess, who has transformed herself into a gigantic monster.

Plot Holes

- "Isn't it fantastic?" Ariel asks, pointing to a shipwreck, probably the sight of untold death and destruction.

- Among her underwater stash of people stuff, Ariel has a book of which she freely flips through the pages. Have you ever submerged a book and tried to turn the pages?

- Perhaps it's because she's been a mermaid all her life and has never had to dress herself, but during a carriage ride Ariel is wearing a giant bow—under her hat.

Bloopers

- In the establishing shot before the concert, the grand chandelier is lit. But seconds later it's out, so Triton can light it during his grand entrance.

- As Ariel swims to the shipwreck, she's not carrying anything. Yet when she arrives at the boat's porthole, she has an orange bag on her left wrist.

- After "Part of Your World," Sebastian gets a thimble caught on his leg. In a rear shot, the thimble disappears, reappears when the angle changes, and finally disappears for good as he exits.

- As Ariel watches Eric's ship, the vessel launches some fireworks from its side portals. The ship sails to the right, followed by an identical flash of fireworks coming from the middle of the ocean—the exact spot where the ship portals were during the first fireworks launch.

- When Max discovers Ariel spying on the festivities on the ship, the dog licks her right cheek. Ariel reacts by wiping her left cheek.

- As Ariel sits in front of the mirror, a blonde and a black-haired sister are on her left and another sister with brown, spiky hair sits to her right. But when the camera pulls back from the mirror, the blonde and brown-haired mermaids have switched places.

- At first glance the seagull appears to have done a lousy job configuring an old tarp into a ragged dress for Ariel. But seconds later the tarp's jagged bottom edge miraculously levels out. And it turns out he's somehow even sewn a pocket into the makeshift dress for Sebastian.

- At the table, just before dinner is served, Ariel, Eric and Grimsby all have empty plates set before them. Just before Grimsby is served, the plate in front of him vanishes. After Sebastian runs across the table to Ariel's plate, the lemon wedges disappear from Grimsby's plate.

- Ariel is barefoot on the dock before she jumps into the water to stop Eric's wedding. On the ship, the shell containing Ariel's voice breaks at her bare feet, but after she regains her voice and is greeted by Max, she's momentarily wearing shoes.

Hidden Stuff

As Ariel spies on the ship at night, the most prominent sailor doing a jig was modeled after layout artist Rasoul Azadani.

Mickey Mouse, Donald Duck and Goofy also make a split-second appearance during the concert at the beginning of the film. The three were drawn in a few frames among the multitude of tiny figures Triton passes by during his entrance.

The Little Mermaid's most controversial hidden image, however, was not in the movie, but on the original movie poster, which depicts Ariel and Eric on a rock in the foreground, with a palace in the background. After the image was duplicated for the cover of the videocassette container, people began complaining that one castle turret, in particular, looked unusually phallic. A Phoenix supermarket chain temporarily pulled the videos off its shelves. A woman from the Midwest even went after Disney, claiming the image traumatized her children.

According to a former co-worker of the guilty illustrator, "The rumor at that time, the one I'd always heard, was that it was a disgruntled employee who did it as revenge. But Disney did its own investigation and found that was completely false. The illustrator was not at all upset, he didn't know what was the big deal. It was just a little thing that got by a couple of art directors. He probably did it as a joke, nobody was really paying attention, and it slipped through the cracks."

In the same illustration, the artist also hid other shapes in the water below the rock, including upside-down Batman wings. "I've worked with these animators, and they paint things all the time," the co-worker added. "It's a boy's club. Most of them are pretty wacko. But to me, it looks like a castle. If somebody wants to, they can see just about anything in anything, but I think that's taking it out of focus."

Strange Reactions

Perhaps the strangest reaction of all was that, for the first time since Walt's death, the studio released a film loved by almost everyone. Clements and Musker seemingly rediscovered the magic formula. For the first time in 25 years, all the key ingredients were combined in one picture: great music, vibrant animation, funny gags, a memorable cast led by an outrageous villain, and exciting storytelling that was relevant to contemporary audiences.

Attraction Offspring

As soon as Tony Baxter previewed *The Little Mermaid*, he knew Disney was back. There was something for everyone, especially— for an Imagineer creating a theme park attraction—wondrous, exotic locations. In designing a Little Mermaid ride, the Imagineers consulted the filmmakers, who were most concerned with, of all things, the film's turquoise and red color scheme. "If you don't have that right, you don't have *The Little Mermaid*," they said.

Like Triton, guests would travel in huge clamshells, through all the major musical sequences and finally to a gigantic, monstrous Ursula. Imagineering devised an amazing water effect so the shells would appear to go above and below the surface, even in the same scene. The opening scene would be Ariel on a rock, calling out in song, then the shells would rise up to view Eric's ship. The water effects were most astounding during the twin-level "Kiss the Girl" sequence, complete with simulated leaves on the surface and ripples from Eric's oars.

Although first considered for Disneyland near Videopolis, the Little Mermaid dark ride was finally slated for Euro Disneyland. The Paris park's Fantasyland was complete, though, but there was room in Discoveryland—until someone suggested the more marketable Space Mountain. As yet, the audio-animatronic Ariel still has not surfaced.

- 26 -

Beauty and the Beast

The Original Tale

Tracing back to Britain in the mid-1700s, the classic fairy tale "Beauty and the Beast" by Marie LePrince de Beaumont tells of a rich merchant with three sons and three beautiful daughters. The two older daughters are spoiled, unlike sweet, lovely Beauty. The sisters mock Beauty for her love of reading and turn down numerous proposals, saying they'll wed no less than a duke or count. Beauty graciously thanks her suitors, but says she is too young to marry and wants to keep her father company.

The merchant suddenly loses his fortune and is left with only a cottage in the country. Beauty awakens at 4:00 every morning to cook and clean; her three brothers plow the fields. Her sisters, whose suitors no longer call, sleep late and mope around. One day, the merchant learns that a ship with his merchandise has docked. The eldest daughters beg him to bring them dresses, furs and wigs, but Beauty wants nothing and asks only for a rose so as not to embarrass her sisters.

Once in town, the merchant is sued over his merchandise and heads home, poor as ever. He loses his way in a dark forest and, fleeing from snow and wolves, stumbles into a palace. He finds the table set for one, eats a great feast and retires to a splendid bedroom. He awakens to find a handsome suit and a nice breakfast. On his way out, the merchant plucks a rose from the trellis for Beauty. A hideous beast appears and accuses the merchant of being ungrateful and stealing his roses. But, upon learning the man has daughters, the Beast gives him three months to see if one will return to die in the father's place.

Returning home, the father explains what happened when he took the rose. Although ridiculed by her sisters for "selfishly" asking for a rose in the first place. Beauty says she will go to the palace in her father's place. There, the Beast provides her with a magnificent bedroom, her own library and a great mirror to keep an eye on her family. Every night she dines with the Beast who, though neither handsome nor witty, is very kind. Every night, he asks her to marry him.

After three months of this routine, Beauty confesses that the mirror reveals her sisters have married, her brothers have joined the army and her father is dying of sorrow. His death would cause Beauty to die of sorrow, which, in turn, would make the Beast die of sorrow, so he allows her to return to her father for one week. He gives her a ring that she is to place on her bedside table when it's time to return.

Beauty's sisters are jealous when she returns home with a beautiful new wardrobe provided by the Beast. One sister has married a very handsome man, but he is in love with himself; the other sister has wed a man of great wit, which he uses to torment her. They conspire to delay Beauty's return to the palace, hoping it will enrage the Beast so he'll devour her. Beauty does stay an extra two days but finally feels too guilty and places the ring on the table. She awakens in the palace to find the Beast unconscious in his garden. Heartbroken, he has decided to starve himself. Beauty promises to marry him, and he suddenly turns into a handsome prince. A wicked fairy had condemned him to Beasthood until a beautiful woman consented to marry him, without him giving even a hint of his true wit. They enter the castle, where her whole family awaits. Before Beauty and the prince marry, the fairy turns her sisters into statues, doomed to witness Beauty's happiness until they admit their faults.

The Disney Version

Disney began work on an animated version of *Beauty and the Beast* in the early Fifties, and scheduled production to begin in 1954 for a 1958 release. But the writers were stymied by the tale's claustrophobic second act when Beauty is imprisoned. Unable to agree on a satisfactory solution, they gave up and concentrated on *Sleeping Beauty*.

More than 30 years later, the studio gave it another try. In late 1988, Katzenberg assigned screenwriter Linda Woolverton, who was working on an unproduced Winnie the Pooh feature, to write a non-musical version of *Beauty and the Beast*. She would be breaking ground. "There were women story artists, but very few, maybe two or three in a room of fifteen or twenty. But I was the first woman writer," Woolverton said. "Early on, it was the Good Old Boys. So here's this female coming in from the outside. There was some resistance, but it's a director's medium, and they really ran with (my ideas)."

The heroine of the story began to reflect Woolverton's own pioneering situation. Unlike the passive princesses that preceded her, Belle would be intelligent, aggressive and would have more on her mind than getting married—in short, the most independent Disney heroine yet. "She was (a strong character) in my early drafts. I wanted someone who speaks to women of today," she said. "She's still a lady, she's just not like heroines before her. After her, the concept of a Disney heroine changed. *Beauty* expanded what women could do and be and changed the nature of the beast, so to speak."

To stress Belle's independence, Woolverton eliminated her brothers and sisters and transformed her rich merchant father into a dependent, near-senile inventor. Ideas to give her a stepmother, a sister named Claire, and a cat were also canned because they started to muddle the plot. The villain would be Gaston, a handsome, overbearing suitor (recalling Brom Bones of "The Legend of Sleepy Hollow" from *The Adventures of Ichabod and Mr. Toad*) who expects Belle to act like Snow White and fall madly in love with him. He started out as a broad, comical character who was the butt of a lot of jokes but, after being given a buffoonish sidekick, became more serious to increase his villainy. The Beast began as brooding and monosyllabic, but slowly became a fuller character.

For amusing supporting players, Woolverton had the castle attendants transform into animated, non-speaking objects when the prince turns into a Beast. She also combined the roles of the magic mirror and ring, and changed the rose's purpose so that when it lost its last petal, the spell could not be undone, heightening the dramatic tension.

After Woolverton completed her first drafts, *The Little Mermaid* was released to tremendous business, with critics pronouncing the rebirth of the great Disney animated musical. Katzenberg realized that *Beauty and the Beast* had better be a musical, too, and reassigned Ashman and Menken to write the music.

Ashman quickly noted that half the cast didn't speak. "We gotta have somebody to sing my songs," he told Woolverton. All of the objects received speaking (and, of course, singing) voices except

Building a Beauty of a Beast

Originally, the Beast was patterned after a mandrill, but evolved into a conglomeration of appendages from various species. Match the animal to the part(s) of the Beast's body it inspired:

(1) Bear

(2) Buffalo

(3) Gorilla

(4) Lion

(5) Wild boar

(6) Wolf

(a) Heavy brow and crest of skull

(b) General shape of head

(c) Nose bridge

(d) Beard

(e) Tusk

(f) Mane

(g) Upper torso

(h) Tail

(i) Legs

Answers:
The Beast has a (1) bear's (g) upper torso, (2) buffalo's (b) general shape of head and (d) beard, (3) gorilla's (a) heavy brow and crest of skull, (4) lion's (f) mane, (5) wild boar's (c) nose bridge and (e) tusk, and (6) wolf's (h) tail and (i) legs.

one, a precocious music box who simply jangled. The music box never made it to animation, though. One scene with Mrs. Potts the tea pot included a little tea cup who spoke one line. As a private joke in a note to Ashman, Woolverton referred to him as "Chip." She recalled, "I faxed it to Howard, and he laughed. I told him I was just kidding, and he said, 'No, leave it in.' And then Jeffrey (Katzenberg) really fell for Chip."

During auditions for Chip's lone line, one boy, Michael Pierce, provided such an endearing performance that everyone tried to find his character more to do. He replaced the music box as the character who stows away with Belle when she returns to her father and, as his part grew, he would completely replace the music box. His expanding role also meant less screen time for a dog-turned-footstool, who originally was going to engage in more funny business—such as sniffing a suit of armor like a tree and having the armor react by kicking the stool away.

Only one Ashman and Menken number went unused, the nearly ten-minute-long "Human Again," sung by butler/candlestick Lumiere and the other objects as Belle and the Beast fall in love. The lyrics didn't match the animated images of awkward romance. The song's focus was on the objects anticipating that they soon might be "human again." This was replaced by a new song, "Something There (That Wasn't There Before)," which focused on the leads. Disney, though, did reinstate "Human Again" in its Broadway stage version of *Beauty and the Beast*.

Cutting Room Floor

As originally animated, Lumiere and the kitchenware sang "Be My Guest" to comfort the castle's first cold, storm-drenched prisoner, Belle's father, Maurice. But during a pre-release screening, a storyman from the back of the room spoke up: "He's singing that song to the wrong person."

Indeed, here was the big production number with only a tenuous connection to the story and nothing to do with either lead character. "Our hearts dropped," Woolverton recalled. "It was like a light bulb went on. The scene had to be repositioned and reanimated. We had to lift Maurice and put in Belle. Howard had to write new lyrics, with 'she' instead of 'he.'"

Plot Holes

• A fairy turns the prince into a Beast because, when she knocked at his castle door disguised as an old beggar woman, he turned her away. With all these servants, what is the prince doing answering the door? She says that he will remain a Beast unless someone falls in love with him before his 21st birthday, but just how long ago did this curse begin? According to Lumiere, "ten years we've been rusting," yet that would mean the prince got cursed when he was 11 (a tad young for the "falling in love" escape clause). He looks much older in the painting he slashes. But how old would that make Chip? And doesn't Chip's mother, Mrs. Potts, appear and sound a bit past her child-bearing years?

• If so much of the Beast's furniture and kitchenware was really his staff, he must have been seriously underfurnished before the spell—and badly in need of shopping after it was broken.

• Even though none of them has ever been there before, Maurice's horse leads Belle to the Beast's castle, and later the mob also has no trouble finding it. The one who gets lost is Maurice, who's the only one who's ever been there before. Then again, how could *anyone* miss a gigantic castle sitting on top of a mountain?

• It's sort of bewildering what Belle sees in the Beast, since for most of the movie he doesn't just look bad, he *is* bad.

Bloopers

• In the opening scene, we first see Gaston with his rifle. His gun suddenly disappears when he starts down the street after Belle, not resurfacing until he climbs out onto a roof, after which it disappears for good. In the same scene, Belle's basket temporarily disappears midway through her walk down the street.

• When Gaston arrives at Belle's house to propose, the cottage door opens *out* and is left open as they walk across the room. Soon after, Gaston backs Belle against the door, which has somehow closed, but she opens the door *out* and slips away, so Gaston falls through. Belle pulls the door shut, then quickly opens the door *in* and tosses out his boots.

Hidden Images

During Maurice's frightful flight through the forest, he quickly passes a sign post with arrows pointing to Newhall (site of the Disney-owned Golden Oak Ranch), Valencia (California Institute of the Arts) and Anaheim (Disneyland).

During the climactic battle between the villagers and the castle furniture, while an axe-wielding peasant chases an endtable across the room, animator Tom Sito (as a tribute to the famous scene in Eisenstein's classic film *Potemkin*) drew a baby buggy bounding down the grand staircase.

Strange Reactions

So beautiful is *Beauty and the Beast* that it became the first animated film to be nominated for the Best Picture Oscar. That didn't stop the chairman of the Malaysian Censorship Board from strongly objecting to one insidious scene, that showed a little pig scurrying around in the background of the courtyard. He said the country's fundamentalist Muslim regime would "find the pigs offensive" and demanded all pig shots be butchered.

Attraction Offspring

To go along with the Little Mermaid ride at Euro Disneyland, the Imagineers completely designed a companion Beauty and the Beast attraction. It would be a Tiki Room-type show that opened with plates and other dinnerware performing "Be Our Guest." Gargoyles would descend to sing "Beware the Beast," a rewritten version of "Kill the Beast." Then an audio-animatronic Beast would appear with a live Belle. "Why have you all come here to stare at me?" he snarls at the audience. But Belle assures him, no, they're friends. She gives a guest a rose to hand to the Beast, there's a puff of smoke and a live Prince emerges from the Beast figure.

The attraction was such a lock for Discoveryland that pictures of Ariel, Belle and the Beast appeared on early maps of Euro Disneyland in the areas where the Little Mermaid and Beauty and the Beast attractions would one day be. But the projects were shelved in favor of Space Mountain.

- 27 -
Aladdin

The Original Tale

"The Arabian Nights" (also known as "The Thousand and One Nights") is a collection of tales assembled over many centuries throughout India and the Middle East. Among the best known are "Ali Baba and the Forty Thieves," "Sinbad the Sailor" and "Aladdin and the Wonderful Lamp."

The latter begins long ago in China with a poor tailor's widow and her lazy son, Aladdin, who spends all his time playing with the other street urchins. One day, a mysterious Moor identifies himself to the 15-year-old Aladdin as his father's brother, returning from 30 years of travels to share his riches. The Moor promises Aladdin's mother he'll turn the idle youth into a merchant with his own shop. He buys him fancy new clothes and says they'll travel to the gardens beyond the city to study how the wealthy act. Instead, they journey to a barren valley, where the Moor starts a small fire. He adds a pinch of magic powder to the flames, the rocks quake and the earth opens, revealing a marble slab. The Moor instructs Aladdin to lift the slab and enter the cave below to retrieve a copper lamp, but not to touch any of the countless other riches. He gives the lad a magic ring for protection.

Aladdin finds the lamp, but for his friends he also pockets jewels, which he has mistaken for colored-glass toys. When Aladdin asks for help out of the cave before handing over the lamp, the Moor becomes enraged, scaring Aladdin back into the cave. Actually, the Moor is not a relative but a sorcerer, who discovered that only Aladdin could open and enter the cave. So the sorcerer shuts the slab and returns to his own country of Morocco.

Imprisoned, Aladdin brushes against the ring the sorcerer gave him, summoning a great black spirit from the ground who offers to do his bidding. Aladdin asks to be freed from the cave, and the spirit obliges. The next morning, Aladdin decides to sell the lamp.

But when he polishes it, a huge black Genie rises out and asks what is his new master's wish. Aladdin is hungry, so the Genie produces silver trays holding golden vessels filled with delicious food. Aladdin grows rich by selling the dishes and discovers his glass "toys" are priceless gems.

One day, the palace heralds are making way through the square for the princess to reach the bath. All are to shut themselves in their homes lest they be killed. But impetuous Aladdin sneaks a peek at the 15-year-old beauty and discovers that under their veils all women do not look like his mother. Determined to marry the princess, he has his mom take the king some gems as a gift. The king is impressed, but his Grand Wazir, who wants his own son to wed the princess, knows the boy is poor and suggests he should first provide a suitable dowry. The king demands 40 gold dishes filled with gems, delivered by a huge caravan. Aladdin asks the Genie, and a minute later the assembly fills the street. Dumbstruck, the king allows Aladdin to marry his daughter and build a palace next to his own, which the Genie does that night.

Meanwhile, the Moor learns that Aladdin, with lamp, is now the son-in-law of the emperor. Furious, the sorcerer heads for China to discover Aladdin is on a hunting trip. The Moor, carrying a basket full of shiny copper lamps, begins shouting, "New lamps for old!" Unwittingly, the princess trades Aladdin's old lamp.

The sorcerer then summons the Genie to transport Aladdin's palace and wife to Morocco. When the King discovers the palace and his daughter have vanished, his Wazir explains Aladdin must be a sorcerer. So when Aladdin returns, the King gives him 40 days to return his daughter or face execution. Aladdin commands the spirit of the ring to transport him to the princess. She reveals that the sorcerer always carries the lamp with him and asks her each day to be his wife. Aladdin has the princess tell the sorcerer she will marry him—after a celebratory glass of wine, into which she slips a sleeping potion. He passes out, Aladdin grabs the lamp and the Genie transports him, the princess and the palace back to China.

The Disney Version

Although an "Arabian Nights" adventure featuring Mickey

Mouse, Donald Duck and Goofy had been considered some years earlier, Howard Ashman first proposed a feature version of *Aladdin* in 1988. He wrote a 40-page treatment, sticking rather close to the plot and characters of the original story, but doing it as a campy 1930s-style musical with a Cab Calloway-like Genie. Ashman had Jafar the wazir disguise himself as Aladdin's uncle and built up the parts of Aladdin's equally lazy friends.

After Ashman and Menken discarded one number for a spoiled princess, "Call Me a Princess," their initial score featured six songs:

(1) "Arabian Nights," sung by a peddler narrator to set the opening scene (which made it to the final version), plus four reprises: to introduce the wicked royal adviser/sorcerer who wants his boss dead, to begin Aladdin and his counterfeit uncle's journey to the cave, to see the boy trapped in a cell waiting to be beheaded, and to close the picture (which almost made it and finally ended up closing the direct-to-video *Aladdin and the King of Thieves*);

(2) "Babkak, Omar, Aladdin, Kassim," an MGM musical-type production number for Aladdin and his buddies to celebrate their laziness;

(3) "Friend Like Me," introducing the generous Genie (the other song that survived);

(4) "Proud of Your Boy," a ballad Aladdin sings to his mother after letting her down again;

(5) "How Quick They Forget," a barbershop quartet a la Bob Hope and Bing Crosby's *Road* picture duets, with Aladdin's friends lamenting his breaking up the foursome, and

(6) "High Adventure," sung as Aladdin, his buddies and the genie of the ring prepare to go after Jafar, who now has the genie of the lamp.

Ashman and Menken moved on to *Beauty and the Beast*, and Linda Woolverton used their treatment and six songs to work up two drafts of *Aladdin*, producing more of "a straight adventure." Then Ron Clements and John Musker, having finished *The Little Mermaid*, took over. They put more of a "cartoony" spin on the story, with unpredictable Robin Williams in mind for the Genie.

Katzenberg, whose opinion could be swayed by only the most persuasive, articulate of arguments, wanted a more realistic Genie.

All it took to change his mind was Eric Goldberg animating a twenty-second routine about schizophrenia from a Williams comedy album. A crazy Genie it would be. During the initial four-hour recording session, Williams did his first scene as the Genie 25 times in 25 different ways. He stopped following the script after the first eight. He did the same dialogue in different voices. Other lines he completely ad-libbed. A scene originally meant to last 30 seconds suddenly went on for ten minutes. Dozens of impersonations ended up on the cutting room floor, including sex therapist Dr. Ruth Westheimer, John Wayne (doing a line later done as Jack Nicholson), and then-president George Bush, who was cut on suspicion he wouldn't be reelected.

To voice the other wise-cracking character, the wazir's parrot, Iago, the filmmakers first considered a John Gielgud-type to offset the hot-tempered Jafar. After Katzenberg suggested a cooler Jafar to make him more sinister, the wilder Danny DeVito was sought to play Iago, but he was not available. A new search of voices turned up the even more overboard Gilbert Gottfried.

As the story evolved, Katzenberg urged Clements and Musker not to feel bound to Ashman's script, but to get something they liked. An anthropomorphic flying carpet made the genie of the ring superfluous. The romance between Aladdin and the princess Jasmine began to take shape.

Joined by screenwriters Ted Elliott and Terry Rossio, the team set about trying to make Aladdin and Jasmine stronger characters. His pals were cut from the picture, placing the spotlight squarely on Aladdin. Instead of having his mother ask the Sultan for his daughter's hand, Aladdin would ask for it himself. Jasmine, though, would wish to choose her own mate.

Reminiscent of the creation of Belle in *Beauty and the Beast*, Elliott and Rossio were particularly concerned with Jasmine's character. "She was yet another princess in an animated film whose basic dilemma centered on who she was going to marry. We had in mind a more active, independent and heroic heroine," Rossio said. "We still both cringe at the section of the movie where Jasmine starts crying, telling Rajah (her pet tiger), 'It's all my fault.' Then, after the sequence in the cave, her father comes to her and she's *still crying*. We argued that at the very least Jasmine needed to go to her father with the declaration, 'We have to talk.' (But) that meant going to the Sultan's bedroom, which meant designing a whole new room, and that was too expensive."

Similarly, the screenwriters lost another battle at the film's climax. When Jasmine is trapped in the giant hourglass, they wanted her to engineer her own escape. Aladdin was doing all sorts of heroic things, they argued, why not let Jasmine do at least one? Elliott's idea was for her to take the jewel from her headdress and use it to cut the glass. But the prevailing opinion was that it was more satisfying for Aladdin to smash open the glass and save her at the last second.

Another major sequence that was proposed, but never story-boarded, involved Jasmine's decision to leave the palace. Rossio was convinced that it was simply wrong to have her run away. "It seemed selfish and silly on her part," he said. "And what a terrible role model for children, I thought, to have the heroine run away from her father, her problems, and go out in the city, without even bringing any money!"

The writers thought it would be better if Jasmine left the palace with a purpose. Yes, she was upset that her father was forcing her to marry. But it also seemed plausible that Jasmine would be smart enough to see that it was because he had been hypnotized. And she also could be heroic enough to leave the palace to go look for help.

This tack dealt with the issue of the Sultan's poor decision making, and allowed Jasmine to leave the palace with a worthy purpose (to find a way to help her father). It also placed the cause of her leaving squarely on the villain's shoulders. Rossio added: "It also set up an interesting scene—Jasmine in the marketplace, getting involved with some shady, fake faith-healer types. That's whom Aladdin would rescue her from, as opposed to the apple salesman, and then the story would proceed the same from there.

"In the end, it was decided that this motivation for Jasmine was too complex, too worked over, and focused too much on the power that Jafar had over the Sultan. So we were left with a princess who didn't want to get married who runs away from home. Sigh."

But as Jasmine's bolder look and personality began to take shape, she started to overshadow Aladdin. In early drawings, Aladdin looked like Michael J. Fox. To give him more sex appeal, the artists beefed him up to look like Tom Cruise. Animators were instructed to always have him look confident, in Cruise control.

Another problem with Aladdin was that his character was a thief who enjoyed being a thief. The public had changed since Alexander Korda's 1940 live action version, *The Thief of Baghdad*, when audiences (who during the Depression had rooted for John Dillinger and Pretty Boy Floyd) could sympathize with the victim of an unfair society who desperately resorts to crime. A Nineties audience might have more trouble accepting a happy thief as the hero, especially in a Disney movie. The writers had to make the audiences understand why Aladdin stole, and consequently the scene that defines his character—in which palace guards pursue him through the marketplace—was one of the last animated. At one point, the scene even included Aladdin with a stick battling a guard with a scimitar. As they locked weapons, the guard was to snarl, "Stealing again, street rat?" Aladdin answered dramatically, "I steal to eat." What worked better was simply having Aladdin give his freshly pilfered food to two hungry children.

Although a "street rat" in appearance (whom the Genie trans- forms into royalty, to the princess' dismay), Aladdin would be good at heart. This way his right to enter the cave with the lamp needn't be dumb luck. It would be too passive for Aladdin to sim- ply be granted entrance, as if he was just destined for greatness due to his innate nature.

It also seemed more heroic and dramatic to have Aladdin do something to prove his worthiness. A sequence was written to let Aladdin earn his access to the innermost reaches of the cave, as recounted by Rossio:

> Just inside the cave mouth entrance, we see Aladdin approaching a spectacularly beautiful lamp. It practically glows, perched on a lovely altar, in a golden room with pictures on the walls. Aladdin is transfixed by the lamp. He moves toward it. He reaches out his hands...
>
> ...but then notices his shadow, on the wall. It's an image of himself, reaching for the lamp. And there are other images on the walls. Other people. A whole series of them, in different dress, from different eras, even. All of them leaning forward, greedily reaching for the beautiful

lamp. The last one in line is the Thief (whom we saw meeting his fate in the film's opening scene). If Aladdin takes this lamp, clearly he's the next one in line to end up on the wall.

So Aladdin backs away from the spectacularly shiny lamp. A "click" is heard, a passageway opens, and Aladdin moves deeper into the cave to meet the carpet and find the real lamp.

This test of worthiness was set up by the original lines spoken by a Tiger Head at the cave entrance:

ONLY ONE MAY ENTER HERE
ONE WHO IS WISE ENOUGH
ONE WHOSE WORTH LIES DEEP WITHIN
A DIAMOND IN THE ROUGH.

These lines are actually clues as to who may enter the cave and how to do it. "A diamond in the rough" describes Aladdin, a thief about to become a hero, but one whose innate goodness will need some time to emerge. "Only one may enter" means that there is someone who is destined to make it into the cave—Aladdin—and all others will fail. "One who is wise enough" refers to the test with the fake lamp in the first chamber. You had to be wise enough to avoid the beautiful lamp, or you'd end up on the walls. And "One whose worth lies deep within" is a dual pun, describing Aladdin and providing a clue to skip the fake lamp and look farther within the cave for the real "worth."

The scene was masterfully storyboarded, but in the end there just wasn't room for it. "There was always a concern that it took too long for Robin Williams to show up as the Genie. Any sequence in front of that event was carefully scrutinized. This was one that didn't make the final cut," Rossio explained. "So when the fake lamp test scene was cut, the line that referred to it in the Tiger Head's rhyme was also cut. This left a rhyme that didn't rhyme, which always bugged me. But the Tiger Head was a CGI (computer-generated imagery) effect, and my understanding was that it would cost too much, and take too much time to change."

By the time Ashman and Menken returned to the picture, the story had changed so much that few of their earlier songs worked.

They wrote "Prince Ali" to welcome the pretend prince's caravan (as the first of his allotted three wishes) and "Humiliate the Boy," in which Jafar cruelly unmasks Aladdin at a public ceremony. The latter, their last collaboration before Ashman's death, didn't work with the story, either.

As the romance between Aladdin and Jasmine became more important, his mother's role continued to decrease and she was finally cut from the story. The filmmakers considered having orphan Aladdin sing "Proud of Your Boy" to his mother in heaven, but they finally gave up on the song.

Suddenly without his long-time partner, Menken's first instinct was to try to write both music and lyrics. He composed "Count on Me" for Aladdin to sing how proud he will make his monkey, Abu. Menken then teamed with lyricist Tim Rice to compose Aladdin's carefree solo, "One Jump Ahead," replacing the carefree buddy song. This song, though, came so close to the spot for "Count On Me," that the latter was replaced with a short reprise of "One Jump Ahead."

Menken and Rice also wrote a romantic ballad, "A Whole New World," and a new song for Jafar, "My Time Has Come," to replace "Humiliate the Boy." Again, they tried to redo the humiliation scene into "Why Me?," a flashback song about Jafar's past. But the material provided a bumpy transition and slowed the momentum of the movie. New lyrics were offered and discarded for the song. Disney even previewed the scene without music and the audience thought it worked great. "Except," noted feature animation president Peter Schneider, "you sort of miss a song there." Finally, they used a sarcastic reprise of "Prince Ali."

To set up the final confrontation, Aladdin had to be forced to use a wish in Act II, leaving him at the end with one wish and two desires: sorting out his own troubles or freeing the Genie. One idea for the second wish was having Jafar devise an impossible test for quasi-prince Aladdin to pass. Hoping to marry the princess himself to gain the power of the throne, Jafar decrees that the only prince who can marry the princess is the one who can pass this test of worthiness. The test would involve ferocious tigers, impossible climbs, dangerous traps, and other thrilling things to animate. Aladdin bravely agrees to do it, uses his second wish to get him through, spoils Jafar's plan, and impresses the heck out of every-body.

This sounded like fun. The artists went to work creating all sorts of elaborate, clever and dangerous-looking contraptions. Everyone put their brains to it for months, coming up with idea after idea... and none of them were any good.

It became a joke after a while: "I'll get to that, right after I fig-ure out the test sequence." "I had a dream that solved the test sequence, but I don't remember it." "Why, there must be a thou-sand clever things to do in the test sequence."

It was finally decided that if twenty clever people couldn't fig-ure out a way to do the idea, maybe it wasn't such a good idea. So they had Jafar just grab Aladdin and throw him off a cliff. When Ted Elliott signed John Musker's copy of a book on the making of *Aladdin*, he wrote, "And I know that someday we'll figure out that test sequence."

The writers also wanted a really big finish to the picture, some-thing as spectacular as the escape from the Cave of Wonders sequence near the opening. Elliott and Rossio proposed that Jafar's wish, once he gets the lamp, was to say: "I wish to be Sultan, to always be Sultan, and to always have been Sultan." Radiating out from him, then, in a huge circle, would be a transforming line, changing the entire city to what it would have been like if Jafar had always been sultan.

It would bring instant poverty for everyone, instant dilapidation for all the buildings, instant misery. Aladdin would be the only character not affected by the change. The carpet would wrap him up as the line went past, protecting him and leaving him alone in this terrible new world. He would also be the only one who remembers how things used to be, how they should be. And only he could fix it, by tricking Jafar into the lamp.

In the end, the idea was deemed just too weird. "Too science-fictiony," Musker called it.

"It became known as the *It's a Wonderful Life* ending and never really caught on," Rossio remembered. "Ironically, though, the art designers and background artists did a version of it, more or less, on their own. The backgrounds, the city, the palace—especially the throne room—are all visually changed during Jafar's rule. The artists executed this to visually support Jafar's rise to power, even if it was too odd an idea for it to be a plot element."

Plot Holes

• To fool Aladdin in the dungeon, Jafar is able to completely alter his face, teeth and body to look like a disfigured old man, yet he still needs Iago to be the hump on his back? It must be a very unique, single-piece disguise because at the entrance to the Cave of Wonders, when Jafar gleefully yanks the beard off, his fake mustache, eyebrows and teeth come off with it.

• To research the look of Middle Eastern architecture, the animators studied Persian miniatures at the New York Metropolitan Museum of Art and the Los Angeles County Museum of Art. The costumes, on the other hand, are decidedly less authentic. It's easy to forgive the Genie for his Ray Bans, tennis shoes and Hawaiian shirt, but Aladdin's character would more likely opt for a droopy desert robe than a shirtless vest that shows off his pecs, harem pants modeled after M.C. Hammer's, and a perky fez that refuses to fall off his head. And a young woman of Jasmine's position would have been shrouded and draped, but our princess sports a bra top, unisex harem pants, hefty gold jewelry and a ponytail with scrunchies.

Bloopers

• After Rajah bites a chunk out of Achmed's pants, the seat of the suitor's pants is torn, but his now visible heart-spotted underwear appear unharmed. Still, Rajah somehow has a sizable swatch of heart-spotted underwear in his mouth.

• During the "Prince Ali" number, the Genie assists a group of onlookers to stand on each other's shoulders to shake the new prince's hand. Five of them fall on top of Ali, but somehow he ends up being buried by seven men. Then the prince hoists them up into an acrobatic arrangement—and there are only six men.

Hidden Images

Not since *Ferdinand the Bull* (1938)—which had a procession of caricatures of animators, directors and Walt as the matador—have

so many animators appeared on screen. *Aladdin* features caricatures of animator Tom Sito as fertilizer dealer Crazy Hakim (self-
animated by Sito); effects animator Dorse Lanpher as one of the 40
thieves summoned by the Genie (tall, pear-shaped, bare feet, small
sword); animators Eric Goldberg, Glen Keane and T. Daniel
Hofstedt (another self portrait) with three-year-old son Daniel in
the crowd watching Achmed; clean-up artist Marshall Toomey as a
jewelry vendor; late designer T. Hee as the fire walker, and produc-
ers/directors/writers Musker and Clements in the crowd when
Aladdin hides behind a posing muscleman. Musker (commenting
"On his way to the palace, I suppose") and Clements ("Another
suitor for the princess") appear again as Aladdin pushes through a
parade. They originally planned to use movie critics Gene Siskel
and Roger Ebert, who would give a thumbs up or thumbs down rating of the new suitor, but were concerned about using the review-
ers' likenesses without permission.

In addition to obvious cameos by Pinocchio and Sebastian the
crab, another Disney character makes a much more subtle appearance. In the scene where the Sultan is stacking little toys, which
collapse after Jafar enters the room, one of the toys is the Beast
from *Beauty and the Beast*.

Animators also included a split-second Hidden Mickey. During
the movie's climax, when Jafar's spells start coming undone, Rajah
turns from a cub back into a tiger. For an instant, just before he
regains his full size, his head becomes the head of Mickey Mouse.

One thing that wasn't hidden is a subliminal message to the
unsuspecting youth of America. Rumors began surfacing first that
in the scene with Prince Ali and Jasmine on her terrace, a subliminal voice uttered "Good teenagers take off their clothes." The
rumor was revised to say that it was Aladdin telling Jasmine to
"take off your clothes." It turns out the offscreen Aladdin, be-
sieged by Rajah, is saying, "Scat! Good Tiger. Take off and go."

Strange Reactions

Although *Aladdin* did record business at the box office, its 1992
release coincided with perhaps the peak of political correctness.
Unfortunately, broad Warner Bros. cartoon-type comedy and irrev-
erence (relatively unfamiliar ground for Disney feature animation)

are sure to insult someone's sensibilities. Sure enough, *Aladdin* did.

The American-Arab Anti-Discrimination League attacked the film for its supposedly demeaning characterizations and, in particular, alleged racial slurs in the lyrics of "Arabian Nights." The group claimed that the slurs made against Arabs would never be accepted if directed at any other ethnic group and demanded the lyrics be rewritten when the movie was released on videocassette. At first, Disney refused to alter Ashman's lyrics, then consented to meet with the group. After obtaining approval from Menken and from Ashman's estate, the studio changed the song's opening words from "I come from a land... where they cut off your ear, if they don't like your face. It's barbaric, but hey, it's home." to "...where it's flat and immense and the heat is intense..."

Arab groups were not satisfied. It was "nowhere near adequate, considering the racism depicted in *Aladdin*," said league president Don Bustany, who also wanted deleted the word "barbaric," the "very sleazy, burlesque" peddler, and the merchant who threatens to cut off Jasmine's hand for taking an apple to give to a hungry child. "Even worse, the supporting characters are all depicted as nasty, mean people. While the Aladdin character, Jasmine and her father speak unaccented, standard Americanized English, all the bad guys speak in foreign accents."

Ironically, the other person steamed by *Aladdin* was Robin Williams, who accused Disney executives of lying to him and breaching an agreement not to use his voice to merchandise products. The feud went on for a year, finally ending after Katzenberg left the studio and his replacement, Joe Roth, formally apologized. It is rather amusing, though, to read in-depth, behind-the-scenes reports of the movie published by Disney that are unable to divulge the name of the star.

Attraction Offspring

Aladdin was welcomed to Disneyland and then to Disney-MGM Studios not by an attraction but by a parade. Despite the studio's recent success, Disney wasn't taking any chances. Countless attractions had been developed for movies before their release, from *Tron* and *The Black Hole* to *Dick Tracy*, only to see the movies fail. "Generally it seems to be the kiss of death. We'd develop an attraction and it'd turn out to be a bad movie," Baxter said. "Things that get prepared beforehand tend to be live entertainment. It's less commitment, it's only a parade, it's not in permanent cement."

Another way to represent newer films at Disneyland without a major financial commitment was to update the Storybook Land canal boat ride with scenes from *Aladdin* and *The Little Mermaid*. In 1994, the Seven Dwarfs' diamond mine was transformed into the Cave of Wonders and the tiny Mr. Toad structures gave way to the sand and spires of Agrabah. Naturally, some Disneyland diehards balked at replacing the charming old miniatures with streamlined fiberglass mosques. Although one Imagineer admitted the Mr. Toad scene was excised because the film was long forgotten, the official excuse—er, explanation—was that when Disneyland first opened, Mr. Toad's Wild Ride had a carnival tent facade. When Fantasyland was remodeled, the ride's entrance became Toad Hall, making the miniature Toad Hall in Storybook Land redundant. Nevertheless, the tiny Toad Hall was preserved backstage, and a little over a year later was resituated as the first new scene in years on the attraction's north shores, home of a languid patchwork quilt that may one day give way to a whole collage of scenes from other under-represented movies.

- 28 -
The Lion King

The Disney Version

The Lion King is about growing up. Disney's new generation in animation was maturing, and hunting for something more challenging than the tried-and-true, prince-and-princess love story. Their choice was an original story, part *Hamlet*, part the Old Testament stories of Joseph and Moses, part *Bambi* and *Jungle Book*. Where the exact idea originated is up for debate. Maybe it was Katzenberg's or one pitched to him by Charley Fink or another idea man. "Many people like to take credit for having the idea for *Lion King*," said Linda Woolverton. "The one I choose to believe is apparently it was Jeffrey (Katzenberg)'s idea. He told us it was based on a personal experience he had."

What's definitely known is that in 1989 Tom Schumacher, after producing *The Rescuers Down Under*, became the first producer involved with *King of the Jungle*, like *Bambi* a coming of age story rooted in nature. Schumacher guided the lion story through its development phase, with George Scribner, assigned to co-direct with Roger Allers, and Linda Woolverton also writing preliminary drafts.

The main characters were there, plus a few who didn't make it:

Simba, the cub who wants to be king but runs away from home after the death of his father, Mufasa; uncle Scar, the one actually responsible for Mufasa's death, who rules over and ruins the Pride Lands in Simba's absence; the encroaching hyenas (also pictured as grotesque cape hunting dogs); Simba's irresponsible friends, meerkat Timon and warthog Pumbaa, and the ones he leaves behind, love interest Nala, her mischievous kid brother Mheetu, and her wisecracking companion, Bhati, a bat-eared fox.

"I worked on *Lion King* about a year, really forming the story-telling, the characters, developing the big picture of it," Woolverton said. "Initially, Nala had a little brother that I included so she could protect him from Scar. There was a lot in the Pride Lands while Simba is away with Timon and Pumbaa, but it was too depressing. How do you animate a concentration camp?"

Instead, the focus switched to the lighter antics of Timon and Pumbaa, who encourage Simba's irresponsibility. At first, the writers pictured the duo as childhood pals of Simba in the Pride Lands who join him in his flight. By making them strangers and fellow outcasts, they could take the impressionable cub under their wing. In the jungle, wild, wacky horseplay may not be realistic, but it's funny. And led to creative differences between Allers and Scribner, who, preferring a more reality-based story, was replaced by Rob Minkoff.

The lighter tone went over well with audiences. Pumbaa and especially Timon were such a hit at preview screenings that the filmmakers tried to enlarge their parts. One idea was for Timon to perform a soft shoe dance to distract the hyenas during Simba's return to the Pride Lands. A funnier suggestion was to dress him in a grass skirt to hula to the "Hawaiian War Chant." But Katzenberg wanted an even bigger laugh: "Why don't we have Timon put on a white John Travolta suit and start singing 'Staying Alive'?" Fortunately, the animators were able to dissuade him.

But Timon and Pumbaa's popularity nearly destroyed the film's romantic high point. Although the movie was first conceived as a non-musical, Tim Rice agreed to write the lyrics and suggested Elton John for the music. John liked the idea of contributing to the long tradition of beautiful Disney love songs, and his first composition was "Can You Feel the Love Tonight." But as the story continued to change, Rice had to keep revising the song's lyrics—fifteen times. First, adult Simba and Nala, who had fallen in love as adolescents in the Pride Lands, sang the song to each other. When the plot changed so that little Simba fled the Pride Lands immediately after his father's death, new lyrics had to reflect Simba and Nala remembering each other yet first discovering love. Then just one character sang the song. Then the other. Then it was sung by a heavenly choir. Then it was moved to different places in the movie and even removed altogether.

Finally, Rice wrote a "goof version" for Timon and Pumbaa to lament the inevitable loss of their lovestruck pal. The animators completely storyboarded the sequence, the voice actors recorded the song, and the storyreel was screened for John. He was horrified to hear his beautiful love song warbled by a warthog. He quickly convinced the filmmakers that the movie fell flat emotionally because it played its most tender moment as a joke. Rice wrote a final, fifteenth set of lyrics, opened and closed by Timon and Pumbaa, but with Simba, Nala and the choir singing the lion's share of the song. John, still partial to the original lyrics, got to sing that very first version over the end credits.

For the fun number, Timon and Pumbaa would boast of their laid-back, bug-eating lifestyle in "Warthog Rhapsody." But the filmmakers wanted the song to move the story along, to show not only the sidekicks' carefree ways, but also Simba turning his back on responsibililty. So, John and Rice replaced it with "Hakuna Matata."

Similarly, the filmmakers were looking for something a little different for Scar's solo. In its first incarnation, "Thanks to Me," the villain gloats to the hyenas of murdering Mufasa and scaring off Simba. A better approach, to build up *to* the murder, would be a song in which Scar plots the evil deed. This time, a whole new song wasn't needed, just new lyrics, and the song became "Be Prepared." Rice also penned a post-stampede reprise during which Scar introduces the hyenas to the Pride Lands. But such a lively number right after murdering Mufasa seemed a bit of overkill.

Another discarded song, "To Be King," was written for Mufasa to bond with his son, but it became difficult to picture Mufasa, voiced by James Earl Jones and regally drawn, singing and dancing in the woods. Also unused was a lullaby, "The Lion in the Moon," about a protective spirit lion, sung by mom to calm Simba after his first encounter with the hyenas.

Plot Holes

• Simba grows up rather fit and beefy for a carnivore on a strict diet of bugs.

• In the finale, a giant fire engulfs the already-burned-out Pride Lands. It could have been worse. The backgrounds were originally drawn so barren, there was nothing to burn (unless, as someone suggested, Pride Rock was made of coal), and the animators had to go back and add some decaying trees and shrubs.

Bloopers

• As Simba descends Pride Rock after Scar's death, Zazu bows and mouths "Your majesty," but no words come out. The words were snipped when they seemed to detract from the solemn moment.

Hidden Images

The controversy supposedly started with a four-year-old boy who, watching his *Lion King* video, noticed something peculiar during the scene in which adult Simba plops to the ground, causing dust to swirl into the sky toward Rafiki. An advanced speller for his age, the lad noted that for a split-second the dust clouds seemed to form the word "SEX." He reported his findings to his aunt, who contacted the American Life League, a Virginia-based media watchdog organization.

The group demanded that Disney remove the videos from stores and formally apologize. Disney denied everything. After a closer look, the group's leader dropped his demands, admitting the image might be accidental or an animator's innocent prank. Nevertheless, when viewed with a freeze frame, it doesn't take too much imagination to identify the cloudy shape. Disney defenders have speculated that the clouds actually form "SFX," short for special effects, since they were drawn by Effects animators.

Strange Reactions

The Lion King didn't spark the furor of *Aladdin*, but it did come under its fair share of scrutiny. First were objections to the disturbing depiction of Mufasa being trampled to death. Then came racism charges, that the villainous, jive-talking, anti-social hyenas who live in the ghettoes on the outskirts of the forest were played by minorities, Whoopi Goldberg and Cheech Marin. Others pointed out that the good lions were cream-colored, while the evil Scar was dark—and played by Jeremy Irons allegedly in a stereotypically effeminate manner.

The Simba-Kimba Conspiracy

Simba, the Lion King	Kimba, the White Lion
Accompanied by an excitable bird, Zazu.	Accompanied by an excitable bird, Pauley Cracker.
Given sage advice by a guru-like baboon, Rafiki.	Given sage advice by a guru-like baboon, Dan'l Baboon.
Bothered by a pack of smart-aleck hyenas.	Bothered by a pack of smart-aleck hyenas.
Lives in concert with all other animals, except the uncooperative hyenas. There are no humans. After mistakenly believing he caused his father's death, the cub flees from the pride.	After his mother dies aboard a ship, the cub escapes by swimming back to shore. While trying to return home, he visits cities and realizes that mankind has created a wonderful civilization of laws, very different from the law of the jungle. He battles poachers, trappers, monsters, "the red menace," "the insect invasion," and "the gigantic grasshopper."
In his absence, evil uncle Scar assumes his throne.	In his absence, evil lion Claw, who has a scar above his eye, assumes his throne.
Is motivated to return to the pride by clouds on the horizon which take the shape of his dead father.	In a memorable scene in the original comic book, the cub sees clouds on the horizon which take the shape of his father, who had just been killed by a hunter.
Grows up to be the king's successor after his father's death.	Grows up to be the king's successor after his father's death.
In a symbolic scene, stands triumphantly on a rock.	In opening scene of the TV show, stands triumphantly on a rock.

Finally, the movie, the most successful animated feature of all time, irked the animation community. Although Disney maintains the idea for the movie originated in its own Feature Animation story department, soon after its release people began noticing an uncanny resemblance to *Kimba the White Lion*, a Japanese-created American television cartoon series of the 1960s (see chart above).

Co-directors Allers and Minkoff said they were not familiar with the TV series, never heard it mentioned while they were on the project and first learned about the controversy while on a promotional trip to Japan. Whenever a story is based in Africa, Minkoff reasoned, it's not unusual to have characters like a baboon, a bird or hyenas.

But Kimba supporters thought it inconceivable that with so many Japanese animation fans currently working in the U.S. animation industry no one at Disney had ever seen Kimba before. Hundreds of American and Japanese cartoonists and members of related fields signed a letter to Disney officials seeking credit for Osamu Tezaka, whose comic book, *The Jungle Emperor*, inspired Kimba.

IX

Disney Diluted
Chef's Surprise

1994-1996

"If this works, it means we will have the license to start making each of these films as different as they can be, and not just adhere to what had been done in the past. I guess we're going to find out whether audiences are willing to accept (from Disney) an interesting smorgasbord rather than the same meal, well-cooked, all the time."

– Eric Goldberg, to the *Los Angeles Times* before the release of *Aladdin*, after starting work on *Pocahontas* (1992)

By the time he was 30, Alexander the Great had conquered the entire known world. So, he ventured beyond Greek geographical knowledge, pressing into mountainous eastern Persia where he thought he would find the last peninsula of the Earth. India would be his final, most difficult battle, and he returned to Babylon, depressed that there might be no place left to conquer. After gorging himself on food and wine, he fell ill and ten days later was dead, less from illness than from exhaustion. He was 32.

In a way, *Lion King* was Disney's India. It's the ideal mix of what animation, specifically Disney feature animation, does well. The story treads deftly between drama and comedy. The music is upbeat, contemporary, accessible. The movie appeals to all audiences—male, female, child, teenager, adult. It was perfectly timed (the other top grossing movie that year was the similarly toned *Forrest Gump*).

But had money become the yardstick of quality? When the crew working on *Pocahontas* heard *Lion King* made $100 million in its first eleven days of release, they were depressed. All they could think was, "We can't make that."

Disney had animated itself into a corner. The studio seemingly had found the perfect mixture of the traditional Disney elements and taken the formula about as far as it would go. Formulas, when mixed in proper measures, can be successful, but, when continually mixed in those same measures, can seem, well, formulaic. The choice was to do either more of the same, at the risk of growing stale, or doing something radically different, at the risk of losing, even offending the legions of fans.

As well, whenever anything grows too popular and becomes a national phenomenon, those who don't care for it are polarized against it. It was high time for the Disney Bandwagon backlash. The company was no longer above reproach. The fascination was over. All the Michael "Prince of the Magic Kingdom" Eisner stories were old news. The seemingly invincible corporation took its first hits.

Eisner announced an American history-themed park to be built in the middle of dozens of historic sites in northern Virginia and, expecting local gratitude, instead encountered statewide protest that sparked a national debate. Plans for Disney's America included a turbulent "Industrial Revolution" ride through mock molten lead, replica Ironclads dueling outside a Civil War fort, and an exhibit designed to "make you feel what it was like to be a slave." Respected historians feared Disney would "commercialize what should be revered, and vulgarize what is noble in American history." Eisner insulted them. Virginians were stunned by his arrogance. Eisner grew more defensive, telling the *Washington Post:* "If the people think we will back off, they are mistaken." Disney backed off.

Amid the controversy, president and chief operating officer Frank Wells died in a helicopter crash. Katzenberg wanted Wells' job, but Eisner wanted someone who would defer more easily as his second-in-command. Katzenberg was squeezed out and later sued Disney for $250 million. Eisner had quadruple bypass surgery; employees throughout the company who weren't bringing in the hundreds of millions of dollars in salary, bonuses and stock options, joked that the doctors went to operate on his heart, opened him up and couldn't find one.

Becoming bigger and more businesslike was forcing the company to become more globally conscious and politically correct. Middle class American adolescents are easier to target than every ethnicity and every age group. "We're facing a multi-ethnic audience that can't speak the language. We're pantomimists. We have always been very careful about that," Joe Grant says. "Plus, there's a new wave of generation after generation of kids who are seeing these pictures for the first time through revivals and videos."

But constantly worrying about offending anyone dilutes the product. At Disney World's Magic Kingdom, one scene in the Pirates of the Caribbean ride was changed so that instead of the pirates chasing the ladies, the ladies chase the pirates. Politically correct maybe, but the new scene doesn't ring true to the rest of the attraction and ruins the scene's punchline in which one pirate is chased by a homely woman. What's next? Replacing the pirates' torches with streamers and their whiskey bottles with Diet Cokes?

For years, people had argued over what was and what was not appropriate for a Disney movie or theme park, only now they were taking it a little more personally. They were worried, yes, about what they might want their children to see, but now they were also concerned about what they, themselves, wanted to see. Like Mickey Mouse, who grew so popular animators could no longer have him do anything outrageous for fear of offending his legions of fans, Disney animation and theme parks as a whole became subject to the expectations of canonization. People know Disney is a business. They just don't want it to act like one.

Twice, Disneyland tried to replace its sparsely attended Great Moments with Mr. Lincoln, sparking public outcries. "Whenever you remove an attraction, you're going to meet some resistance from the die-hards," says writer/creative director Ryan Harmon. "The Lincoln theater sits at the park's main entry and exit. People walk right by on their way in and out. The hat shop next door does better than Lincoln! But when it got out that we were going to put Muppetvision 4-D in its place, people freaked. So I was asked to write a new show for an intimate space next to the Disney Gallery (above Pirates of the Caribbean in New Orleans Square). One concept was a Lincoln-Douglas debate that included a period campaign train car parked outside. It would have been a better show, but people started writing letters. So Lincoln's still there, playing to crowds of seven."

What people forget is that Disneyland and its sister parks were always meant to change. Walt was always experimenting. He added a streamlined Viewliner train in 1957 and removed it in 1958. He changed the Jungle Cruise three times. He tore down Tomorrowland. The consensus is the parks stayed stagnant for too long, and those who loved them grew overly sentimental.

Quite telling is when Disneyland decided to tear down its Skyway tram ride in 1994. The park gave nostalgic fans a few days notice to come pay their final respects. On the final day, adults jockeyed for position to be the *last* ones to ride (although the final bucket was saved for Mickey and Minnie). One rider, a woman about 40, couldn't believe that her teenage son chose to stay home and do homework. The teenager was the one who didn't want to go to Disneyland.

Disney, though, will reach out to profitable markets. For the late Nineties revamp of Disneyland's Tomorrowland, Imagineers designed a Planet Hollywood-type restaurant to replace the Mission to Mars attraction; it would display artifacts and show movie clips not from Hollywood's past but from Disneyland's. Old Flying Saucers and Rocket Jets would adorn the halls, PeopleMover cars and Skyway buckets would be turned into booths, and one of Mission to Mars' two spacecrafts-in-the-round would become a dining room.

As well, in 1996, the marketing department turned the final season of the park's popular Main Street Electrical Parade into a hype-heavy farewell tour. Hopefully, the next time they need a good promotion, they won't kill off another beloved attraction. However, it's certainly easier than building a new one.

As the Disney admirers held tighter to the past, the Imagineers and animators were maturing and getting their own visions of new things they wanted to do. The conflict didn't seem headed for the traditional happy ending.

- 29 -

Pocahontas

The Original Tale

Pocahontas, or "Playful," was the youngest daughter of Powhatan, the stern chief of the Algonquin confederacy of Indian tribes in the tidewaters region of Virginia. In 1607, a group led by John Smith and other investors of the London Company settled in Jamestown. According to legend (first recounted by Smith years after Pocahontas was no longer around to corroborate it and later romanticized in the 1805 novel *Captain Smith and Princess Pocahontas*), braves captured Smith and were about to bash in his skull, when the smitten 12-year-old Indian maiden laid her head upon his. Powhatan spared Smith's life, and Pocahontas helped to establish trade between the Indians and the settlers that would sustain the first permanent English colony in America.

In 1612, a British captain took Pocahontas hostage, but before she could be returned, she caught the eye of John Rolfe, a planter ten years her senior. They married in 1614 and two years later sailed to England, where she met the king and queen. On the eve of her return to America in 1617, Pocahontas died of smallpox.

The Disney Version

When Mike Gabriel suggested taking on the legend of Pocahontas he saw it as the logical next step in Disney feature animation. It still offered the classic princess love story, but for the first time it would pack the power of being based on actual characters and events and places. Going for a greater sense of realism could provide it with the greatest depth of emotion animation had ever seen.

One of the unwritten laws of animation is that there must be a reason for animating the story as opposed to producing it in live action—whether it's because of extraordinary characters or places, it has to be the antithesis of realism. Disney's goal for *Pocahontas* became creating a fantastic, magical "real" world. Nature would come alive, swirling with vibrant, wind-swept colors and mystical spirit forms.

One of Gabriel's early ideas was to have Pocahontas' mother embodied in a certain star in the sky; by the end of the film she would help Pocahontas find her path to Smith. Eventually mom's spirit became integrated into the swirling wind that occurs throughout the film.

Animating historical events provided the background artists with an unusual advantage: they could visit the actual sites where everything happened. But, in scouting out Jamestown and researching the period, the filmmakers quickly discovered that historical accuracy was out of the question. It turned out that Smith was a ruthless killer and unrepentant scalawag. Most of his men died of disease or starvation. Women of Pocahontas' tribe went topless and sported half-shaven heads. Pocahontas' husband, John Rolfe, introduced the cultivation of the tobacco plant to America (which was plenty to keep him out of the story, even though he never really fit in, despite pleas from Rolfe's descendants that he be included).

Head storyman Tom Sito said the writers boiled history down to the least common denominator: "Of all that exists, what does work is whenever John Smith ran the colony, it functioned and there was peace with the Indians. Whenever the English aristocrats ran the colony, it didn't (function)."

From there, the story team began employing and embellishing the legend more than the truth. Pocahontas faced the dilemma of her princess predecessors: does she choose the safe path her father expects her to by marrying the dull brave Kocoum or does she take her own, more adventurous route? Smith becomes the diamond in the rough she helps to shine. The villain, who tries to keep the lovebirds apart for his own selfish gain, would be John Ratcliffe, an amalgamation of actual British captains, including Martin, Newport and Wingfield. The one who really hated Smith the most was Wingfield, but the filmmakers preferred the sinister sound of "Ratcliffe."

Eisner even wanted to give Pocahontas a mother. "We're always getting fried for having no mothers," he explained. The writers countered that Powhatan was polygamous and formed dynastic alliances among the neighboring tribes by impregnating a local squaw and giving away the child. Although Powhatan was especially fond of her, Pocahontas was something like Daughter Number 149. "Well," Eisner conceded, "I guess that means we're toasted."

The story crew tried to work in more actual events—Pocahontas warning Smith that the Indians were after him so he can escape in the middle of the night, Powhatan ordering the captured Smith to make bead necklaces to humiliate him, Pocahontas kidnapped (though by Ratcliffe)—but none of them worked with the story.

Still, they tried to make the movie look as realistic as possible, sometimes a little too realistic. One of the first screen tests showed a bare-chested Smith moving in to kiss Pocahontas. "It was *very* steamy," Gabriel recalled. "We played it for the staff and everyone was howling and hooting. So we put a shirt on him."

But after the public relations nightmare of *Aladdin*, Disney realized it was stepping onto sensitive ground with a story about Native Americans. The studio, whose last animated Indian was the ridiculous "red man" in *Peter Pan*, would do everything in its power to treat the subject reverently. It hired historians and Native American consultants and cast Indians in all the Indian roles, notably activist Russell Means as Pocahontas' father and Irene Bedard, whose father is Cree, as Pocahontas' speaking voice.

"The picture was politically correct," said old-timer Joe Grant, the first to begin developing story ideas with Gabriel. Grant admitted that the pervasive atmosphere tied the writers' hands. "We lost out on some great opportunities for caricature, especially with the Indians. We didn't want to be offensive in any way."

Sito also wanted to include more and broader jokes, but "the higher-ups wanted it more winsome, more gentle," he said. "Some of the folks were so concerned about political correctness, they didn't want to be cuckoo-wacky about it. Everybody knows what happened to the Indians, so they thought it would be like making slapstick out of a Jew in pre-war Nazi Germany. But all the best drama has comic moments. Look at Shakespeare."

Executive paranoia reached a ridiculous peak over the final scene, after the Indians and settlers have made peace, for which

Grant had drawn Percy, Ratcliffe's pampered pooch, wearing an Indian feather. The animators took the concept one step further by placing a Spanish ruff on Meeko, Pocahontas' raccoon. "This doesn't make sense!" protested one executive. "Animals don't have the intelligence to switch their clothes! They don't even have opposing thumbs!" Yes, the animators argued, but it's funny.

Early in development, the animal characters were going to talk. Percy was to be voiced by Richard E. Grant (*The Player*) or Steven Fry (*Jeeves and Wooster*). John Candy was suggested as the voice of Pocahontas' original pal, the jittery turkey Red Feather. The character would always be on the run, with lines like, "You guys gotta remember—I'm edible!"

After much debate, it was decided to take a more realistic approach and have the animals pantomime. That put the turkey on the chopping block, replaced by the rascally raccoon. "A turkey doesn't have hands," co-director Eric Goldberg explained. "Once he loses his voice, there's not much he can do."

Although they proved to be the highlights of the picture, the comedy scenes involving the animals were reduced because they were most expendable to the story. "There were a lot more scenes with Meeko," Grant recalled. "Another scene was Percy's first encounter with the outdoors. Percy had come in with Ratcliffe and he had never seen the wild, and we had a scare sequence where he finally confronts wild turkeys and such." Instead, after Percy chases Meeko into the forest, he reappears a short time later clearly battered by the unfamiliar surroundings.

Although the animals wouldn't talk, a tree would. According to legend, Pocahontas had a mystical grandmother who was full of stories and magic, and who told her about the spirits that lived in the sun, in trees, rocks and animals. So, to help Pocahontas with her decision and accentuate the Indians' connection to the earth, the filmmakers gave her a Grandmother Willow. The movie was supposed to start with a present day prologue of granny as a stump with branches for arms and fingers. "At one time, the tree was going to be the narrator," Joe Grant said. "She points to the rings of the tree and says, 'Right here, about 400 years ago was when I first met Pocahontas...' She was both wise and motherly, but we had to add some puns. I was hoping for an Edna May Oliver-type, and the woman we got (Linda Hunt) was very good, but she didn't have that fussiness."

Composer Alan Menken and lyricist Steven Schwartz wrote three songs that were cut entirely from the picture. After Pocahontas runs off to see John Smith, the filmmakers wanted a happy moment for the couple to enjoy life together before Kocoum shows up and they are torn apart. Menken and Schwartz composed the peppy "Powerful Magic," but it seemed silly to have a happy, smiley number just before Kocoum appears brandishing a knife like Norman Bates.

"First to Dance" was another attempt at a happy song, while "Middle of the River" was a pretty little ballad replaced by "Colors of the Wind."

For the wrap up, the story seemed too realistic to have a typical fairy tale ending, with Pocahontas and John Smith in each other's arms and the colonists and the Indians living happily ever after. Everybody knows that didn't happen, yet Disney still wanted to stress the message, "why can't we all just get along?" The only probable course seemed to be separating the lovebirds: shipping Smith out and having Pocahontas unselfishly stay behind to help her tribe and the settlers get along.

A Disney animated feature had never before had an unhappy ending, and this worried everyone. They knew the press and the public would make a big deal about it, so how were they going to defend it? Their best defense was to make it as believable as possible. "Good tragedy has to be inevitable," said Sito. "If there's a way out, it's not a tragedy; the protagonists are just stupid. The tragedy has to be complete and hopeless. John Musker and Ron Clements looked (the sequence) over and said, 'It's not gonna work unless Pocahontas has no other choice but to stay and John Smith has no other choice but to go.'"

So, they had John Smith heroically take a bullet, which will kill him if he doesn't return to England. And Pocahontas must stay behind to keep the Indians and settlers from killing each other. Her betrothed has been killed, her lover is dying; at least Pocahontas gets to keep Ratcliffe's dog.

Cutting Room Floor

To tighten the picture, a number of gags that had been fully animated were clipped. After the storm, Wiggins opens his umbrella, starts to blow away and then quickly whips the umbrella over Ratcliffe's head. Deleted was a short sequence of Wiggins flying around the deck, struggling with the umbrella.

When the ship arrives at the New World, Wiggins asks if they will meet any savages, and Ratcliffe answers that if they do, they'll be sure to give them a proper English greeting. As initially animated, Wiggins replied, "Oh, I love a fracas!" He placed a silver tray on his head for a helmet and, using a soup ladle as a rifle, shot at Percy. As he carried on, he tripped over a stool and crashed into a suit of armor with an axe that swung down between his legs. Instead, in the final version, Wiggins responds by holding up two gift baskets, followed by Ratcliffe's same response ("...and he was so highly recommended.").

Wiggins' and Percy's roles were also shortened during the skirmish between the settlers and the Indians. In the final film, the frightened Wiggins dives behind one of his topiary creations, while Percy is covered by a flying helmet. Additional footage was animated of Wiggins who, having shaped one of the bushes into the likeness of Ratcliffe, accidentally cuts off its head. He later tries to chase the runaway helmet with Percy underneath.

Other scenes were trimmed after receiving unexpected reactions from preview audiences. Originally, after the song "Mine, Mine, Mine" (which in the finished film ends on a close-up of Ratcliffe's face), the camera pulled back to a wide shot of the desolated forest, with smoke rising from the ground. The area looked like Hiroshima after the bomb. Instead of being amused by the rollicking number, the test audience gasped, and the closing shot was cut.

Also animated was a sequence in which Pocahontas visits John Smith imprisoned in an Indian hut the night before he is sentenced to die, and she sings the reflective "If I Never Knew You." The beautiful ballad had Grammy written all over it, but presented a big challenge for the animators. "The entire song was not lyric-specific. There were no visuals, and they weren't doing anything. It was just her saying, 'I love you,'" Sito said. "Smith is tied to a stick in a hut that's empty with her kneeling in front of him. Ed Gombert did the storyboards and said, 'I keep trying to get out of this room...'" Gombert finally resorted to a montage of flashbacks.

Another thing working against the song was its placement. Typically, the last third of every Disney movie has no music, except maybe a march to the big fight ("Kill the Beast"). The story's picking up steam for a big finish and no one wants to stop for a song. So at preview screenings, test audiences began to groan. They'd hear the piano begin tinkling and they'd begin thinking, "Oh, no! They're going to sing!" Not only did it seem to bring the whole picture to a dead stop, it was also a pretty preposterous time for her to start singing. But the song was so good no one knew what to do—or, even worse, everyone knew what had to be done. Fortunately, Menken was the first one to stand up and say, "We've got to cut the song." Everyone heaved a sigh of relief. The scene was cut and the song wound up being played over the end credits.

Plot Holes

• Disney went for something new with its not-so-happy ending, with John Smith forced to return to England for medical attention. However, I fail to see the therapeutic value of having a dying man spend months at sea.

Bloopers

• As soon as the storm hits, the British flag on the ship's mast is shredded, but the second the harsh weather subsides, the flag is restored.

Strange Reactions

As hard as Disney tried to appease sensitive audiences, there was no way to please everyone. Historians, Native American and otherwise, faulted the film for blatantly straying from the truth, whatever that actually might have been. "What got me was the people who said we didn't stick to history," Sito recalled, annoyed. "I mean the girl was 13 and running around naked—remember it's 90 degrees and humid and she has no Judeo Christian sensibilities.

John Smith was much older and a notorious social climber who never married. He was 52 when he died and he left his money to the woman he was living with. John Smith didn't speak Algonquin. The reason he went back (to England) was a powder horn exploded on his hip. I think half his men wanted him to die, so they put him on a boat. The Indians nailed the real Ratcliffe to a tree and skinned him alive."

Attraction Offspring

As much as the film celebrates nature, in the end, *Pocahontas'* green message had nothing to do with the environment. To provide a more woodsy feel for the Spirit of Pocahontas stage show, five massive sycamores were planted in the outdoor theater at the Disney-MGM Studios theme park. Yet the trees grew so fast that they couldn't be removed without tearing up the theater's concrete floor. The morning after the show's eight-month run ended, hours after the last strains of the lyrical plea to respect and care for the earth, Disney chopped down the 40-foot-tall trees.

- 30 -

The Hunchback of Notre Dame

The Original Tale

Victor Hugo's *Notre Dame de Paris* (1831) was soon retitled *The Hunchback of Notre Dame*, recognizing its most memorable if not its most central character. The historical romance begins in 1482 in Paris, where gorgeous gypsy La Esmerelda spellbinds the audience with her dancing and the tricks of her goat, Djali, during the Festival of Fools. Each year, the gypsies recognize the ugliest visitor as the Pope of Fools; this time they crown the hideous hunchback Quasimodo. Having become deaf after years of ringing Notre Dame's bells, he thinks it's a compliment.

While walking home late that night, penniless poet Gringoire, whose play the gypsies disrupted, notices a hooded figure seizing Esmerelda. The assailant's accomplice, Quasimodo, strikes Gringoire, but captain of the guard Phoebus rides to the rescue and the attackers flee. Wandering on, Gringoire finds himself in a bad part of town called the Court of Miracles because here the beggars and thieves return at night to shed their phony bandages and crutches. The thugs capture the poet and threaten to hang him if no one will marry him. At the last second, out of pity, Esmerelda volunteers. But no glorious wedding night awaits Gringoire, for Esmerelda's heart now belongs to Phoebus. Instead, the poet takes interest in the goat.

The hunchback's hooded companion was archdeacon Claude Frollo, who is obsessed with the dancer. Quasimodo slavishly obeys the priest, since Frollo not only adopted his own orphaned little brother, Jehan, but also took in the disfigured baby Quasimodo left at the church gates. Quasimodo is charged with abducting Esmerelda, tried and flogged. When he cries out for a drink, the crowd responds with jeers and stones. Even Frollo abandons him. Finally, Esmerelda mounts the scaffold and puts her flask to Quasimodo's lips. He weeps.

One day, Phoebus is entertaining four ladies on a balcony overlooking the square where Esmerelda is performing. They call her up and Djali shows a trick Esmerelda has taught her: to spell "PHOEBUS" in blocks. The ladies call her a witch, but the captain follows her and arranges to rendezvous the next night.

Gringoire later tells Frollo he has married Esmerelda, but she cares only about Phoebus. The hooded Frollo trails Phoebus and bribes the captain to let him secretly watch his date. When Frollo sees it is in fact Esmerelda, he leaps from his hiding place and stabs Phoebus. Esmerelda faints. Frollo flees. A crowd, thinking the sorceress has slain Phoebus, takes her to prison. She is convicted of witchcraft and is about to be hanged. Frollo whispers he can save her if she'll be his, but she refuses. Quasimodo suddenly appears and carries the girl to sanctuary within the church, where he hides her in his cell. One night Frollo gets a key and menaces the gypsy girl, until Quasimodo drags his master away.

Frollo then tells Gringoire to save Esmerelda because officials are plotting to storm the cathedral. The poet rallies the gypsies to break in first and save her. But Quasimodo, thinking the gypsies mean her harm, throws down stones, pours molten lead on them, and pushes away their ladders, killing Jehan and hundreds more. When the king's guards join the fray, killing among others gypsy leader Clopin, Quasimodo thinks they're going to protect Esmerelda. But the girl and Djali have already escaped with Gringoire to a boat where Frollo, again hooded, waits.

When the priest starts acting peculiarly, Gringoire flees with the goat. Frollo asks once more if she'll be his, and Esmerelda refuses. So, while he fetches the guards, he leaves her in the hands of a jailed madwoman, who hates gypsies because years ago they took her only child. The hag discovers Esmerelda is her long-lost daughter and attempts to hide her. But when Esmerelda spots the now engaged Phoebus among the guards, she calls to him. The guards hang Esmerelda and kill her mother. Back at the church, still searching for Esmerelda, Quasimodo happens upon Frollo, shaking with laughter as he looks down on the gypsy's hanging. The bellringer pushes him off the top of the tower. Two years later, inside a vault are found the skeleton of the gypsy and, with its bony arms wrapped tightly around her, that of the hunchback.

The Disney Version

The Hunchback, of course, had several movie credits to his name long before Disney came along. These films always had Quasimodo as the central character but they were always, as well, horror pictures. Disney junior development executive David Stainton was a big horror movie buff, fascinated with Hugo's tale since first reading the illustrated comic book version as a child. But, for Disney, Stainton saw the story as a romantic vehicle, with Cyrano de Bergerac undertones—out of love, the kind-hearted yet disfigured hero delivers the shallow yet handsome rival to his beloved.

Reversing the fate of the star-crossed lovers also meant reversing their traits that predetermined it. Esmerelda traded in her ignorant trust for street smarts. Instead of instantly falling in love with Phoebus and blindly clinging on to the delusion that he loves her, which causes her downfall, she would seriously doubt his intentions, and even attack him. Phoebus, instead of being a gigolo who disappears when the witch hunt heats up, would be a gentleman who becomes an outlaw out of love and righteousness.

Quasimodo, the unthinking brute, would be a gentle, introspective outcast, who in true Disney fashion, just wants to be part of the outside world. He became the ugly, lonely freshman in love with the prom queen. As the star of a musical, he could no longer be deaf or practically mute, and, as the star of a Disney musical, he could no longer be hideous to behold. His looks had to make him a believable outcast, yet provide a certain appeal. Artists came up with countless different designs that made him look like everything from a teenager with bad posture to one of the Seven Dwarfs. In the end, he would be misshapen yet endearing, like the favorite doll that's been loved a bit too hard a bit too long.

The biggest writing challenge then became creating an active story in which the principal character was its most passive. One nice touch was Quasimodo's opening scene, in which, expressing his own difficulty and desire to leave the nest and revealing that he's his own worst enemy, he coaches a little bird to fly. The scene, although identical in message, is opposite in execution to how it was first conceived by story supervisor Will Finn: "My idea was the little bird spent all his life there and then died. It was too grim."

Tab Murphy wrote the original outline, playing up the Cyrano angle to the extent that Quasimodo even wrote poems for Phoebus to read to Esmerelda. In June 1993, Murphy drafted the first script; in fairly rapid succession, he then wrote three more complete, more polished drafts. The filmmakers would stick faithfully to the structure of the outline, while changing all the details and sublimating the Cyrano angle.

One potential problem detected early on was the story's perceived similarity to *Beauty and the Beast*. The misunderstood monster is isolated from and hated by the crowd but kept company by the objects around him. He's befriended, initially out of pity, by a beauty and falls in love with her. But the crowd storms his fortress, and the objects help him fend them off. Finally, not for his own sake but for his beloved, he rebels against the villain, who falls off the top of the castle.

Michael Eisner figured the people who knew best how *not* to remake *Beauty and the Beast* were the ones who had made it. So he enlisted co-directors Kirk Wise and Gary Trousdale, who tried to steer away from Belle's storybook surroundings and make Quasimodo's a much more realistic, gritty, hard-knocks world, colored by such adult themes as sexual obsession.

Therein lay a new challenge, trying not to make the movie too adult and scare Disney's established juvenile audience. "There was a lot of discussion. It was a gamble. We were walking in with our eyes open on that one," Finn said. "It was a real concern, but Michael Eisner felt strongly that this was a new direction for Disney, a progressive gamble, a risk he was willing to take."

The filmmakers, still cautious not to offend religious sensibilities, would have to secularize Frollo. Unfortunately, his not being a priest robbed the story of its central dichotic theme (that a priest, who was supposed to control his passions, be all virtuous and opposed to the hedonistic, pagan gypsies, would become sexually obsessed with a virtuous gypsy). Even though Frollo was recast as part of the judiciary, the writers set out to establish his disdain for gypsies from the start. As first envisioned, a prologue would show Frollo as a younger man graduating from law school, pledging to rid Paris of gypsies, but as he left a tavern, an old gypsy cursed him, promising he would come to some evil end. To intensify the drama, the storymen changed this introduction to a scene in which Frollo condemned a witch to burn. The witch, tied to a stake, curses him before being set on fire. The second idea was more exciting, but too grim.

The solution came after the writers asked themselves: What linked Frollo to Quasimodo? How does a character pursuing the life of a judge relate to a bellringer of a church? The answer, in Disney fashion, was having Frollo kill Quasimodo's gypsy mother and a kindly archdeacon force him to raise the disfigured orphan.

For the obligatory sidekicks, Murphy took a cue from the original novel, which briefly mentions that the hunchback talked to his bells and the cathedral walls. Murphy's original screenplay gave Quasimodo some bats, spiders, a talking stained glass window, and two quasi-imaginary gargoyles (named Bela and Boris after his favorite horror movie actors, Lugosi and Karloff). After the gargoyles became his only companions, the stone statues were expanded to three, dubbed Chaney, Laughton and Quinn, after three actors who played Quasimodo in earlier film versions. But the legal department was afraid of potential lawsuits, so the gargoyles were renamed Victor, Hugo and, after the third Andrews sister, Laverne.

The gargoyles represented Quasimodo's inner voices: Victor, professing the safe thing to do; Hugo, advocating the lunatic, crazy path, and Laverne, the moderate straight-shooter. The latter, first envisioned as a sassy young female, became an older mentor, like Ruth Gordon in *Harold and Maude*. But, argued some of the crew, isn't a third gargoyle superfluous? If you have the two extremes, wouldn't Quasimodo himself proffer the moderate point of view? The answer came back, if Quasimodo can figure all this out for himself, why does he need any of the gargoyles?

The biggest change in the middle of the story was making Phoebus a fugitive. Early on, feature animation president Peter Schneider suggested the change, but the story team resisted because they thought it would take too much focus off their main characters. Phoebus remained Frollo's henchman who sneaks away secretly to help Esmerelda. Still, if he was going to get the girl, at some point he would need to break from Frollo. The story crew finally gave in, after realizing the second act reached a certain pitch and just hung there; it needed another dramatic high point to take the narrative to a new level.

The sequence that got the most revisions was The Court of Miracles. Everyone wanted to take the characters to this exciting, colorful location, but no one could quite figure out what they should do once they got there. At first, it was the locale where Phoebus comes to read one of Quasimodo's poems to Esmerelda; he confesses his love, Esmerelda returns the sentiment, and Quasimodo is heartbroken. Menken and Schwartz wrote three different songs for the scene, first a song fantasy, "In a Place of Miracles," then a rewrite as "Court of Miracles."

To make Quasimodo's heartbreak even more devastating, the writers considered borrowing Hugo's account of Esmerelda's gypsy wedding, only the groom would be Phoebus. So, Menken and Schwartz wrote a wedding song based on gypsy traditions, "As Long as There's a Moon." Unfortunately, every idea seemed to stop the story cold. After all, this was the hunchback's story, not Phoebus and Esmerelda's. The writers finally decided to quickly get the heartbreak out of the way when Esmerelda aids the wounded Phoebus. Quasimodo would have to reunite them, knowing it was Phoebus she loved.

But that made going to the Court of Miracles seem even more extraneous. Quasimodo, Frollo, Esmerelda and Phoebus were already at the cathedral. It seemed silly to send them all across town to the Court of Miracles, then right back to the cathedral for the big siege. So, through the beginning of the movie, the writers laced in the idea of Frollo's obsession with locating the nest of gypsies so he could use Quasimodo to find it. That way, Quasimodo doesn't just lead Frollo to Esmerelda, but to *all* the gypsies. One thought was having some of the gypsies escape, but it seemed more powerful to have Frollo capture them all. With the film nearing a close, the villain would have absolutely everything.

As in *Pocahontas*, the more serious approach suggested a more believable, more bittersweet, more responsible finale, with Quasimodo giving his blessing to Esmerelda and Phoebus. A "Rolling Stones" ending, as Will Finn calls it. Quasimodo may not get what he wants (Esmerelda), but he gets what he needs (accepted by the world). Some suggested that as long as they were completely negating all the tragedy in the book, why not just let Quasimodo get the girl, too? But that seemed too far fetched even for a Disney fantasy.

Also as in *Pocahontas*, the predicted break-out single almost didn't make it into the movie. Menken and Schwartz originally wrote "Some Day" as the prayer Esmerelda sings while trapped in the cathedral. It was a prettier song than its predecessor, "God Help the Outcasts," but its lyrics were less specific. So, once again, perhaps the best song in the picture wound up playing over the end credits.

Cutting Room Floor

Early into production, the filmmakers could see how intense the film was progressing and considered shooting for a PG rating. They finally decided to try for the safer G rating, meaning Schwartz had to rewrite and tone down the lyrics to Frollo's song, "Hellfire."

Kathy Zelinski had also animated a brief scene in which Frollo grabs Esmerelda and lustily sniffs her hair (interestingly, a scene both animated and storyboarded by women). The scene was so graphic, it made viewers uncomfortable, and was cut down. In the final version, Frollo makes the same moves, but in about half the screen time.

Hidden Images

During Quasimodo's song "Out There," the camera pans over the rooftops of Medieval Paris and atop one building near the lower left is a tiny satellite dish. The camera then briefly zooms in on a small crowd of people, among them two men carrying a pole from which hangs *The Lion King*'s Pumbaa, a merchant shaking out *Aladdin*'s Magic Carpet, and, most conspicuously, *Beauty and the Beast*'s Belle strolling down the street, her face buried in a book. She originally was animated even more obviously, but the filmmakers were concerned people's laughs of recognition might stop the picture.

Bloopers

• At the end of the Festival of Fools, Esmerelda leaps onto the stage and cuts Quasimodo's ropes. A second later, he's still tied, then freed again in the next shot.

• Phoebus is struck in the back by an arrow, but later we see it's torn the *front* of his shirt and Esmerelda stitches up his chest. Phoebus keeps us further guessing as to the location of his wound by hobbling around and clutching his arm.

Strange Reactions

Critics, in general, loved the movie. General audiences were more critical. As expected, many parents felt outraged, even deceived that Disney would present such adult material under the guise of a cartoon. On the opposite end of the spectrum were the literary purists, disgusted that Disney had made a mockery of another piece of classic literature.

"The challenge of the movie was to serve two disparate masters: to turn this dark, almost nihilistic adult story into an animated Disney musical comedy. But, they say, sometimes mixing disparate elements makes for genius," Finn said. "We knew we would be treading on literary toes. But Rudyard Kipling, Lewis Carroll, J.M. Barrie, those are all children's literary authors; we were dealing with a very adult story. We were prepared for a certain amount of backlash."

By now you'd think Disney would automatically be afforded a certain amount of artistic license. "Disney has always been fairly irreverent with its source material," he explained. "They typically make it more contemporary, fashion it for current tastes. They've always been fairly clear about it. It's doing what Disney does, the Disneyfication. And the book's still there. It doesn't dissolve. You can go back and read it. In fact, what I would do as a child was see the Disney movie and then want to go read the original."

After *Hunchback* fared disappointingly at the box office, there were more theories than Aladdin has fleas: Poor timing. Stiff competition. People thinking it's too much like what they've seen before. People thinking it's *not enough* like what they've seen before. "The new regime wants a picture every year," explained

Finn. "Films like *Fox and the Hound* and *Black Cauldron* were made without any deadline at all. It didn't matter if they were finished in 1979 or 1981 or whenever. Now they're taking something that was once a novelty and releasing them one after another. You wonder if maybe we're squeezing the golden goose too hard. Only time will tell."

Or maybe, just maybe, Disney was growing up, and audiences didn't want it to.

X

Disney's Destiny
Conclusion

1997-

"Anybody can make you enjoy the first bite of a dish, but only a real chef can make you enjoy the last."

– Francois Minot,
in the *New York Times* (1964)

Katzenberg's last months at Disney were difficult ones, filled with hard meetings, heavy politicking and flared tempers. One day near the end, he sat with a group of animators and confessed, "I think this is the only room I can sit in where everyone doesn't want to tear my throat out." He didn't want to go, but he knew it was best. "It's time for me to go," he admitted. "I've done just about everything I can do before it gets stale. How do you top *Lion King*?"

Before he left to start DreamWorks SKG with S (Steven Spielberg) and G (David Geffen), Katzenberg had provided invaluable direction in helping to develop *Hunchback*, furious that after six months of story work he had no idea what it was about or who the main character was. Still, many felt saying goodbye to Katzenberg was like removing their training wheels, and were glad he was gone. Finally, they could have the feeling that they were making their movie their way.

Dozens of others, like Will Finn, left to work for Katzenberg. "You have to be confident about collaborating with him. People can be very intimidated," Finn says. "I always found the collaboration with Jeffrey stimulating. He was a force of nature that I missed. At the end of the day, he always wanted the same thing we all did, to make the best picture possible. He absolutely loves feature animation, absolutely understands it, and is nuts about getting it right."

Tom Sito left as well, sold on the idea of blazing trails and starting a new, homier studio. "I think everybody wants an alternative studio," he says. "I trust Jeffrey's instincts; his motivation is to make animation as good as Disney. He has a real hunger. He understands and respects artists. Jeffrey understands the potential of animation."

So many defected to DreamWorks (not to mention new animation studios opened by Fox and Warner Bros.), that everyone's value went up. For a while, Disney animators referred to Katzenberg as "St. Jeffrey." A handful of the best in the business were now commanding more than $1 million a year.

Animation in general had reached a high water mark, the product never before so popular nor the industry so busy. Sito, the Cartoonists Union president, notes that in 1979 the animation industry had 1,850 union members, 55 percent of them technical. By 1983, with more and more Saturday morning TV jobs going overseas, the member count had dropped to 750. In 1996, there were 2,500 members, 8 percent technical. He explains: "For years everyone thought animation offered too low a profit and took too long to make. All attempts to do it on the cheap with impoverished Third World slave labor have failed; only the most qualitative succeed. Now we're kicking Tom Cruise's and Arnold Schwarzenegger's butts."

Most see the competition as good for all of animation, even Disney. "They're like the 1970s Yankees; they've got a lot of depth on the bench," admits Sito. "Disney will always have the rep(utation). For animators, it's still the Tiffany's, the Rolls Royce you want to be associated with. It would take decades of gross mismanagement to change that."

But will it get stale, since so much of being Disney is giving audiences what they expect? If someone had an idea that was too progressive, Katzenberg would find himself or Eisner reining them back in because "that's not what Disney is about." With his new studio, there are no preconceived notions, no artistic straitjackets. It was enough of a temptation for Finn to direct his first feature for DreamWorks instead of Disney. "I've been a Disney fan all my life," he says. "I worked there for nine years. I kind of knew if I would direct there, it seemed less challenging. I would know at least how to turn Property XYZ into a good Disney picture. With *El Dorado* (DreamWorks' second animated feature), I'm working without a net, without the previous 35 features to gauge what works, yet to do something with the same commitment to quality."

But the Disney influence is so pervasive, he says, "it's hard to imagine doing anything else. I'm very conscious to try not to reference what we did at Disney in story design, color, effects, and to try to find new influences, new raw material to draw from. I know what the Disney style is; I don't know what the non-Disney style is, and the Disney style is hard enough to get right."

Not long ago, amusement parks were divided into two groups: Disney's and all the others. So evident was the difference that the competition routinely acknowledged Disney's supremacy in design and execution. They're finally starting to learn.

Around the world, amusement parks are more popular than ever before. New non-Disney parks and attractions are opening at a record pace, from Missouri to Malaysia, featuring Disney-like thrills, attention to detail, integrated merchandising, and, best of all, vivid theming. Although they began with generic amusement parks filled with roller coasters and carnival rides, Time Warner (Batman: The Ride, Superman: The Escape, Bugs Bunny World) and Paramount (*Star Trek, Wayne's World, Days of Thunder* attractions) have come to realize the value of building upon their latest movies and classic characters. Says one spokesperson for Six Flags: "We want to be the Number One theme park company in the world."

For Disney, it has become a race for the latest technology. "At one time you could just do 80 audio-animatronic figures and people would be impressed. People were so impressed with the animated pirates that they didn't think about this ride being all about raping and pillaging and looting," says Tony Baxter. "That's missing now. Now they'll say, 'Really? So what's the story?' So (the Indiana Jones Adventure) is all effects."

Disney has come a long way since the days of *Snow White*. Its size, its scope, everything has grown and evolved, except the goal to provide the best entertainment possible. Joe Grant has seen it all. "There's no difference today with the original Disney set-up. It's the same bitching and complaining. We gather in groups of who knows each other. With 600 people in here now, we're all among strangers," he says. "The revelation is that there's an audience out there. To think the animated feature is an established idea, what started as a novelty. But some new medium will come, like 3-D, and we'll have to start all over again, to remake *Casablanca* and everything else in 3-D."

For animation, for theme parks, for the next medium they invent, Disney has the recipe for success. The challenge will be finding new and surprising ways to prepare it.

Ingredients

In addition to deep, occasionally disturbed insight garnered from more movie screenings and visits to Disneyland and Disney World than I'd care to admit, this book is based on the following sources:

Interviews

Tony Baxter (1-29-96)
Carol Connors (1-12-96)
Will Finn (7-16-96)
Vance Gerry (1-21-96)
Joe Grant (3-7-96)
Terry Gilkyson (3-25-96, 4-11-96)
Ryan Harmon (4-22-96)
Huston Huddleston (8-15-96, 8-28-96)
Mrs. Richard Huemer (8-14-96)
Steven Hulett (12-27-95)
Al Kasha (1-28-96)
Earl Kress (10-17-95)
Peggy Lee (8-26-96)
Mel Leven (1-11-96)
James Lopez (11-25-95)
Fred Lucky (1-9-96, 1-12-96)
Malcolm Marmorstein (1-23-96)
Jeffrey Price (1-26-96)
Maurice Rapf (3-3-96)
Terry Rossio (c.2-28-96)
George Scribner (9-4-96)
Peter Seaman (1-26-96)
Tom Shaw (9-96)
Richard M. Sherman (2-22-96, 4-11-96)
Robert B. Sherman.(2-22-96)
Tom Sito (6-7-96)
Linda Woolverton (2-6-96)

General References

Art of Walt Disney (1942), Robert D. Field, McMillan
Bill Peet: An Autobiography (1989), Bill Peet, Houghton Mifflin Co.
Cinderella & Other Tales from Perrault (1989), Henry Holt & Co.
Disney Animation: The Illusion of Life (1981), Frank Thomas & Ollie Johnston, Abbeville Press
Disney Films (1973), Leonard Maltin, Crown
Disney Studio Story (1988), Richard Holliss & Brian Sibley, Crown Publishers
Disney That Never Was (1995), Charles Solomon, Hyperion
Disney's Art of Animation (1991), Bob Thomas, Hyperion
Enchanted Drawings: The History of Animation (1989), Charles Solomon, Alfred A. Knopf
Hogan's Alley, No. 1, "Seldom RePeeted," (1994)
L.A. Times, "Beauties of the Beast," (6-23-95)
L.A. Times, "Stalking the King of Animation," (6-20-96)
McCall's (1-55)
Music & the Magic: The Musical Artistry of Alan Menken, Howard Ashman & Time Rice (1994), Walt Disney Records
Music of Disney: A Legacy in Song (1992), Walt Disney Records
Orange County Register, "Rivals Aim to Take Disney on a Scary

259

Ride," (7-19-96)

Rec.Arts.Disney Newsgroup (Some of the Bloopers and Plot Holes and Bloopers were suggeted by various Internet postings)

"Recollections of Richard Huemer: Interviewed by Joe Adamson: An Oral History of the Motion Picture in America (1968-9)," Department of Special Collections, University Research Library, UCLA

Since Eve Ate Apples (1994), March Egerton, Tsunami Press

Treasures of Disney Animation Art (1982), John Canemaker, Abbeville Press

1. Snow White & the Seven Dwarfs

Complete Grimm's Fairy Tales (1944), Brothers Grimm, Pantheon Books

E-Ticket (Summer 1992, Winter 1995)

Life (4-87)

Register (3-31-89, 3-31-93, 10-22-94)

Snow White: Making of a Masterpiece laser disc

Variety (3-23-92)

Walt Disney's Snow White and the Seven Dwarfs & the Making of the Classic Film (1989), Richard Hollis & Brian Sibley, Simon & Schuster

2. Pinocchio

Adventures of Pinocchio: Tale of a Puppet (1983), Collodi, translated by M.L. Rosenthal, Lathrop, Lee & Shepard Books

E-Ticket (Summer 1991)

Film & Radio Guide (10-45)

News (7-11-41)

Pinocchio press release (1940)

"Pinocchio" synopsis (8-10-38)

"Pinocchio" synopsis (8-19-39)

Redbook (2-40)

Register (6-26-92)

3. Fantasia

Fantasia press release (1990)

Fantasia theater program (1940)

Fantasia: The Making of a Masterpiece laser disc

Film Music Notes (3-42)

Long Beach Press-Telegram (11-28-91)

L.A. Times (11-9-80, 2-8-82, 3-14-82, 12-16-88, 8-26-90, 3-19-92)

MPAA production code files (11-24-39)

Variety (11-13-70, 7-8-91)

4. Dumbo

"Dumbo" synopsis (10-22-40)

Time (12-29-41)

5. Bambi

Bambi pressbook (1942)

"Bambi" synopsis (c.1939)

"Bambi" synopsis (1941)

Bambi: A Life in the Woods (1928), Felix Salten, Simon & Schuster

Citizen-Views (4-13-66)

N.Y. Times (7-19-42)

Walt Disney's Bambi (1990), Ollie Johnston & Frank Thomas, Stewart, Tabori & Chang

6. Song of the South

Complete Tales of Uncle Remus (1955), Joel Chandler Harris, Houghton Mifflin Co.

MPAA production code files

7. Cinderella

Cinderella: The Making of a Masterpiece laser disc

"Letter to Dick Huemer" (1948), by Cap Palmer

8. Alice in Wonderland

"Alice in Wonderland" script (7-23-45) by Milton Gunzberg
"Alice in Wonderland" script (8-29-45) by Milton Gunzberg
"Alice in Wonderland" script (12-28-45) by Cap Palmer
"Alice in Wonderland" script (3-1-46) by Cap Palmer
"Alice in Wonderland" casting possibilities (1-18-46) by Cap Palmer
"Alice in Wonderland" episode board (1-18-46) by Cap Palmer
"Alice in Wonderland" song ideas (1-18-46) by Cap Palmer
Alice in Wonderland: Making of a Masterpiece laserdisc
Alice's Adventures in Wonderland and Through the Looking Glass (1965), Lewis Carroll, Airmont Publishing Co.
"Cinema Texas" program notes (1-20/21-76)
N.Y. Times (4-21-74)
Persistence of Vision (Spring 1993)

9. Peter Pan

Newsweek (2-16-53)
Peter Pan (1980), James M. Barrie, Charles Scribner's Sons
Peter Pan production notes (1953)

10. Lady & the Tramp

Hollywood Reporter (3-21-91)
L.A. Examiner (6-5-55)
L.A. Times (2-19-91, 10-8-92)
Lady and the Tramp program notes (1955)
"The Lady and the Tramp" script (c.1945) by Cap Palmer

11. Sleeping Beauty

Disneyland: The Nickel Tour (1995), Bruce Gordon & David Mumford, Camphor Tree Publishers

12. 101 Dalmatians

"101 Dalmatians" synopsis (1960)
MPAA production code files (6-16-60)
One Hundred and One Dalmatians (1957), Dodie Smith, Viking Penguin
Too Funny for Words (1987), Frank Thomas & Ollie Johnston, Abbeville Press

13. Sword in the Stone

Sword in the Stone (1939), T.H. White, G.P. Putnam's Sons
Sword in the Stone program notes (1963)

14. Mary Poppins

Mary Poppins (1981), Pamela L. Travers, Dell
Storyboard (Sept./Oct. 1989)

15. Jungle Book

"Jungle Book" song demos (c.1963) by Terry Gilkyson
Jungle Book pressbook (1967)

16. Aristocats

Hollywood Studio Magazine (4-70)
L.A.Times (12-24-80)
Variety (11-11-81)

17. Bedknobs & Broomsticks

Bedknob & Broomstick (1957), Mary Norton, Harcourt Brace & World
N.Y. Times (4-6-66)

19. Rescuers

Miss Bianca (1962), Margery Sharp, Little, Brown & Co.
Miss Bianca in the Antarctic (1971), Margery Sharp, Little, Brown & Co.

The Rescuers (1959), Margery Sharp,
Dell Publishing Co.
"The Rescuers" song demos (1974)
by Floyd Huddleston
Variety (12-6-78)

20. Pete's Dragon

"Pete's Dragon" script (3-29-76)
"Pete's Dragon" script (4-30-76)

21. Fox & the Hound

The Fox and the Hound (1967)
Daniel P. Mannix, Dutton
Hollywood Reporter (8-6-73, 7-26-
78, 9-17-79, 3-16-94)

22. Great Mouse Detective

Back Stage (6-20-56)
Great Mouse Detective press notes
(1986)
L.A. Times (6-29-86, 7-4-86)

23. Who Framed Roger Rabbit

Esquire (8-94)
L.A. Times (3-17-94, 3-18-94)
Rolling Stone (8-25-88)
Variety (11-3-81, 3-14-94)
Who Censored Roger Rabbit?
(1981), Gary Wolf, St. Martin's
Press
"Who Shot Roger Rabbit?" script:
4th draft (10-15-86)

24. Oliver & Co.

L.A. Times (12-18-88)
"Oliver and the Dodger" script (3-30-
87)
Oliver Twist (1838), Charles Dickens

25. Little Mermaid

Hans Andersen's Fairy Tales (1979),
Hans Christian Andersen, Schoc-
ken Books
Hollywood Reporter (7-30-90)

L.A. Times (1-28-90, 7-30-90)
Little Mermaid press kit (1989)
People (12-4-89)

26. Beauty & the Beast

Beauty and the Beast (1990), Marie
LePrince de Beaumont, Simon &
Schuster
Beauty and the Beast press release
(1991)
Fantasy & Science Fiction (7-92)
Hollywood Reporter (5-5-92)
L.A.Times (9-1-95)
Long Beach Press-Telegram (4-4-94)
N.Y.Times (4-25-54, 11-17-91)

27. Aladdin

*Aladdin: The Making of an Animated
Film* (1992), John Culhane,
Hyperion
Buzz (Dec./Jan. 95)
DramaLogue (11-26-92)
L.A. Times (11-8-92, 12-6-92, 12-11-
92, 7-10-93, 10-24-94, 8-19-95)
N.Y. Times (11-8-92)
Register (5-22-93, 9-29-93)
TV Guide (10-2-93)

28. Lion King

A Masterpiece: The Lion King laser-
disc
Art of the Lion King (1994), Chris-
topher Finch, Hyperion
Disney Magazine (Spring 94)
GQ (5-95)
Hollywood Cinefile (3-20-92)
L.A.Times (7-13-94, 8-9-94, 2-9-95)
Lion King production notes (1994)
London Times (7-20-94)
N.Y.Times (9-2-95)

29. Pocahontas

Art of Pocahontas (1995), Stephen
Rebello, Hyperion
Entertainment Weekly (6-23-95)

The Light and the Glory (1977) Peter
    Marshall & David Manuel, Flem-
    ing H. Revell Co.
Orlando Sentinel (2-27-95)
Pocahontas press release (1995)

30. Hunchback of Notre Dame

Hunchback of Notre Dame (1831)
    Victor Hugo
L.A. Times (6-16-96)

Index

– Order Form –

Quantity   Amount

_____   **Mouse Under Glass: Secrets of Disney Animation** _____
                  & Theme Parks (hardcover) @ $23.95

_____   **Mouse Tales: A Behind-the-Ears Look at** _____
                  Disneyland (softcover) @ $13.95

_____   **Mouse Tales: A Behind-the-Ears Look at** _____
      Disneyland (hardcover, *personally autographed*
                  by the author) @ $25.95

Total for book(s) _____

Postage: Add $2 for first book, _____
$1 for each additional

Sales Tax: **California residents only** please add _____
7.75% tax

Amount enclosed (U.S. funds) _____

Ship Book(s) to:

_____

_____

_____

_____

IF THIS IS A LIBRARY COPY,
PLEASE PHOTOCOPY THIS PAGE

BONAVENTURE PRESS

P.O. Box 51961
Irvine, Ca. 92619-1961